No Place for a Lady

NO PLACE
FOR A LADY

The Life Story of Archaeologist Marjorie F. Lambert

SHELBY TISDALE

THE UNIVERSITY OF
ARIZONA PRESS

TUCSON

The University of Arizona Press
www.uapress.arizona.edu

We respectfully acknowledge the University of Arizona is on the land and territories of Indigenous peoples. Today, Arizona is home to twenty-two federally recognized tribes, with Tucson being home to the O'odham and the Yaqui. Committed to diversity and inclusion, the University strives to build sustainable relationships with sovereign Native Nations and Indigenous communities through education offerings, partnerships, and community service.

ISBN-13: 978-0-8165-4972-6 (hardcover)
ISBN-13: 978-0-8165-4971-9 (paperback)
ISBN-13: 978-0-8165-4973-3 (ebook)

Cover design by Leigh McDonald
Cover photograph of Marjorie Ferguson at Pueblo Bonito – Neg. No. 70.849, courtesy of the Museum of Indian Arts & Culture, Lab of Anthropology Archives
Typeset by Sara Thaxton in 10/14 Warnock Pro with Good Headline Pro and Bullshorn WF

Support for this publication was provided by the Arizona Archaeological and Historical Society.

Library of Congress Cataloging-in-Publication Data
Names: Tisdale, Shelby J., author.
Title: No place for a lady : the life story of archaeologist Marjorie F. Lambert / Shelby Tisdale.
Description: Tucson : University of Arizona Press, 2023. | Includes bibliographical references and index.
Identifiers: LCCN 2022034816 (print) | LCCN 2022034817 (ebook) | ISBN 9780816549726 (hardcover) | ISBN 9780816549719 (paperback) | ISBN 9780816549733 (ebook)
Subjects: LCSH: Lambert, Marjorie F. | Women anthropologists—Southwest, New—Biography. | Women museum curators—Southwest, New—Biography. | LCGFT: Biographies.
Classification: LCC GN21.L246 T57 2023 (print) | LCC GN21.L246 (ebook) | DDC 301.092 [B]—dc23/eng/20221025
LC record available at https://lccn.loc.gov/2022034816
LC ebook record available at https://lccn.loc.gov/2022034817

This book is dedicated to the women anthropologists, archaeologists, and museum professionals who found their place in the Southwest and to those who choose to follow their paths.

Contents

Part III. In Recognition of a Legacy

Illustrations

Acknowledgments

In the course of writing this book, I have benefited from the knowledge, advice, and kindness of many scholars and colleagues. I am especially indebted to Nancy J. Parezo for giving me the opportunity as a graduate research assistant to work on her important volume *Hidden Scholars: Women Anthropologists and the Native American Southwest* (University of New Mexico Press, 1993) and for encouraging me to write this biography on Marjorie Ferguson Lambert. I also want to thank her for generously sharing her thoughts and research materials with me during the early stages of my research.

I would like to thank Allyson Carter, senior editor; Alana Enriquez, editorial assistant; editorial, design, and production manager Amanda Krause; art director Leigh McDonald, and the staff at the University of Arizona Press for believing in this project and shepherding me through the process. I am also indebted to Rachel Paul for her careful and skillful copyediting of this manuscript and Linda Gregonis for her skill at indexing. I especially want to thank the peer reviewers who made helpful suggestions, thus making this a much better book.

Funding is always a major part of any research project. I am indebted to the Arizona Archaeological and Historical Society (AAHS) in Tucson for providing the seed money to a starving graduate student so she could pursue her dream of writing a biography on this amazing woman archaeologist. A scholarship given to me in 1990 enabled me to travel to Santa Fe for two weeks to interview and tape record Marjorie and some of her colleagues, most of whom are no longer with us. Knowing that I would not get back to this project until I completed the doctoral program at the university, the interviews with these individuals were timely. I am also extremely grateful to the AAHS for their additional funding to support the publication of this book.

In 1997 I received a grant from the Southwestern Foundation for Education and Historical Preservation to continue with my recorded interviews with Marjorie and to have the tapes transcribed. I want to thank Boleyn Baylor of Tucson, who patiently and meticulously transcribed all of the interview tapes. Funding from the Southwest Foundation also covered my travel and living expenses while at the School of American Research (SAR) in Santa Fe, New Mexico, where I was an Ethel-Jane Westfeldt Bunting Foundation Summer Resident Scholar. I was provided with an apartment and office space for almost two months in the summer of 1997. This enabled me to spend valuable time with Marjorie, where I continued to record in detail many of her life experiences. This also gave me time to take advantage of the archival materials in the SAR library and at the Indian Arts Research Center. Without the opportunity to spend this time in Santa Fe, many important details would have been left out.

This book was decades in the making and there are numerous people who assisted along the way. Many have moved on to other institutions, retired, or sadly are no longer with us. Several SAR staff assisted me during the early years of my research, including Catherine Cocks, former editor of SAR Press, who read early outlines and drafts and made important suggestions. Several SAR staff helped when I was a summer scholar in 1997—Douglas Schwartz, retired president: Duane Anderson, former vice president; Joan O'Donnell, former director of SAR Press; Christy Sturm, former collections manager of the Indian Arts Research Center; Cecile Stein, director of the Resident Scholars Program; Deborah Flynn Post, former director of the photo archives; Jane Gillentine, former librarian; Peter Palmieri, who took care of computer problems; and my old friends Ray and Jim Sweeney. More recently Katherine Wolf, SAR's Catherine McElvain librarian and archivist, assisted in tracking down my photo requests.

Other institutions and individuals helped along the way as well: Gloria Bird, former photo archivist; Laura Holt, former librarian; Lou Haecker, archivist for the Archaeological Records Maintenance System at the Laboratory of Anthropology in Santa Fe; Lee Goodwin, senior archivist at the State of New Mexico Records Center and Archives; Beth Silbergleits, archivist; Louis Hieb, former director of the Center for Southwest Research; Joyce Raab, archivist; and Francis Joan Mathien, retired director of the Chaco Archives at the University of New Mexico. More recently I was assisted by Diane Bird, archivist, and Allison Colborne, librarian, at the Laboratory of Anthropology; Janelle Weakley at the Arizona State Museum Photo Archives; Hillary Mannion, archivist at the Colorado Springs Pioneers Museum; Catie

Carl, digital imaging archivist at the Palace of the Governors Photo Archives; Andrea Hanley, chief curator at the Wheelwright Museum of the American Indian; Elena Perez-Lizano, archives bureau chief at the State Archives of New Mexico; and David Grant Noble, who gave me permission to include his beautiful photo of Marjorie.

I want to thank the many anthropologists and archaeologists who were colleagues and friends of Marjorie. In 1990 I interviewed Bertha Dutton, Sallie Wagner, Albert Schroeder, Charles Lange, Douglas Schwartz, Stewart Peckham, and Curtis Schaafsma; and in 1997 I interviewed Edwin Ferdon, Nancy Fox, Courtney Jones, Katherine Halpern, Winifred Creamer, and Cordelia Snow. They all shared wonderful stories about Marjorie and their own experiences. I am also indebted to Louise Stiver, Nancy Fox, Marianne Kocks, Andrew Darling, and Andrew Hunter Whiteford for sharing copies of taped interviews they had conducted with Marjorie. And a huge thank you to Nancy Parezo for sharing the transcripts from the interviews that Jennifer Fox conducted with several women anthropologists for the Daughters of the Desert Project.

Lastly, I would like to thank some of Marjorie's family members who shared information with me. Patricia Hilbert, Jack Lambert's granddaughter, shared some of her memories and sent me copies of some of Jack's mother-in-law's diaries of her time at San Gabriel Ranch. This gave me insight into what life was like on the ranch for Jack and the Pfäffle family. Geoffrey Ferguson called now and then to see how the book on his Aunt Marjorie was coming along. I am grateful for his patience and for his keeping the rest of the family informed of my progress.

There are some I have left out of this acknowledgment, especially my family, friends, and colleagues who no doubt got tired of me talking about "the book" I was writing on Marjorie Lambert. Thank you for listening and lending your encouragement and ongoing support.

Abbreviations

AAA	American Anthropological Association
AAHS	Arizona Archaeological and Historical Society
IAF	Indian Arts Fund
IARC	Indian Arts Research Center
LAB	Laboratory of Anthropology
MIAC/LAB	Museum of Indian Arts and Culture / Laboratory of Anthropology
MNA	Museum of Northern Arizona
MNM	Museum of New Mexico
MOIFA	Museum of International Folk Art
NAGPRA	Native American Graves Protection and Repatriation Act
NMAIA	New Mexico Association on Indian Affairs
NMHM	New Mexico History Museum
POG	Palace of the Governors
SAA	Society for American Archaeology
SAR	School of American Research / School for Advanced Research
SWAIA	Southwestern Association for Indian Arts
UNM	University of New Mexico

No Place for a Lady

Introduction

"No Place for a Lady"

Marjorie has a remarkable range and number of achievements in her long career, not only in archaeology, but also in the history and ethnology of the Southwest and its relationship to Mesoamerica.

— CYNTHIA IRWIN WILLIAMS[1]

Marjorie Ferguson Lambert is one of a handful of women who left their imprint on the study of southwestern archaeology, anthropology, history, and museology during the first half of the twentieth century. Throughout her remarkable career spanning more than sixty years, Marjorie devoted her life to the study and advancement of our understanding of the ancient past in the American Southwest. She cared deeply about the preservation of the arts and cultures of the living Native Americans and Spanish Americans of New Mexico. At a time when there were relatively few women establishing full-time careers in anthropology, archaeology, or museums, Marjorie became a professional archaeologist and museum curator. Nevertheless, she was among hundreds of women who were marginalized in academe and museums. Her story adds to the growing literature on feminist archaeological historiography.[2]

As a woman in a profession dominated by men, Marjorie struggled throughout her life against the male biases that limited women's recognition and advancement in scientific circles. She forged strong and enduring friendships with colleagues, acquaintances she met along the way, and the Native Americans she studied with and worked alongside. She was viewed by many as a warmhearted and generous friend. Like numerous others, I found Marjorie to be an intelligent, strong-willed, courageous, and talented field researcher and museum professional. She had an amazing sense of humor and was especially quick-witted and known for her puns and funny stories about her mentors and colleagues. She had an intense love for her second husband, Jack Lambert, who shared her interest in the Southwest, anthropology, and archaeology, and New Mexico's diverse cultures and landscape.

Marjorie was a fighter who demanded to be treated as an equal by her male colleagues, even when it was obvious they were working against her. She was one of the young women who broke through barriers and blazed a trail for the next generation of women anthropologists, archaeologists, and museum professionals to follow. She set high standards for many young women to aspire to, especially those of us working as professional and/or academic archaeologists, or as museum curators and administrators.

A Chance Meeting

I first met Marjorie Ferguson Lambert in 1984 while I was working for the School of American Research, now the School for Advanced Research (SAR), in Santa Fe, New Mexico. As the assistant collections manager at the SAR's Indian Arts Research Center (IARC), I was periodically asked to transport Marjorie to meetings and "Brown Bag" lectures at the School. During these travels back and forth between her home and the SAR, we would talk about southwestern archaeology, and she mentioned her frustration with her failing eyesight and how difficult it was to keep up with her professional reading and writing. On one of these trips, I offered to read archaeological reports and other anthropological publications to her, and we agreed to get together on Wednesday evenings.

I would go over to Marjorie's apartment after work, and she would fix a light dinner or we would go out to eat at one of her favorite restaurants. Afterward, I would read whatever was on her list. I mostly read archaeological reports and book chapters. Marjorie was also fascinated with primates, so we sometimes ventured away from archaeology and anthropology to articles or books on the study of mountain gorillas in Rwanda by Dian Fossey or Jane Goodall's study on chimpanzees in Tanzania. Marjorie contributed to organizations such as the Jane Goodall Institute, which focuses on the conservation and protection of primates and their habitats throughout the world.

Marjorie and I discussed what was in the reading each evening, and sometimes our discussions turned to the issues faced by women in archaeology specifically, and in anthropology and museums in general. It was during these reading sessions that Marjorie started to share her experiences as a young female archaeologist in the 1930s. As these spirited discussions progressed and we got to know each other, we compared my own experiences as a 1980s anthropologist with hers, and we both realized that the position of women in anthropology and archaeology had improved little over the years despite the attempts by feminists during the women's liberation movement of the 1960s and 1970s. Fortunately, this has changed as more women entered archaeology and anthropology and started taking on leadership roles at universities and in museums in the late twentieth and early twenty-first centuries.

Throughout the years, Marjorie and I continued to keep in contact with one another and we found that we shared many common interests. We especially shared a love for the Southwest, its diverse cultures and landscapes, and its deep history. In 1989 I left New Mexico for Tucson, Arizona, to study for my doctorate at the University of Arizona. Shortly after I started my studies, Nancy Parezo hired me as a graduate research assistant to work on the *Hidden Scholars* volume that she was editing.[3] This project was an outgrowth of the papers delivered at the Wenner-Gren sponsored "Daughters of the Desert" conference held in Tucson in 1986. The conference was related to a traveling exhibition and publication by the same name organized by Barbara A. Babcock and Nancy J. Parezo.[4]

Nancy and I discussed the women in these two publications at length, and I felt that the history of anthropology and archaeology would benefit from more complete biographies of some of these "daughters." I approached Marjorie about the possibility of writing a biography on her. I proposed it as a cross-generational collaboration, which would be a significant contribution to the intellectual history of women's roles in southwestern archaeology. There is much to gain from the experiences of others, and those of us following a similar path could benefit from Marjorie's willingness to share her personal and professional experiences with us.

Why a Biography on Marjorie Lambert?

Ann Axtel Morris's *Digging in the Southwest* is one of the earliest autobiographical publications on southwestern archaeology from a woman's point of view. This book inspired numerous young women to become Southwest archaeologists. Autobiographies and biographies by and about southwestern women archaeologists serve as useful tools in telling us something about the role gender played in the early development of the discipline. In her introduction to a collection of articles on women in archaeology, Cheryl Claassen states that "gender directly and significantly influences the state of knowledge in archaeology, our perception of our knowledge both about our own history and about the past for various regions and ethnic groups." Biographies tell us much about what was done but also about what Claassen argues is "the exclusion of data, hypotheses, explanations and practitioners or the usurping of those perspectives by others."[5] Biographies are important to anthropological history and scholarship because they demonstrate "some of the ways in which person, discipline, and society articulate in particular ways at particular times, to create science and scholarship."[6] This biography of Marjorie Ferguson Lambert provides a lens by which we can examine changes occurring in society over a sixty-year period, particularly in the American Southwest, as well as in the professional development of anthropology and archaeology at both the micro and macro levels.[7]

Most often biographies are written posthumously and the writer must depend on archival materials in addition to the remembrances of family members, students, and colleagues. Working in the context of a living biography provides many advantages in terms of the accuracy of information and the extraordinary amount of detail that can be included. While living in Tucson, I traveled back to Santa Fe between 1990 and 1996 to visit Marjorie. She and I talked about her life and experiences, which I tape-recorded and later had transcribed. After obtaining my doctorate in anthropology in 1997, I returned to Santa Fe, where I was an Ethel-Jane Westfeldt Bunting Summer Resident Scholar at the SAR. During this time, I was able to conduct research in the archives at the SAR and the Laboratory of Anthropology (LAB) and search through the photo archives at the Palace of the Governors (POG). Marjorie and I spent numerous hours together, where I continued to tape-record her recollections. That summer I interviewed and tape-recorded sessions with Katherine Halpern and Courtney Reeder Jones, who also had interesting stories to share about some of the obstacles and harassment they experienced trying to break into a field dominated by men.

I was fortunate that I was able to read drafts of chapters to Marjorie while she was still alive. She often provided helpful edits and corrected some of her quotes. However, it did present some challenges when she wanted to

FIGURE 1 Author Shelby Tisdale, an Ethel-Jane Westfeldt Bunting Summer Resident Scholar, with archaeologist Marjorie Lambert at the School of American Research in July 1997. Photo by Katrina Lasko. Courtesy of the School for Advanced Research.

edit out certain personal details, for one reason or another. Sometimes this was out of concern for the reputation of certain individuals and their living descendants. Yet this approach did have its advantages as well. One of the benefits of working with a living person on their biography or memoirs is that it enables us to initiate new directions that integrate women's voices into the intellectual history of anthropology and archaeology.

The Southwest: A Place for Women to Learn and Work

Born in the wake of a major shift in the status of women in science and the changing role of women in society in general, Marjorie challenged the stereotypes of the day and carved out her own path in the field of southwestern archaeology.[8] It was also a time when American archaeology was developing as a science and becoming professionalized.[9] The Southwest proved to be an excellent training ground for numerous students.

Southwest archaeology at the turn of the twentieth century was supported by large collecting museums in the East, which were essentially well-funded treasure hunts.[10] This prompted the enactment of the American Antiquities Act of 1906 (16 USC 431–33). Marjorie's interest in archaeology was sparked during high school, but her career as a southwestern archaeologist didn't begin until she started her graduate training in the Department of Anthropology and Archaeology at the University of New Mexico (UNM).

As Nancy Parezo documents in her conclusion to *Hidden Scholars*, "The lure of the Southwest was so strong that one group of women remained, forgoing mobility and increased salaries. Their acceptance in western institutions, the perception that these were humane places to work, their desire for intellectual freedom, and the love of place held people in the Southwest."[11] Marjorie Lambert was one of those women who found her place in the Southwest.

Throughout her career, there were many obstacles that she had to overcome and maneuver around that would have, and probably did, discourage many young women from pursuing a career in southwestern archaeology. It took courage for Marjorie to stay the course in the Southwest instead of mentoring with well-known women anthropologists and taking advantage of the prestige offered by the well-established departments in the East. She has pointed out on numerous occasions that she had become enamored with New Mexico, and when her male colleagues encouraged her to leave, she said, *I didn't want to leave the Southwest. . . . I loved the contacts with the Indians, which I knew I would lose. I knew that I could lose close and immediate contact with the archaeological sites . . . so I didn't consider leaving.*[12]

Several women anthropologists and archaeologists who conducted fieldwork in the Southwest in the early twentieth century were primarily from well-established eastern institutions.[13] At the time, the Southwest was growing academically, and the museums recognized today for their excellence in research and outstanding collections were in their infancy. Edgar Lee Hewett in the West and Frederic Ward Putnam in the East were patrons of women in archaeology and facilitators of their participation, although they often worked in minimally prestigious roles as lab assistants rather than active fieldworkers.[14]

By the time Marjorie entered the field, archaeology was becoming increasingly professionalized. Unfortunately, this operated against women because it was harder for them to obtain the graduate credentials that were increasingly necessary for academic employment.[15] Oftentimes women were discouraged from going on to obtain their doctorate. The issue of young women trying to gain a higher education and employment in the fields of anthropology and archaeology drew the attention of scholars beginning in the 1980s with publications such as Barbara A. Babcock and Nancy J. Parezo's *Daughters of the Desert: Women Anthropologists and the Native American Southwest 1880–1980* (1988); Ute Gacs, Aisha Khan, Jerrie McIntyre, and Ruth Weinberg's edited volume *Women Anthropologists: Selected Biographies* (1989); Nancy J. Parezo's edited volume *Hidden Scholars: Women Anthropologists and the Native American Southwest* (1993); Alice B. Kehoe and Mary Beth Emmerich's edited work *Assembling the Past: Studies in the Professionalization of Archaeology* (1999); and more recently Shirley A. Leckie and Nancy J. Parezo's edited volume *Their Own Frontier: Women Intellectuals Re-Visioning the American West* (2008) and David L. Browman's *Cultural Negotiations: The Role of Women in the Founding of Americanist Archaeology* (2013).

Southwest Archaeology: No Place for a Lady

In the early twentieth century, the archaeology profession was dominated by men, and very few women were able to gain entry. Considered the sacred domain of rough, tough, adventurous men in the early 1900s, archaeological fieldwork was considered no place for a lady. In his introduction to Charles Amsden's *Prehistoric Southwesterners from Basket-Maker to Pueblo* (1949), Alfred V. Kidder compares the popular myths of the two types of archaeologists: "the hairy-chested" type who is portrayed as "a strong-jawed young man in a tropical helmet, pistol on hip, hacking his way through the jungle in search of lost cities and buried treasures" and "the hairy-chinned" type who is absent-minded and "his only weapon is a magnifying glass, with which he scrutinizes inscriptions in forgotten languages." Interestingly, the women, if mentioned at all, end up being the daughters who are "rescued from savages by the handsome young assistant."[16] Dime store novels and the Indiana Jones movies have played on this popular myth, where women are portrayed as the beautiful assistant who creates additional problems for the archaeologist to overcome. This popular view, or myth, is not that far off in the Southwest, where the "self-image of the archaeologist as cowboy" that is "marked by other facets of *machismo*, including hard-drinking and womanizing" is more readily apparent.[17] As Linda Cordell points out, "The myth portrays the male archaeologist as the active fieldworker who is also comfortable with high-tech analyses. The female archaeologist of the myth is engaged in simple sorting of materials, basic laboratory analysis, and library research."[18]

These images of archaeologists were detrimental to women trying to break through the barriers and roadblocks that were intentionally put in their way. Some women made it, while others worked in the field laboratories and behind the scenes taking care of the collections, tasks which were undervalued and compared to housework. Joan Gero illustrates this disparity when comparing the expected roles of male versus female archaeologists:

> We can expect archaeologists to conform in their professional roles to the same ideological constructs they adopt to explain the past. We are alerted to certain strong parallels between the male who populates the archaeological record—public, visible, physically active, exploratory, dominant, and rugged, the stereotypic hunter which likes his data raw. . . . Corresponding, then, to the stereotyped male, we expect to find the female archaeologist secluded in the base-camp laboratory or museum, sorting and preparing archaeological materials, private, protected, passively receptive, ordering and systematizing, but without recognized contribution to the productive process. The-woman-at-home archaeologist must fulfill her stereotype feminine role by specializing in the analysis of archaeological materials, typologizing, seriating, studying wear or paste or iconographic motifs. She will have to do the archaeological housework.[19]

The ability of a woman to direct men in the field also became an issue for women supervising field crews. This has been raised by several women archaeologists, and Cynthia Irwin-Williams noted that when Marjorie was given responsibility for a project that had been initiated under the direction of male colleagues, these colleagues claimed that the "native laborers would probably refuse to work for a woman."[20] Despite their assumptions, Marjorie successfully completed her projects with all-male excavation crews.

By the 1930s women archaeologists were finding positions in newly created anthropology departments and museums in the Southwest. Some of Marjorie's female colleagues who chose to stay and work in the Southwest became close friends throughout their careers. Marjorie met Florence Hawley Ellis at Chaco Canyon in New Mexico when both worked there in the early 1930s. Florence received her doctorate in anthropology at the University of Chicago and worked at Chaco Canyon from 1929 to 1933, excavating and collecting dendrochronological samples. During this time, she was also an instructor at the University of Arizona. Ellis was one of the few women to find a full-time academic position in the Southwest when she was hired as an assistant professor in anthropology at the University of New Mexico (UNM). She went on to become a full professor. While at UNM, Ellis directed the archaeological field schools in 1956, 1959, 1960, and 1962–64. She returned to Chaco Canyon in 1985 with her own field school. While well known and highly respected as a professor and archaeologist, Ellis is recognized for the work she did on Pueblo land claims and water rights. She is quoted as saying, "I wanted to live out here and be with my Indian friends and the archaeology that went with them."[21]

Even though Florence Hawley Ellis is credited with pioneering ethnoarchaeology in the Southwest, Marjorie was very much on the frontier of incorporating this approach into her archaeological work. One of the early practitioners of ethnohistorical and ethnoarchaeological techniques, Marjorie hired Native American and Spanish American men as crew members on her excavations. She consulted with her crew members about her findings and incorporated their oral traditions and histories into her analyses and interpretations of the past. This was a practice that differed from most of her colleagues at the time.

Other women archaeologists who trained in the Southwest continued to conduct research in the region while living and working elsewhere. Some of these women went on to be well known for the work they did in the Southwest and their contributions to archaeology. One of these women is Anna O. Shepard, who is best known for her work in ceramic technology in the Southwest and Mesoamerica. She participated in the SAR field school at Gran Quivira and at Jemez, New Mexico; the UNM Field School at Chaco Canyon; Harvard University's Awatovi expedition in Arizona; and at Mesa Verde in Colorado. She also did archaeological and ethnological ceramic research in the northern Rio Grande region. Shepard was one of the early anthropologists to undertake an ethnoarchaeology approach to her work as well. She was the curator of ethnography at the San Diego Museum of Man (now the Museum of Us) from 1926 to 1930 and held a research position in ceramics at the Laboratory of Anthropology in Santa Fe from 1930 to 1937, where she specialized in petrographic analysis of the ceramics excavated at Pecos Pueblo by A. V. Kidder. In 1936 Shepard would take the position of ceramicist at the Carnegie Institute of Washington, where she stayed until 1968.

Another colleague of Marjorie's who attended Edgar Lee Hewett's UNM field school at Chaco Canyon in 1931 was Dorothy Keur. She developed an interest in southwestern archaeology and went on to combine her interest in Navajo (Diné) origins and acculturation with her archaeological and ethnographic work at Big Bead Mesa and in the Gobernador area from 1939 to 1940. After receiving her doctorate in anthropology from Columbia University in 1941, she returned to Hunter College, where she had received her bachelor's and master's degrees to take a position as an instructor in anthropology. She would eventually become a full professor. According to Babcock and Parezo, Keur spent thirty-seven years teaching and expanding the anthropology department at Hunter College. Regarding her fieldwork, Keur is quoted as saying, "Here were these great marvelous ruins, and here were Navajos living their own kind of life."[22] Even though she had a tremendous impact on our understanding of early Navajo history, Hunter College continued to be her home base.

Other women not described here—for example, Jean McWhirt Pinkley, Jane Holden Kelley, and Cynthia Irwin-Williams—also made their mark on southwestern archaeology. Linda Cordell provides brief biographies on these women in her contribution to Parezo's *Hidden Scholars* volume. There are numerous other women pioneers who found their niche in southwestern archaeology; some are well known while others remain invisible.

Women Archaeologists Working in Museums

A number of women archaeologists who were unable to obtain university positions found museums to be a viable alternative. Nancy Parezo and Margaret Hardin point out that "women entered museums in the 1920s, when museums were expanding across the country, primarily as collection assistants and support staff, i.e., in technical rather than elite scientific positions. As the Great Depression intensified and university professorships became almost nonexistent for everyone, women who wanted to work in anthropology, especially archaeology, were drawn to and hired by museums. This was partly because they were willing to accept less pay, to work in western rather than eastern museums and in small rather than large institutions."[23]

When Marjorie joined the Museum of New Mexico (MNM) staff in 1937, she was one of the earliest women to occupy a major curatorial position in the country.[24] The first woman curator in a southwestern museum was Katherine Bartlett. After spending the summer working with Harold S. Colton doing archaeological fieldwork in northern Arizona, Bartlett was hired as the curator of anthropology and archaeology at the Museum of Northern Arizona (MNA) in Flagstaff in 1930.[25] She remained at MNA for another twenty-five years. Work in the museum included numerous duties, as Bartlett opined in a 1985 interview, "I was the jack-of-all-trades. In the beginning there were so few people and we really did everything. We had to stop what we were doing and all help put up an exhibition."[26]

In 1935 Hannah Marie Wormington was hired by the Denver Museum of Natural History (now the Denver Museum of Nature and Science). She was first hired as a staff archaeologist before being appointed to curator of archaeology in 1937. Wormington held this position for thirty-one years, in spite of a museum director who continually threatened to remove her from her position because of her gender. Nevertheless, Wormington became recognized as a leader in the field of Paleoindian archaeology both nationally and internationally. Like so many other women who were attracted to the field of archaeology, Wormington recalled, "Once I discovered there was such a thing as archaeology, I just never looked back."[27] It's a sentiment that continues to be shared by young women entering the field today.

In 1937 Marjorie joined these women curators when she was appointed curator of archaeology at the Museum of New Mexico (MNM). She would later be joined by Bertha Dutton, who started out as Edgar Lee Hewett's administrative assistant in 1933. In 1939 Dutton was appointed as curator of ethnology at the MNM. While Dutton worked on exhibits and publications at the MNM, she is best known for her series of archaeological mobile camps for senior Girl Scouts, which is well-documented in Catherine S. Fowler's recent publication *Dutton's Dirty Diggers: Bertha P. Dutton and the Senior Girl Scout Archaeological Camps in the American Southwest, 1947–1957*. Bartlett, Wormington, Lambert, and Dutton were among the first women to be recognized as professional archaeologists, to gain meaningful and engaging positions in museums, and to continue to live and work in the Southwest. There were several other women who ventured into southwestern archaeology and ethnology; some stayed and many left. Marjorie Lambert is one of the ones who stayed and carved out a niche for herself.

Jennifer Fox writes about the many women anthropologists and archaeologists who opened doors in the early years while being confronted with the inequities in pay and gender discrimination in terms of promotions and keeping their jobs in both academe and museums.[28] Many women also found that when they entered academic and museum positions they were not offered paid time to conduct research or time to write, unlike their male counterparts. As Marjorie recalled, *When I went into the museum, we were told we would spend half the time doing curatorial work and half the time on our own research. It never did work out that way. The duties you had just took too much time. I sometimes thought that if I was in a [university] department I would get time to do fieldwork. I think maybe I missed it because they do have summers free to do fieldwork.*[29] It would be another five decades, however, before women would start to gain some parity with their male counterparts in salaries and recognition. Despite the inequities, women chose to stay because they loved their work and found their lives as anthropologists and archaeologists fulfilling and rewarding.[30]

Marjorie's contributions to the development of the Museum of New Mexico and New Mexico archaeology were often overlooked as her male colleagues gained recognition through their publications and written histories. Marjorie was not the only woman, however, to be overlooked for her contributions to southwestern anthropology and archaeology. Florence Hawley Ellis stated in a 1985 interview that these women "have not been widely recognized and that other people [male colleagues, administrators, and husbands] are just as likely to claim that they discovered this or that. There's a tendency to not pay attention to [the] publications of women."[31] Part of the problem with this recognition is that women often tend to write for a more popular audience. Throughout her long and productive career, Marjorie penned almost two hundred scholarly and popular articles for *American Antiquity, El Palacio, New Mexico Anthropologist,* and *New Mexico Magazine*; two monographs for the School of American Research; and several review articles and forewords to books (see appendix C).

Carving Out Her Own Niche

It was important to Marjorie that anthropology and archaeology be relevant and accessible to the general public. To accomplish this, she organized several exhibits at the Palace of the Governors in Santa Fe and gave numerous lectures introducing archaeology and anthropology to a wide audience.[32] Unfortunately, this form of popularizing the discipline was generally undervalued in academe, and those who attempted to introduce anthropology to a nonprofessional audience generally tended to be marginalized by their male colleagues and the discipline as a whole.[33]

Marjorie was determined to make it as an archaeologist despite the blatant male prejudice that she had to contend with throughout her career. Florence Hawley Ellis noted that gender discrimination "is, of course, discouraging when you stop to think of it. So you just don't dare stop to think of it. All you do is see what you can do to get around the situation at the moment and go ahead with your work."[34] Part of the reason that Marjorie was able to balance her feminine side with her professional career so easily had much to do with her family background and the intellectual atmosphere she was raised in. Later it would be her high regard for scholarship and professionalism that would raise her up in rank with her numerous male colleagues.

By the beginning of World War I, anthropologists had collected hundreds of thousands of pieces of ethnographic and archaeological art and material culture from groups throughout the Greater Southwest. These men and women published hundreds of scholarly analyses, descriptive monographs, exhibit catalogs, and popular accounts of the objects made and used by Native Americans.[35] Women anthropologists working in museums and universities began to specialize in art and material culture—for example, Clara Lee Tanner and Kate Peck Kent. Marjorie shared an interest in the arts and material culture through her work in the museum as well. Her sense of place in the Southwest compelled her to support the arts of the Native Americans and Spanish Americans of New Mexico and to be an activist for the Santa Fe community, as well as the Pueblo communities and Spanish villages sprinkled throughout New Mexico.

Throughout the years, Marjorie was recognized for her contributions to both the profession and the northern New Mexico community (see appendix A). She also has several excavations to her credit that she worked on and/or supervised (see appendix B). When asked why she chose a career in anthropology and archaeology, Marjorie often replied, *I just like the challenge that prehistory seemed to give, the mystery of it, and finding out about people— why they think the way they do and what makes history.*[36]

When not excavating archaeological sites, Marjorie was digging through books and research materials in her quest for information that would add to her unquenchable thirst for knowledge of the anthropology, archaeology, and history of the Southwest. To her, there was nothing more interesting than how the American Southwest, Mexico, and Mesoamerica were interconnected. Her keen interest and enthusiasm for anthropology, and especially southwestern archaeology, informed her professional career as a

FIGURE 2 Studio Photo of Marjorie F. Lambert, ca. 1945. Courtesy of the Palace of the Governors Photo Archives (NMHM/DCA). Neg. No. 048007.

southwestern archaeologist, assistant professor, and museum curator. Marjorie loved the Southwest, and there was nowhere else in the world that she would rather be.

Within these pages, we not only learn about Marjorie's life as a New Mexico archaeologist and museum curator, but we have the opportunity to discover what it was really like for a young woman to go against the expectations of women's roles in society during the first half of the twentieth century and the many obstacles and barriers that she had to overcome. May her words inspire young women considering careers in archaeology and museums today.

PART I

A Time of Discovery

CHAPTER 1

In the Shadow of Pikes Peak

1908–1930

> I grew up in Colorado Springs. So, I was born, you might say, in
> the shadow of Pikes Peak on Pikes Peak Avenue.
>
> — MARJORIE F. LAMBERT[1]

Born in Colorado Springs on June 13, 1908, Marjorie Elizabeth Ferguson came into a world where women had been playing acceptable roles in scientific discovery and in anthropological research for over two decades. By 1910, however, as Margaret W. Rossiter discloses, these roles were rapidly changing, and as Marjorie began to pursue her own interests in history and archaeology, as well as an academic career, she faced numerous obstacles and barriers based strictly on her gender.[2] More than likely it was her proud Scottish upbringing and the early support of her father that gave Marjorie the strength to pursue her interests.

A descendant of one of Colorado's oldest pioneer families, Marjorie had firsthand knowledge of the importance of history. Born in 1860 in Missouri, Marjorie's maternal grandmother, Mary Ann (Molly) Wilson, was among the early pioneers who moved west in the mid-nineteenth century. Lured by the discovery of gold, the Wilson family joined other argonauts in a wagon train and crossed the tallgrass prairie to the Colorado Rockies. Marjorie's maternal grandfather, Henry Anthony Wattson, born in 1847 in Australia, was a pioneer resident of El Paso County, Colorado, and was one of the first members of the Colorado Springs City Council. He became prominent in mining, ranching, and construction in the Cripple Creek–Colorado Springs–Leadville area.

Three years after the establishment of Colorado statehood, Mary Ann and Henry were married in Fairplay, Colorado, on March 3, 1879. The Wattsons had five children. Their second child, Elizabeth, born during a blinding snowstorm in California Gulch outside of Leadville in December 1882, was Marjorie's mother. Marjorie's father, John Ferguson, born in Sanquhar, Dumfries and Galloway, Scotland, in December 1874, immigrated to the United States in 1889. He married Elizabeth Wattson on November 20, 1905, in Colorado Springs.

Five years after John and Elizabeth Ferguson were married, the Wattsons moved to Los Angeles, California, in 1910, where Henry and his son-in-law Carroll Atchison Spicer founded Wattson and Spicer, a contract-engineering firm that worked on large-scale building projects, such as the Hill Street Tunnel. The Fergusons stayed in Colorado Springs and became active members of the El Paso County Pioneers Association. Elizabeth was a charter member of the Daughters of the Colorado Pioneers, and throughout her adult life she was actively involved in the Colorado Springs Pioneers Museum and the Society of Colorado Pioneers. The Fergusons owned and operated the Diamond Mercantile & Grocery Store for forty-two years.

Raised by his grandmother after both parents had passed away, John Ferguson valued education and was considered an authority on the great Scottish poet Robert Burns (1759–96) and British writer born in Scotland Thomas

Carlyle (1795–1881). Mr. Ferguson was the last surviving member of the Caledonian Society of Colorado Springs, an international organization composed of native-born Scotsmen living abroad. Marjorie took great pride in her Scottish heritage and noted that *Colorado Springs was originally built up primarily with native-born English and Scots, and you had to be a native Scot in order to be a member of the Caledonian Society.*[3] The Colorado Springs chapter played an important role in the history of this small city.

The Caledonian Society of Colorado Springs was organized by Andrew Green in December 1898. The purpose of the society was to promote friendly relations among the people of Scottish birth and descent in the city and to keep their shared love for the music,

FIGURE 3 Photo of John Ferguson. Date unknown. Courtesy of the Colorado Springs Pioneers Museum.

literature, and ancient games of Scotland alive. The society also assisted any Scot through sickness or misfortune and raised the funds to build a cottage located in a suburb of Edinburgh, Scotland, to assist the disabled at the close of World War I. The meetings of the Colorado Springs Caledonian Society were held at the Acacia Hotel, where bagpipes were played and haggis was always on the menu. Selections of works by Robert Burns were read and the meetings were known as the "Robert Burns Banquets," after the famous poet.[4] Marjorie's father was the chief (president) during the last twenty years of the Caledonian Society's existence in Colorado Springs.

Growing up under the azure skies and towering ponderosa pines of the Rocky Mountains, the Ferguson children gained an appreciation for their surrounding environment and became nature lovers and conservationists. Marjorie, her older sister Helen Mary (Mrs. Joel Jensen), and her younger brother, John Allen Ferguson, also grew up in a literary environment. The whole family enjoyed reading, and Marjorie often walked the five blocks between her home and the library to search out obscure books for her father. Marjorie recalled that as a child and particularly during her teenage years, *I came across some books on Egyptology in my grandfather's library, and it never occurred to me that I would ever be anything but an Egyptologist. [When] I was in high school . . . I wrote a letter to [James Henry] Breasted, the great Egyptologist and Orientalist. At the time, he was connected with the Field Museum and the Oriental Institute in Chicago. It's amazing that he even took the time to write to me. I had no idea how much would be involved in order to become an Egyptologist. But I still thought that I probably would be an archaeologist.*[5] The more she read about Egyptology, the more interested she became in the subject of archaeology.

FIGURE 4 Elizabeth Wattson Ferguson with her two daughters. Marjorie Elizabeth is on her lap and Helen Mary is standing, ca. 1908–9. Courtesy of the Colorado Springs Pioneers Museum.

While still in high school, Marjorie came across A. V. Kidder's *An Introduction to the Study of Southwestern Archaeology*,[6] which, according to James Snead, "was both a landmark effort to pull together information about the southwestern past and a symbol of the rise of a new generation of archaeologists."[7] This was one of the first scientifically written archaeological publications about the Southwest that Marjorie had ventured upon, and it made a significant impression on her. Another publication that captured her attention was Sylvanus Griswold Morley's *The Inscriptions at Copan*.[8]

Marjorie graduated from General Palmer Colorado Springs High School in 1926 and was officially placed in its Alumni Hall of Fame in 1995. An early interest in the Southwest had been kindled, and it would eventually lead her to a lifetime of achievement in and dedication to southwestern archaeology. It was a path she would follow from her first years of study at Colorado College to her long association with the Museum of New Mexico and the School of American Research in Santa Fe, New Mexico.[9]

Colorado College: An Introduction to Southwestern Archaeology

In the early decades of the twentieth century, young women generally were not encouraged to seek a higher education in colleges or universities. Those who did generally attended normal schools and women's colleges, where they focused on the traditional studies of education, social studies, and the domestic arts. As Alice B. Kehoe observes, "Scientists, including archaeologists, were modern heroes exploring vast phenomena of the universe to capture facts," whereas "people hobbled by skirts could not fit the image." She continues to point out that "women's colleges perpetuated the stereotype by orienting their students toward careers designed to alleviate social problems, where women's nurturant proclivities would be appropriate."[10] Unlike most young women at the time, Marjorie had a very different experience than what was expected of her.

Coming from a well-read and educated family background, it is no surprise that Marjorie and her siblings entered college upon graduating from high school. As Marjorie noted,

An education was paramount as far as my father was concerned. I think my mother wanted her daughters to be raised as ladies and eventually marry and be housewives and mothers. I'm sure that's what she had in mind because

that was her background. . . . I think my father was very, very proud of me.
He's the one [who] encouraged us to be scholars. . . . They both wanted us to
get good grades and amount to something. They wanted us to have a college
education. I would say that they probably had the equivalent of a junior
college education. . . . My father was a very scholarly and well-read man. . . .
My mother, who gave up her interest in painting to raise a family, felt that a
young woman should be a librarian or a teacher.[11]

Of course, being a librarian or a teacher was considered a culturally and
socially acceptable career choice for young single women at the time. Despite
this, Marjorie chose a different career path.

Mr. Ferguson had planned to send his three children away to college, but
money was tight. It was the beginning of the Great Depression, so instead, all
three of the Ferguson children lived at home and attended Colorado College
for their undergraduate degrees.[12] At the time that the Ferguson siblings
were attending Colorado College, it was a small liberal arts college in the
Harvard Exchange Program, which included lectures by visiting professors
from Harvard University and other institutions. W. W. Postlethwaite, the
college bursar and business manager, was the director of the college's small
museum, where Marjorie worked part-time. He knew several archaeologists
and invited them to give lectures at the college, in private homes, and at
other public places in Colorado Springs.

While attending Colorado College, Marjorie was introduced to Edgar
Lee Hewett and Sylvanus Griswold Morley, by Lewis Abbott, a social anthropologist and head of the department. Abbott thought that his students
should have courses in archaeology, so he would invite Hewett and Morley
to be guest lecturers in his anthropology classes. At the time, Hewett was
the director of the School of American Research (SAR) and the Museum of
New Mexico (MNM) in Santa Fe, and was teaching courses on southwestern
archaeology and ethnology at the University of New Mexico (UNM). Morley,
the famous authority on the ancient Maya, was also with the SAR.

Morley, who was fascinated with lost civilizations and archaeology, met
Hewett while he was studying the Maya at Harvard University. Morley
learned of Hewett's archaeological field school in southwest Colorado, and
in the summer of 1907 he and two other Harvard students, Alfred Vincent
Kidder and John Gould Fletcher, left the East Coast to conduct archaeological fieldwork there.[13] On their first day, Hewett took them to the confluence

of Yellow Jacket and McElmo Canyons, where they were told to conduct an archaeological survey and map the area. Morley returned to the Southwest the following year as a field assistant, along with John Peabody Harrington, to work at the large archaeological site of Tyuonyi in the Canyon de los Frijoles in New Mexico. In 1909, Hewett hired both Morley and Harrington as part of the staff of the School of American Archaeology, which would become known as the School of American Research in 1919, in Santa Fe.[14]

Postlethwaite, who was also on the Board of Managers of the SAR, encouraged Marjorie to keep in touch with Hewett and to think about going into archaeology. It was this series of guest lectures by Hewett and Morley on southwestern and Mayan archaeology and ethnology that steered Marjorie away from Egyptology or social studies, another area of interest, and instead toward a career in southwestern archaeology. Even though Marjorie's father had a tremendous influence on her earlier years, it would be Edgar Lee Hewett who would have the most profound impact on the direction that her life and career would take.

At Colorado College, Marjorie was a member of Pi Gamma Mu, an interdisciplinary social science honor society. She earned a little extra cash while working in the Colorado College Museum for twenty-five cents an hour.[15] She received her bachelor's degree in Social Anthropology in 1930. During her senior year at Colorado College, she received the Alice Van Diest Award for Excellence in Social Studies, and in 1988 the college presented Marjorie with the Louis T. Benezet Award. Louis T. Benezet was the eighth president of Colorado College (1955–63). The college's alumni association presents the Louis T. Benezet Award to recognize outstanding achievement in one's chosen field, and excellence through unusual success in innovation or research that has advanced a cause or improved the quality of life.

Next Step: Graduate School

Upon graduation from Colorado College, Marjorie had to decide what to do next. While reflecting on the choices available to her as a young woman at the end of the 1920s, Marjorie made this observation:

I can look back now and see how different my life could have been. I had three fellowships offered to me. One was from the University of New Mexico in Archaeology, as they called the department then, and History, which was a separate department. Or, I could have gone to Smith College and majored in social welfare work. Or, I could have gone to New York and studied at [Columbia University's] School of Social Work. Of course, I have always been a great admirer of people like Ruth Benedict, and I look back now and think of what life would have been like if I had gone to New York and become attached to Ruth Benedict when she was so prominent in the field. I probably would have met Franz Boas too because he was still alive then. I just somehow had the feeling that if you're going to be any good in the world, you'd better get to the basics of things. So I took the fellowship at the University of New Mexico.[16]

During Hewett's visits to Colorado Springs, Marjorie had opportunities to discuss her future educational and career possibilities with him. He was a powerful and intimidating man, so Marjorie was surprised to find that she had made such a favorable impression on him. She recalled, *After I had my first interview with Hewett, I was amazed to receive from him, three or four months later, an invitation to join the graduate school at the University of New Mexico.*[17]

Hewett, Morley, and Postlethwaite were insistent on the Southwest as an ideal locale for Marjorie's future studies and clearly influenced her decision. She accepted a research-teaching fellowship at UNM and began her graduate studies there in the fall of 1930. She didn't realize at the time that there was only one fellowship available and that she was the top contender when the fellowship was offered to her. This presented her with a problem that surprised her. Some of the students reacted negatively toward her for receiving this fellowship—all the other applicants were men. She clearly noticed some resentment toward her and remarked, *I didn't know why two of them didn't like me very well. I found out soon enough though. They were jealous.*[18] This attitude toward Marjorie would haunt her throughout her career as she faced ongoing sexism and discrimination, whether intentional or not.

Hewett, much like Boas in the East, was instrumental in opening doors for women to study and work in southwestern anthropology, archaeology, and museums. Other male mentors at the time were Byron Cummings, known as the dean of southwestern archaeology, who provided opportunities for Florence Hawley (Ellis) and Clara Lee Frapps (Tanner) at the University of Arizona, and Harold Colton at the Museum of Northern Arizona, who gave Katherine Bartlett her start in a museum career.

On the other hand, there were few women mentors in anthropology other than Ruth Benedict, Elsie Clews Parsons, and Ruth Bunzel at the time. Although these early pioneer women in southwestern anthropology influenced Marjorie a great deal, she points out their lack of visibility: *They were never around when I was in the field. They never came to any of the field camps that I was in. They never came to any of my excavations. I just never had any opportunity to really work with any women archaeologists or ethnologists. It really was sort of a beginning science as far as stratigraphy and excavation and so on were concerned.*[19]

Marjorie reflected on her long-term relationship with Hewett:

> *I think if I was to classify Hewett in the beginning . . . I think that Hewett was a leader and a pioneer and I also think he had a vision. A lot of people have criticized him because they think that he extended himself probably too widely, and perhaps he did, but if you stop and think of the organizations that he backed or that he thought of during his career, he was fantastic. The first field schools in the training of anthropologists in New Mexico, and coming from Washington, D.C., to be the director of the School of American Archaeology . . . with the backing of Alice Fletcher and Adolph Bandelier and so on. He just went on from there. At the time of his death, Hewett was even talking about opening a branch in South America and in Mexico. . . . He was the first director [of the Museum of New Mexico and the School of American Research] and a professor in the Department of Anthropology at the University of New Mexico, and that's why I came here. It was to study archaeology, I thought. It turned out to be something much bigger than that!*[20]

With her bachelor's degree in hand, she left Colorado Springs to begin her graduate studies at UNM.

Prior to attending classes at the University, however, Marjorie got her first hands-on experience as a "dirt archaeologist" in August 1930. When Hewett became the first head of the University of New Mexico's Department of Archaeology and Anthropology in 1927, he instituted a program of highly successful field schools under the sponsorship of the SAR and UNM. Hewett set up a summer field school for beginning archaeologists at Battleship Rock in the Jemez Mountains in northern New Mexico in 1921 and initiated a program for advanced students at Chaco Canyon in western New Mexico in 1929. Many of the next generation of leaders in Southwest and Mesoamerican archaeology trained and/or taught at Chaco Canyon, including Marjorie Lambert, Bertha Dutton, Florence Hawley Ellis, Anna O. Shepard, Stanley Stubbs, Gordon Vivian, and Paul Reiter.[21]

Marjorie has often commented that once she got her hands in the dirt, she never looked back. Her life and career as a New Mexico archaeologist began with a trowel in her hands at the Battleship Rock Field School. She went on to make a major contribution to the history of archaeology in New Mexico, and to the growth of the Museum of New Mexico and the School of American Research. She shares her experiences and memories of her life as a young woman excavating, working, and living among the sage and piñon of New Mexico's high desert throughout these pages.

CHAPTER 2

"I'm Going to Be an Archaeologist!"

> I just like the sort of challenge that prehistory seems to give, the mystery of it . . . and finding out about people, why they think the way they do, and what makes human history. . . . Digging is the part that's fun, being outdoors and digging. I don't think there is anything I love more.
>
> —MARJORIE LAMBERT[1]

Marjorie Ferguson's career as a southwestern archaeologist began with an invitation from Edgar Lee Hewett to attend an archaeological field school at the Battleship Rock Field Camp in the Jemez Mountains in 1930. Already accepted into the graduate program at the University of New Mexico, her interest in archaeology was redirected as she learned more about the Southwest and experienced hands-on training in excavation techniques in the field. At the same time, her interest in Pueblo Indian cultures and ethnology was sparked as she was trained by, and worked alongside, some of the Pueblo men that Hewett hired as laborers on his archaeological projects.

Institution Builder, Teacher, and Mentor

Much has been written about Edgar Lee Hewett, who was a key figure in southwestern anthropology and archaeology for forty years. He trained several archaeologists who went on to gain recognition in the profession. He also played a pivotal role in Marjorie's professional life.

Hewett founded the School of American Archaeology in 1907 and the Museum of New Mexico in 1909. He directed both until his death in 1946 at the age of eighty-two. He also organized the exhibits at the San Diego Panama-California Exposition in 1915 and was a professor of anthropology at San Diego State Teachers College from 1915 to 1928. As part of his ongoing efforts at institution building, Hewett became a professor of anthropology at the University of New Mexico in 1929 and helped found the Anthropology Department at the University of Southern California in 1934.[2]

The New Mexico Territorial Legislature granted the School of American Archaeology the use of Santa Fe's historic Palace of the Governors as its permanent home on February 19, 1909. Hewett, along with Frank Springer, a prominent citizen and attorney from Las Vegas, New Mexico, and others lobbied for use of the building for this purpose. The legislature stated that Hewett's sponsor, the American Institute of Archaeology, was to use the Palace "for the seat of the School and the Museum of American Archaeology which museum shall be the Museum of New Mexico."[3] According to Malinda Elliott, "Hewett and his supporters saw the School and its Museum as part of a cultural complex that would some day evolve into a sort of 'Smithsonian of the West.' The School was the administrative, research, and academic center of the institution; the Museum of New Mexico served as the interpretive, public education branch."[4] Hewett and his supporters felt that by having the School, a private organization, serve as the administrator of the Museum of New Mexico, it would be protected from the machinations of state politics. The complexities of this relationship are still being worked out over a century later. It was during this period at the height of Hewett's powerful career that Marjorie left Colorado for New Mexico.

The school and the museum were intricately connected in the beginning by one director and a shared staff. As the director, Hewett hired John Peabody Harrington and Sylvanus Griswold Morley on the staff of the school and Kenneth Chapman and Jesse Nusbaum on the staff of the museum.[5] From the start, Hewett was stubborn and contentious, and his management style was highly personal and authoritarian. His staff and adversaries referred to him as "El Toro." Between 1904 and 1930, Hewett often clashed bitterly with members of the eastern establishment and was vilified and slandered by his enemies in both the East and in Santa Fe.

In her history of the School of American Research, Malinda Elliott noted, "The work of numerous young archaeologists, many of whom later became giants in the field, augmented the School's early activities. Among these scientists were Hewett's students and staff as well as archaeologists and anthropologists from institutions cooperating with the School under the name of the Archaeological Institute of America."[6] Many of the students in the School of American Archaeology Summer Field School at El Rito de los Frijoles in 1910 included such renowned archaeologists and anthropologists as John P. Harrington, Frederick Webb Hodge, Neil Judd, Barbara Friere-Marreco, Sylvanus Morley, Kenneth Chapman, Jesse Nusbaum, Nathan Goldsmith, Junius Henderson, W. W. Robbins, Donald Bearegard, Maude Woy, and J. P. Adams. Adolph Bandelier was also an early member of the school's staff, and he continued to support Hewett until his death in 1914.

Ten years after its founding, Hewett changed the name to the School of American Research—a name he believed covered the broad scope of inter-disciplinary scholarship that he considered to be its wide-ranging mission. Hewett is remembered as a flamboyant, innovative figure who left his mark on the preservation of ancient and historic sites and the development of southwestern archaeology. He promoted the artwork of Native Americans in particular the work of Maria and Julian Martinez of San Ildefonso Pueblo. Hewett trained numerous archaeology students and was especially encouraging to young women. Marjorie not only was introduced to southwestern archaeology by Hewett and Morley but she was also trained by them and eventually worked side by side with them.

SAR-UNM Archaeological Field School in the Jemez Mountains in 1930

Some of Marjorie's happiest memories were of the early archaeology field schools she attended. *The first archaeological field camp I attended was in the Jemez Mountains. The museum, SAR, and UNM were excavating the little site of Unshagi in the Jemez Mountains and that's really how I happened to come to New Mexico. Once I got my hands in the dirt, I never left.*[7]

Getting to the Battleship Rock Field Camp in August 1930 was the first of many adventures Marjorie would experience as she struck out on her own.

They sent the instructions to me from the office of the University of New Mexico. I was told to report for the first field session. I was scared to death. I had never done any archaeology in my life. Hewett said, "Whatever you do, you are going to have to learn how to dig." He said that I could come to his dig up in the Jemez Mountains. This was the rock-bottom Depression. My father had one child through college, my sister. She was in graduate school by then in Michigan. Here I was, and then I had a younger brother that still had to be educated and Colorado College was a very expensive school. There was really very little money. . . .

So, I came on the train and my mother was so naïve that she didn't even have any idea what it would cost or anything. They bought my ticket, a lower berth, and my clothes had been sent on to the university, which I was to pick up in the fall. I had a bedroll, and I had some field clothes that they bought for me. I had fifteen dollars. [My mother] said she didn't want me going to a hotel because it is very dangerous for a young girl alone. She told me to go to the YWCA.

I got off the train in Albuquerque. It was my first real sight of the Alvarado Hotel. . . . I looked around the Alvarado Hotel and wondered, Well, where is the YWCA? Then I thought, I'm not going to go there. I'm just going to take my suitcase and start walking. I thought I surely could find something near the university. I asked someone which direction the University of New Mexico was in and they pointed way out east toward the Sandia Mountains. I started up Central. It was a very hot day. It was early August.[8]

Marjorie had walked for quite some time when she came across a little house with a sign saying, "Room and Breakfast, $1.50."

I went up to the house and rang the doorbell and the sweetest old lady came to the door. I told her who I was and that I was looking for the University of New Mexico, but that the trucks wouldn't be going to camp until the next morning. She told me to come in and that she would take care of me. It was a very tiny house. It was spotlessly clean. She gave me a little front bedroom and she fed me that night, a very simple meal but good. She told me she wanted me to be nice and clean so she heated the water so that I could have a bath that night. She asked me about my parents and where I was from and so on. And then she sent me on my way at a quarter to eight the next morning.

Marjorie described the scene that met her when she arrived at the university: *They were out on the main part of the campus with all the camp equipment. I climbed up on one of the trucks with the bedrolls and went to Jemez.*[9]

The annual archaeological summer field school at Jemez Springs opened on August 4, 1930.[10] Prior to arriving at their field camp, Hewett took the UNM students to a Corn Dance at Santo Domingo Pueblo, where he provided a lecture on the ceremony they were witnessing. The next day they stopped at Sandia Pueblo and the ancient Tiguex Pueblos across the Rio Grande from Bernalillo that had been invaded by Coronado. Afterward, they stopped at Zia and Jemez Pueblos and some archaeological sites before arriving at the Battleship Rock Field Camp in time to set up camp and settle in before starting their fieldwork the next morning.[11]

The field camp at Battleship Rock was in the vicinity of Unshagi (LA 123), Nanishagi (LA 541), and Giusewa (LA 679), which were archaeological sites located six miles north of Jemez Springs. The field camp was in an open area below Battleship Rock. There was a series of two-person tents around the perimeter that were equipped with army cots, study tables, camp chairs, a wash basin, and water pail. Edwin Ferdon, who attended the SAR-UNM Field School, recalled that the "toilet facilities consisted of two outhouses situated at the top of a rather abrupt rise. After a heavy rain, it was always a question whether one could make it to the top . . . without skidding down in the mud."[12] The field camp would often flood when there was a heavy rainfall, and the food was limited and not very tasty.

Arriving at the SAR-UNM field camp was unlike anything Marjorie had experienced before. *The first thing they did was put us in pairs. It was kind of a big camp. The students were from all over. Some of them were very interesting.*[13] The field camp housed about a hundred students, along with faculty members and assistants. The UNM enrollment in the archaeology camp was

FIGURE 5 Field camp, Battleship Rock, Jemez, New Mexico, ca. 1925. Photo by Sam Hudelson. Courtesy of the Palace of the Governors Photo Archives (NMHM/DCA). Neg. No. 127882.

about fifty students; the other students came from "Bryn Mawr, Columbia, Leland Stanford, Monticello Seminary, North Texas College, Ohio State College, Pomona College, San Diego State College, Scripps College, University of Arizona, University of Illinois, University of North Carolina, University of Southern California, University of Wisconsin, Vassar College, New Mexico Normal University."[14] Marjorie's tent mate was Jane Howard, who later penned *Margaret Mead: A Life.*[15]

Marjorie recalled what the average day was like: *We would go down to the dig in the morning, and then we would have lectures in the afternoon and then lectures around a big bonfire at night, or if it happened to be a ceremonial day, we would go to the nearest Pueblo. The first day I was told to take Jose Rey Toledo with me to the site. He was one of the boys in the Indian camp. We had about ten or twelve Indian boys to help us because it was a big excavation.*[16] The field school included classes in geology, biology, anthropology, and archaeology, of which the latter two were of most interest and attended by more than half the students.[17]

During this field school, Marjorie had her first introduction to Pueblo ceremonies when she attended dances at Santo Domingo and Jemez Pueblos.

FIGURE 6 Marjorie in front of one of the Battleship Rock camp tents with colleagues Doc Penny (left) and J. Webb (right), 1930. Courtesy of the Archives, Museum of Indian Arts & Culture, Lab of Anthropology. Neg. No. 70.842.

FIGURE 7 Edgar L. Hewett (in pith helmet) giving a lecture to students during the excavation at Unshagi, Jemez, New Mexico, ca. 1928. Courtesy of the Palace of the Governors Photo Archives (NMHM/DCA). Neg. No. 090141.

It wasn't long before the students developed their own memorable culture, with songs and stories that they recorded in a journal called *Digs*. Some of these were published in *El Palacio*.[18]

Marjorie's first exposure to field archaeology was at the fourteenth-century Jemez ancestral site of Unshagi that summer. As reported by Paul Reiter,

> [Unshagi] is situated on a little hill at the foot of the steep west talus slope of San Diego Canyon, 150 feet from the Jemez River, and more than twenty feet above it. Its altitude varies from 6,726 to 6,755 feet. The site is three-eighths of a mile below the junction of the Jemez and East Fork. Bounded on the east and west sides by small arroyos, which are dry except in the event of heavy rain, the site conforms to the contours of the original slope with room floors varying considerably in their elevation. The pile of debris, which marked the site before the beginning of partial excavation, accentuated these contours.[19]

Prior to excavation, the Jemez Springs-La Cueva highway had cut through the lower parts of the site separating the rooms on the riverbank from the main portion of the site.

The SAR and UNM were involved in excavations at Unshagi from 1928 to 1934. Michael Elliott best summarizes Reiter's 1938 report on Unshagi with the following description of the site:

Unshagi consists of several room blocks enclosing a rough quadrangular plaza area. Approximately two-thirds of the site and 101 rooms were excavated. Reiter estimated portions of the site had three stories. Using his story estimates, and extrapolating them to the unexcavated areas, the site would have contained 263 rooms. Three kivas, some detached rooms, and several midden areas where numerous burials were also excavated. . . .

The masonry at Unhasgi was constructed of unshaped, uncoursed, and uneven-sized elements, using large amounts of mortar, spalls, wedges, and chinks. The walls were constructed primarily from flow breccias, sandstone and other conglomerates, and rhyolite. The most exterior walls of the pueblo had no openings. Entry was probably by ladders and through roof openings. Features within rooms included the floor features . . . (bins, vents, firepits, deflectors, and benches), and small crypts or cavities in the walls, postholes, and sub-floor cists. One of the cists was jar-shaped, 4 feet 10 inches deep, and 3 feet 7 inches in its maximum diameter. The opening on the floor was 2 feet in diameter. The cist was filled with large, damp boulders. Reiter believed the cist was used for water storage. The cist could have held 145 gallons of water.[20]

While Marjorie was excited to learn about southwestern archaeology, the first couple of days at Unshagi proved to be more challenging than she had expected. It was there that she encountered blatant sexism and discrimination for the first time. Marjorie quickly discovered that there were some male students in the camp who clearly did not want women in the field and considered archaeology to be their sacred domain. When she first arrived at the site, Marjorie recalled that

Paul Reiter and Gordon Vivian were in charge of the work at Unshagi. Sid Stallings was there doing tree ring work too. It was very difficult in the Jemez Mountains. But they didn't seem to want to help us. I had no instruction on how to use a trowel or a shovel or anything. When are you supposed to shovel? When are you supposed to pick? What do you do? How do you find what you're going to work on? What Reiter said to Jose [Jose Rey Toledo] was,

"You pick out a room for her and let her go to it." Well, it was a rock pueblo, of course, and very hard to dig. I think he [Jose] was my real instructor. I think that whole summer working with Indians of different sorts and in different types of situations is how I really learned to be an archaeologist.[21]

Not only did the site supervisors refuse to teach field techniques to the female students; Marjorie also claimed that

the men would see to it that you got the dirtiest jobs! They played the dirtiest tricks on me, but . . . I caught on pretty quick. They would sit up under the ramada and talk about archaeology and leave someone like me to take out the baby burials and say, "Oh, she is so maternal. Let's get her to take out the baby burials." I did that about three times and then I realized what they were doing. They were leaving these little things with tiny bones that moved. They are the hardest things to uncover and not move a bone.[22] *I caught on and I said, "I am not maternal! You're paternal! You uncover that. I will take out my burials and you take out your own." I would say it in a nice way and they would laugh at me.*[23]

As frustrated as she was at times, she never let these incidences in the field discourage her.

During that first season, female and male students were treated differently in the field camp as well. Marjorie recalled:

[The males] kind of chummed around with Paul Reiter. I think he liked the men students around him. In that first season we also had a pair of physical anthropologists, Drs. [George and Edna] Woodbury. . . . They were very standoffish. They didn't give lectures at night. . . . They wanted to excavate the skeletal materials, but they wouldn't show us how to do it. But Jose Rey Toledo and I found a skeleton, a burial, in the room we were working in. Jose, with my tools, which I'd been told to buy, showed me how to do it. The Indians are so careful and so sensitive about things like that. So, I think I really had my basic instruction from an Indian. We also had a kiva, which was in the process of being excavated. . . . [Hewett] didn't come down on the dig. He didn't participate really, but he would give us instructions or give the background of the purpose of the kiva and what it came from, the Sipapu and Mother Earth.[24]

In addition to training students in archaeological field techniques, Hewett's field camps introduced university students and paying participants to professors and scientists in other fields. Marjorie recalled:

Those camps of Dr. Hewett's in the Jemez Mountains were internationally famous. He had participants from all over the world. He had a perfectly wonderful faculty. He had geologists. He had mythologists and philosophers. There was [American philosopher] Hartley Burr Alexander, the mythology of all races expert.[25] *He was there. Dr. Stuart Northrop for geology. We had several different botanists and biologists. Hewett himself lectured on the prehistory of the Southwest and provided background information particularly on the Zia Indians. And then Jemez Pueblo with the Jemez and Pecos Indians. Those were the first Indians that I met and worked with. . . . I knew from that early work that that's where I wanted to be. [I told myself] "I'm going to be an archaeologist. I'm not going to go on into social anthropology or anything else, I'm going to be an archaeologist!"*[26]

It was at the Battleship Rock Field Camp that many of Marjorie's lifelong friendships began, both professionally and personally. During the summer of 1930, Marjorie met Edwin N. Ferdon Jr., an archaeology student from Ohio. Marjorie and Ed danced on the tables in the mess tent that first year and became lifelong friends. Jose Rey Toledo also became a lifelong friend. Born in Jemez Pueblo in 1915, Toledo would have been about fifteen years old when he worked at Unshagi in 1930. He went on to the University of New Mexico, where he received both his bachelor's and master's degrees in arts education and taught and practiced the art of painting. He received numerous awards for his paintings, which can be found in the collections of museums and universities throughout the nation.[27]

Despite some of the difficulties Marjorie experienced with some of the male crew members, this first field experience had a dramatic and positive impact on her. She often said, *Once I got my hands and feet in the dirt that was it. I knew that I had come to the place that I wanted to be.*[28] It was this first experience in the field as a "dirt archaeologist" that led her down a very different path than she had anticipated or that was expected of her as a young woman in the early 1930s.

After leaving the Battleship Rock Field Camp, Marjorie headed to Albuquerque to begin her graduate studies at the University of New Mexico.

While at UNM, Marjorie majored in anthropology and minored in southwestern and Latin American history, which were taught by France Scholes. She also took a course on Indian art from Kenneth Chapman.

Second Field Season in the Jemez Mountains, 1931

Hewett ran two archaeology field schools in New Mexico during the summer, one in the Jemez Mountains and the other at Chaco Canyon. As a graduate student, Marjorie was able to take advantage of both field camps. She recalled:

> *The way the field camps worked, the undergraduates, the ones who hadn't had fieldwork before, went up into the Jemez Mountains. The ones who had a little bit more experience and had been in the field at Unshagi went to Chaco. And then they went back and forth. Each summer it was six weeks in each camp. Of course, we got to the point where we realized we loved staying at Jemez because, heavens, there was a nice big river to bathe in and wash your clothes and it was cool and rained a lot. . . . And we got to go down to Jemez Pueblo quite a bit and trade with the Indians and get familiar with them and the Pueblo.*[29]

Marjorie returned for another field season in the Jemez Mountains in 1931, which proved to be a somewhat different experience for her. It was during this field season that preliminary work under the supervision of Gordon Vivian was carried out at Nanishagi.[30] The purpose of excavations at Nanishagi was to compare this site to Unshagi. That summer, Vivian focused on stratigraphic work and the removal of burials. During the SAR-UNM Field Schools at Nanishagi in 1931, 1936, and 1938, "nine rooms and one kiva were excavated, and two midden areas were test excavated. The site was found to be very similar to Unshagi architecturally."[31]

This second field school experience offered more opportunities for Marjorie and the other students to explore the area. *In connection with Nanishagi we were allowed, with supervision at first and then on our own, to do quite a bit of climbing there. There were great big sites up on the sides of San Diego Canyon. . . . These were very hard climbs. Several thousand feet up to some of them . . . most of them were refugee sites. The Indians set those up when they learned that the Spaniards had discovered Jemez Hot Springs. Of course, that was a sacred place to the Indians. They came there from all over for their [religious] rites.*[32]

Marjorie recalled that *the students just loved that next season. . . . We had Clyde Kluckhohn as our physical anthropologist. By that time Dr. Hewett had let me graduate to being in charge of the tent, where we washed potsherds and cleaned the bone material. We did do a little bit of work with the skeletons, but we left that mostly to Clyde and his group. Also, I taught them how to restore pottery. I was pretty good at it and they loved doing that.*[33]

Hewett didn't want the students to leave his field camps at night, but Marjorie and some of her fellow campmates would sneak off to visit with the Indian crew members camped out in the Jemez Mountains. *We would go over there at the Indian encampment at night and, if we could, we would swipe a little food from the kitchen, which I managed to do on one occasion. Then we would lay everything out and the Indians would lay out what they had. They always had cornmeal or tortillas or something. But it didn't matter; even if we just had water, we would sing, and they'd teach us all the Indian songs that they thought we could remember and play the drums softly.*[34]

Marjorie shared a story about one night when she and another raided the camp kitchen:

The students thought I was a little bit elevated because Hewett had appointed me to be in charge of the tent . . . [and] they said, "You look so innocent . . . you go down to the kitchen. They made pies late this afternoon." One of the kitchen boys told me this. So, I went down there in the dark and I got a pie. And then I looked over because I thought I heard something on the other side of the mess tent. There was the shadow of a man standing there and I thought they'd come down to spy on me and I was going to get kicked out of camp. So, I stood there absolutely frozen. I hid the pie in back of me, hoping I wouldn't drop it, and suddenly this man moved forward a little bit and he said, "Is that you, Marjorie?" And I said, "Yes, I'm afraid it is." And I thought, Well here it goes. *He said, "I didn't mean to scare you. I was just leaving. Everything's all right. You go first and then I'll go." I noticed he kept his hands in back of him, the way I had mine in back of me. So, I said, "You won't see me down here again, Clyde." I left and I knew I was in trouble. Anyway, I had the pie. I went over to the Indian encampment and who should be on the other side of the fire but Clyde Kluckhohn. He'd stolen a ham! . . . We could have gone on a raid! We both just laughed. And the Indians laughed too. They thought*

that was awfully funny. . . . We had a wonderful relationship, and they were
my friends to their deaths. They would often come to the university or the
museum to see me.[35]

A number of clay objects interpreted as having a ceremonial purpose
were excavated at Unshagi and Nanishagi, including miniature clay vessels,
effigies, and pipes. Marjorie reported on one of these items that was later interpreted as a pottery bell in 1958.[36] In addition to her ongoing training at the
Battleship Rock Field School, Marjorie now had the education and required
field experience to work part of the summer at Chaco Canyon as a graduate
student. After working at Nanishagi for about six weeks, she went to Chaco
Canyon to work on Hewett's ongoing excavation at Chetro Ketl for the rest
of the 1931 SAR-UNM summer archaeological field school.

CHAPTER 3

Chaco Canyon Archaeology Field School

1931

> There is a real mystery about Chaco Canyon, the kind on which archaeologists thrive.
>
> —DOUGLAS W. SCHWARTZ[1]

I open this chapter with a quote from Douglas Schwartz, who was president of the School of American Research when "New Light on Chaco Canyon" was published in 1984.[2] This was the first publication I read to Marjorie as she was rapidly losing her eyesight. As I read, Marjorie recalled her field experiences at Chaco Canyon in the 1930s, and we discussed various topics about southwestern archaeology, her relationship with Edgar Lee Hewett, and what it was like being a woman in the field of archaeology and in museums. But before we go into Marjorie's experience, I provide a brief overview of the importance of Chaco Canyon and what it means to our understanding of the ancient Southwest and the early years of Americanist archaeology.

A Brief Overview of Excavations and Research at Chaco Canyon

Chaco Canyon, a center of intellectual debate and rivalries among archaeologists, is a mysterious place rich in cultural history. Between 850 and 1250 CE, Chaco Canyon served as a major urban center for the Ancestral Puebloans.[3] Remarkable for its monumental public and ceremonial structures, engineering projects, astronomy, artistic achievements, and distinctive architecture, it served as a hub of ceremony, trade, and administration for the Four Corners area of the Southwest for four hundred years. Since people left the area around 1250 CE, members of culturally affiliated clans and religious societies from the present-day Hopi and New Mexico Pueblos have continuously returned to Chaco Canyon on pilgrimages to honor their ancestral homelands.

The Pueblo Revolt of 1680 briefly unified the Pueblo peoples of New Mexico and their allied neighbors, and they expelled Spanish settlers from the Southwest. Twelve years later in 1692, the Spanish reentered New Mexico, forcing many Puebloans into exile, with some finding refuge with the Navajo (Diné) living in the Dinetah region northeast of Chaco Canyon. These cultural interactions resulted in intermarriage, the exchange of ceremonial knowledge, as well as conflict and competition. By the 1700s, Navajo (Diné) settlement patterns were well established in Chaco Canyon. Soon Spanish and American explorers would follow.

A map produced by Don Bernardo de Miera y Pacheco in 1774 identified the Chaco Canyon area. In 1823 Jose Antonio Viscarra led a military force west from Jemez Pueblo onto Navajo lands and noted many fallen Chacoan-style buildings along the way. His route became a well-used trail for forty years. The Washington Expedition, a military reconnaissance under the direction of Lt. James Simpson, surveyed Navajo lands in 1849 and wrote accounts of Chacoan ancestral sites. On a U.S. Geological Survey led by Ferdinand Vandeveer Hayden in 1877, William Henry Jackson photographed ancestral sites and produced expanded descriptions and maps of Chaco Canyon. Victor and Cosmos Mindeleff of the Bureau of American Ethnology spent six weeks in Chaco Canyon surveying and photographing the major ancestral sites for a monumental study of pueblo architecture in 1888.

It is no surprise that Chaco Canyon became a major site for looting and scientific exploration. After excavating Mesa Verde cliff dwellings and other Ancestral Puebloan sites in the Four Corners area, Richard Wetherill moved to Chaco Canyon in 1896 to excavate sites there. With Wetherill's assistance, the Hyde Exploring Expedition, led by George H. Pepper from the American Museum of Natural History in New York City, carried out full-scale excavations at Pueblo Bonito between 1896 and 1900. The primary focus of the Hyde Exploring Expedition was the accumulation of artifacts for the museum collection, and numerous crates packed with artifacts from Pueblo Bonito were shipped to the museum in New York City, where they remain today. In 1901 Richard Wetherill homesteaded land in Chaco Canyon that included Pueblo Bonito, Pueblo Del Arroyo, and Chetro Ketl.

Soon Edgar Lee Hewett became involved in archaeological excavations at Chaco Canyon. Hewett with his wife, Cora, and a small group of students and faculty from the New Mexico Normal School (now New Mexico Highlands University) in Las Vegas, spent a week at Pueblo Bonito in 1902. Assisted by Navajo laborers, his group excavated and made maps of the ancestral sites that had been extensively excavated previously by the Hyde Exploring Expeditions.[4] It wouldn't be long, however, before Chaco Canyon and the Southwest in general would attract anthropologists and archaeologists from other eastern institutions. It seems that anything having to do with Hewett met with controversy, and his field school and excavations at Chaco Canyon were no exception.

Between 1904 and 1930, Hewett was a dominant figure in southwestern archaeology. Don D. Fowler aptly summarizes the contest that emerged for control of southwestern archaeology during this time period. Hewett and "his supporters clashed with various archaeological and other members of the 'Eastern Establishment' over policies, professional standards, and control of key institutions and the funds to operate them."[5] Competition between eastern institution archaeologists and Hewett, with his institution building and archaeological field schools in the Southwest, became especially fierce over Chaco Canyon in the 1920s. But before this, Hewett worked to prevent easterners and locals, such as the Wetherills, from looting the archaeological sites in the Southwest to fill museums in the East.

Hewett, among others, pushed Congress to enact the Federal Antiquities Act of 1906, which was the first law to protect antiquities and archaeological sites in the United States. The Antiquities Act forbids the unauthorized excavation of archaeological materials on or the removal and collection of archaeological materials from federally controlled lands and was a direct consequence of the controversy surrounding Wetherill's work and that of the Hyde Exploring Expeditions. The law also granted new powers to the president of the United States to declare by public proclamation historic and prehistoric landmarks as national monuments. Under this act, President Theodore Roosevelt established Mesa Verde National Monument in southwest Colorado in 1906 and Chaco Canyon National Monument in 1907. Richard Wetherill relinquished his claim on several parcels of land he held in Chaco Canyon and continued to homestead and operate a trading post at Pueblo Bonito until his controversial murder in 1910. On December 19, 1980, Chaco Canyon National Monument was renamed Chaco Culture National Historic Park and was designated a UNESCO World Heritage Site in 1987.

In the early twentieth century, numerous anthropologists supported by eastern museums and universities were working in the Southwest. The independently wealthy Elsie Clews Parsons was conducting ethnographic research in the Southwest by 1915. Franz Boas, who much like Hewett supported young women anthropologists, had a number of his students conducting ethnographic work in the Southwest, including Ruth Benedict, Ruth Bunzel, Gladys Reichard, and Esther Goldfrank.[6] As Don Fowler points out,

> Hewett had few objections to ethnographic research in the Southwest. But the continued influx of eastern archaeologists was troublesome. In 1920–21, some of the easterners staged an invasion of Chaco Canyon, which Hewett regarded as his private preserve since he had helped run out the Wetherills and the Hyde Expeditions in 1902. The invasion was doubly offensive to Hewett because it was engineered by three of "his" former students, Neil M. Judd, A.V. Kidder, and Sylvanus Griswold Morley, aided and abetted by former employees Earl H. Morris and Jesse Nusbaum. Kenneth Chapman, a current employee of the Museum of New Mexico, helped from behind the scenes in Santa Fe. Furthermore, Hewett had in place an elaborate cooperative agreement in 1916 with the Smithsonian Institution and the Royal Ontario Museum of Toronto, Canada, to work in Chaco Canyon. The plan was delayed by World War I.[7]

Despite Hewett's efforts and objections, Neil Judd was granted an antiquities permit and he started work at Pueblo Bonito in Chaco Canyon in May 1921. Judd wanted to work at Chetro Ketl, but Hewett had already secured the permit to work there. After Judd left at the end of August, Hewett sent a crew to work at Chetro Ketl; however, he did not return until after Judd completed his project in 1927. After being appointed as a professor of anthropology at the University of New Mexico, Hewett was finally able to return to Chaco Canyon and start excavations at Chetro Ketl in 1929.[8]

The field school at Chaco Canyon was limited to twenty graduate and advanced graduate students. As Joiner recounts from the *Field School Announcements* of 1929, "Registration cost $12.50 for residents, $20.00 for nonresidents, and both had to pay a $5.00 matriculation fee. Students were required to live in tents supplied by the school and to eat in the commissary, at a cost of no more than $2.00 daily. All personal equipment was to be supplied by the students, who were reminded to bring many blankets because of the cold nights. They would be provided with the 'usual camp conveniences'—army cots, water pails, wash pans, and tables and chairs. Firearms were not allowed, but students with cars should by all means bring them."[9] Hewett would continue to train students at Chaco Canyon until 1940.

Young Women in Training

As it had in the late 1800s, Chaco Canyon continued to attract a number of students, scholars, and celebrities in the 1920s and 1930s. Hundreds of students participated in research there during the pre- and post-Hewett years.[10] The field school at Chaco Canyon had a tremendous impact on the training of both staff and students, many of whom were at the beginning of their careers. The excavation work at Chetro Ketl, in particular, was the archaeological training ground for several young women who were able to continue on and have a career in archaeology.

Even though they came to archaeology later than to ethnology as a field of study, women have made important contributions to archaeological theory

FIGURE 8 Chaco Field School headquarters with students' tents, ca. 1929. Courtesy of the Archives, Museum of Indian Arts & Culture, Lab of Anthropology. Chaco Photo Collection, Box-B-1, 70.4, Series 70.4/1835–1844.

and method, as well as southwestern cultural histories. One of Marjorie's colleagues, Florence Hawley Ellis, worked on archaeological excavations in Chaco Canyon while at the University of Arizona. Florence applied the new technique of tree-ring dating, known as dendrochronology, developed by A. E. Douglass at the University of Arizona, to Chetro Ketl in the 1930s. She also pioneered the dating of charcoal samples from cooking fires.[11]

Other young women had training opportunities at Chaco Canyon. One in particular was Katherine Spencer Halpern, an ethnologist and applied anthropologist best known for her Navajo work with Clyde Kluckhohn in the late 1940s and her later fieldwork on Navajo health and welfare in the late 1960s and early 1970s.[12] Katherine attended the University of Chicago, where she started her graduate studies in social welfare research. Discovering that this was not what she wanted to do, she switched to anthropology her second year. She recalled:

> As soon as I got into the anthropology department, I just went head over heels into anthropology. The first summer of my work in anthropology, an invitation came from the University of New Mexico Field School with a one-hundred-dollar scholarship for someone who wanted to come and join the archaeology field school at Chaco Canyon. There were three of us girls who were interested so we got together and went to the department chairman . . . and proposed to him that we split it into three. We all were allotted $33 for summer field school. We just wanted to get there that was all.[13]

This was in 1937 and the other two students were Malcolm Carr, who later married Donald Collier, and Dorianne Wooley. They all wanted to do ethnology, and the UNM fellowship opened the door for all three to work with Clyde Kluckhohn from Harvard University. While attending the Chaco Canyon Summer Field School, these three young women persuaded Kluckhohn to allow them to study kinship and clans in the Navajo community of Pueblo Alto.[14]

Katherine took the train from Chicago to Albuquerque, where she and another student were to be picked up by Kluckhohn. Like Hewett, Kluckhohn was very supportive of women in anthropology and provided advice and assistance to young struggling students. Katherine recalled her trip to Chaco Canyon with Kluckhohn at the wheel. "He picked me up in Albuquerque with another student in a little fliver, an open Ford. The way he raced across that desert! I swear that in the course of our trip to Chaco we had two blow-outs. He would not let us help. He'd get out, fix the tire, and climb back in. It was a very hectic drive. Bumpy. He asked me what I wanted to do at Chaco and I told him 'ethnology.' He said, 'Ethnology? There isn't ethnology at Chaco.' We let that drop for a while. He asked me a lot of questions too."[15]

"When we got there, he set it up so that he would teach us at night. . . . He suggested the kind of project that we would undertake, which was on Navajo kinship, learning their kinship terms and also their clan affiliations . . . simple introductory fieldwork. We gathered enough data on the kinship system and particularly the clan system in the Chaco area to get published, with the three of us as authors, by the American Anthropological Association. Within two years it was published as an article."[16] Katherine was especially grateful for the guidance she received from Kluckhohn and said, "He was just wonderful. He was very good, and he was especially good with women students."[17] Katherine Spencer later married Abraham M. Halpern, known for his ethnographic work among the California and Colorado River Indians.

Courtney Reeder Jones had a different experience. She was attending the University of Nebraska and was the first female student from there to go on an archaeological field trip. It was 1934 and her anthropology professor was known to have a reputation for sexually harassing young female college students, and Courtney was no exception. While attending a street party in South Dakota, he told Courtney, "You know, if you want to get a real good grade like a 99 . . ." and she replied, "If I got a 99 I'd never dare show my head around there again! Don't be silly."[18] Fortunately, she never had any more problems with him. The following year he sent her off to the University of Arizona to study with Byron Cummings, director of the Arizona State Museum and chair of the Department of Archaeology. Cummings, affectionately known as "The Dean," and his students were working on an excavation at Kinishba in the White Mountains in east-central Arizona.

Assuming that Courtney was a male, the camp was not prepared for a young woman when she arrived. She recalled their reaction:

Boy, were they surprised! Then when I got there to the dig . . . I went down to dinner and there was a lot of whispering and it turned out that the boys all bet on how long I'd stay. Davey [Jones] bet that I would stick it out. Now that's interesting because I later married him. But I did stick it out. Of course I did. It was fun. We lived in tents. I met a lot of people who later became quite well known, like Gordon Willey. He'd make up stories every night and tell them to us. He said that he was going to be a famous archaeologist and wear a pith helmet and sit in a high place and direct all the people that were doing the digging. And he did![19]

Cummings took his field school students to Chaco Canyon, and the trip was a memorable one for Courtney. "We had to push those cars all the way from Thoreau because the mud was practically up to our knees. It had been just pouring. We pushed the cars in."[20]

Courtney did not have the money to return to Nebraska that fall so she stayed in Tucson and set up a dress design shop. Davey Jones, who was Byron Cummings's assistant at the university, was working on a preliminary ethnological study of the Yaqui. The two later married, and Davey Jones went to work for the National Park Service. At their first post, they lived in Ancestral Puebloan rooms that had been converted into living quarters at Wupatki National Monument outside of Flagstaff, Arizona. Davey worked part of the year as a park ranger at Casa Grande Ruins National Monument at Coolidge, Arizona, and part of the year as superintendent at Wupatki. When they were at Wupatki, Courtney worked at the Museum of Northern Arizona in Flagstaff. Courtney's experience at Wupatki is detailed in the book *Letters from Wupatki*.[21]

On Being a Student at Chaco Canyon

Now back to Marjorie, who attended the Chaco Canyon Field School as an advanced graduate student in 1931. In the 1932 annual report of the School of American Research, Hewett reported on the 1931 excavations at Chetro Ketl. The staff included Hewett as director and W. W. Postlethwaite from Colorado College as an associate and assistant in excavations. Florence Hawley from the University of Arizona oversaw the stratigraphic study and tree-ring work. Others included Reginald Fisher, in charge of engineering, surveys, and cartography; Paul Reiter, in charge of excavations and installation of the field museum; and Sam Hudelson, in charge of construction and repairs. The student assistants and auditors were Ruth Blackwell, Marshall Clinard, Fletcher Cook, Marjorie Ferguson, Grace Fisher, Margaret Foraker, Sara Goddard, Ann Kent, Susan Kent, John Linkins, Fern Johnson, Lydia J. Towbridge, Richard Vann, Gordon Vivian, Janet Woods, and Margaret Woods.

Marjorie spent the second half of the UNM Field School at Chetro Ketl in Chaco Canyon. Even though she enjoyed her experience there and learned a lot about archaeology, she didn't feel that it was that well organized. She recalled:

Paul Reiter and Reginald Fisher were in charge of the main excavation in the house block proper. A whole crew was there in the Big Kiva. That was the main thing they were digging. But I worked in the East Tower Kiva with Fletcher Cook and a Navajo. All three of us were down there for about two weeks. One nice thing about it though: the sun went around, and it was halfway shady in there. We didn't get very much, but one of the things that I wanted to do was learn something about the pottery from Florence [Hawley Ellis], who roomed with Sara Goddard, a high school teacher from Albuquerque. Goddard would help her wash potsherds. I asked if I could help, so I did a lot of sherd washing.[22]

The Chaco Canyon field camp was not as pleasant as the one at Battleship Rock, but Marjorie had fond memories of her summers working at Chaco Canyon.

I liked Chaco very much. It was quite a rugged camp. . . . We had one tap in the canyon. . . . We were instructed to go down and fill our water bags and a bucket of water. We didn't have canteens. Each one was rationed. That's what you had per day. We would put our water outside our tent in the morning because it got very hot, of course, and you could have a pretty good lukewarm bath by the time you got home. I hated those water bags. They smelled like rotting canvas. . . . We'd take our water bags down to Chetro Ketl every day with us. . . . Our tents were all set up in back of Pueblo Bonito with Threatening Rock right up above us. They had geologists out there all the time and Stewart Northrup himself estimated that it would be a good 20 years or maybe longer before anything fell down.[23]

On January 21, 1941, after a year of heavy rains, Threatening Rock fell and destroyed about thirty rooms at Pueblo Bonito that had been excavated by Neil Judd in the 1920s.

The students learned the different aspects of archaeology, and Marjorie recalled that *Hewett did a lot of walking too, so-called surveying. He would take us all up and down the canyon. You know, they carried on so about these roads, whatever they were, in Chaco Canyon. He knew about them. He walked us over I don't know how many miles of different ones he knew. . . . He wouldn't let us even suck on an orange. He wouldn't let us take water along. He said the Arabs said you were better off in the desert without water, but to drink lots of water and tea at night.*

Water was scarce, and the students learned to use it sparingly. *On Sunday morning, we had an opportunity to wash our hair and our clothes. Reginald Fisher found an old tin tub somewhere and we pooled all our water and we washed our clothes in that. Then we took a bath in it.*[24] Food was also in short supply and often rather questionable in the Chaco Canyon field camps. It was quite different from the cuisine served at the Battleship Rock Field Camp in the Jemez Mountains.

Marjorie described the typical meals at Chaco:

The food was served by Indian girls who were absolutely untrained. Their thumb was always in everything that they brought in. Have you ever heard of case eggs put in a water glass? They are eggs that are put in these crates of spinning water in glass—horrible looking stuff that keeps them from spoiling. They have a perfectly awful taste. We'd get one of those for breakfast, burnt cornbread, and oleomargarine that was uncolored. It was white and it was greasy. You had either coffee or tea and you would get half an orange, and they were very small oranges. Then for lunch, you would get the same thing over again. You'd get watery beans and burnt cornbread. Once in a great while there might be some kind of fat put in, maybe a side of meat or salt pork or something.

On the dig we had a goat that got run over. We had a little mining railroad setup there that took these dump carts down and the goat ran across and got killed. So the Indians butchered it and we had cabrito stew for several meals. One night at dinner I remember Gordon Vivian looking at this kind of gray-looking stuff in front of us. "You know," he said, "I've seen animals hurt worse than this that lived." We supplemented our diet by going over to the trading post [near Pueblo Bonito] and getting some boxes of prunes. Some of them would be dried out and hard and maybe wormy, but we thought they were great.[25]

When Marjorie got to Chaco during the latter part of the summer, it was extremely hot. Once the sun went down and the canyon cooled off, the students would find ways to keep themselves entertained.

Our entertainment at night for the most part was to go to the trading post. We'd go through all the dead pawn, which was wonderful to look at. Of course, we didn't have any money. We did all the blankets, which some of us did buy for very little. Little saddle blankets and stuff like that. And then we were supposed to attend lectures by Hewett or one of the scholars he had invited. One night Clyde Kluckhohn lectured on physical anthropology and the Navajos, which we liked. Many scholars would come to Chaco. Mr. Postlethwaite was always there. He loved the Great Kiva. He came down from his post at Colorado College. He was actually in charge of the dig in the Great Kiva. Gordon Vivian was working on Casa Rinconada, "Garbo" was what we called him. He excavated a large kiva there too.

Other than the night lectures and going over to the trading post, we would go down to the Great Kiva at night. I don't think Hewett liked for us to do this. But when Mrs. Thomas Curtin, who had homes in southern California and Santa Fe, would come to Chaco with Mr. Postlethwaite, and some of the others to visit, or when Dean Cummings and his students would come over from Arizona, he didn't say anything.

Mr. Postlethwaite and Mrs. Curtin would bring in a great big container of ice cream on dry ice. One of those tall ones that they have in the drug store. And a box of Benson and Hedges cigarettes. Of course, everybody smoked, but we didn't have fancy cigarettes. We were smoking Wings, which were terrible cigarettes. Students didn't drink then. Maybe they did elsewhere, but they did not drink in the camps. Hewett's rule was, "No firearms. No pets. No liquor." But we would go down to the Great Kiva, especially if there was a full moon, and sit on one of the bancos and have our feast and sing. . . . Sometimes some of the Navajo workmen, who certainly didn't associate with us, would be standing off to one side sort of watching us.[26]

The Great Kiva that Mr. Postlethwaite helped excavate was at Chetro Ketl. Marjorie described the excavation:

They took it down several levels. I was astounded at the masonry. I had never seen masonry like that. It was just incredible. Down on one of the lower benches . . . we noticed that the stonework around the bench varied here and there. It was pretty regular. Each one would be equidistant, but there'd be something about eight to ten inches long that didn't fit the rest of the masonry. One of the first of these features was opened by Hewett and James F. Zimmerman

*[President of UNM from 1927 to 1944],
Ernest Thompson Seton, one of the celebrities who was there, and Mr. Postlethwaite. They opened the first of the
niches and it was filled with a beautiful
necklace, as well as black and white shell
and turquoise pendants. The same sort
of thing was found in each of the niches.
We didn't take out all of them. They were
taken out later. I wasn't there when the
rest of them were taken out, but I was
so glad that I was allowed to sit by the
first one that was opened because they
wanted my hand for contrast.*[27]

As with just about any archaeological field school, there is the possibility for accidents to happen. Marjorie
recalled this one from her first year at
Chaco Canyon:

FIGURE 9 Marjorie Ferguson as a young graduate
student standing in a room at Pueblo Bonito wearing
a silver concha belt she purchased at the trading post
during the 1931 SAR-UNM summer field school at Chaco
Canyon. Courtesy of the Archives, Museum of Indian
Arts & Culture, Lab of Anthropology. Marjorie Lambert
Collection. Neg. No. 70.849.

*We were all working one afternoon after
lunch in the hottest sun, I think, of the season, and Fletcher Cook, one of the men in
camp, had borrowed these dump trucks
and these little railroad cart things from
a mining company to take the dump way
off from where the excavation was going
on. He had little signs put up, "crossing
here" and so on and he really had a lot of fun with that. Those dump trucks were
a big addition to the work we were doing. One of the men accidentally threw a
big stone the wrong way and it sort of over-balanced the cart. It got partly off
the track. This Navajo lifted it but he cut one of his fingers off. Another Navajo
walked up, picked up the finger, and threw it over the dirt. . . . He wanted him
to go on working and wrapped a dirty piece of cloth around it. Hewett would
not have it. Hewett took charge and got a truck and two of his best drivers and
another Navajo to go to Crownpoint to the Indian hospital. I remember Mr. Pos-*

tlethwaite said that if there was any additional expense for him or his family, he'd be glad to contribute and other people said the same thing.

So, they took him to the hospital and they took off his clothes and put him in a white gown, which he did not like. He fought that. They tried to clean up his arm and hand the best they could without him bopping everyone. He asked for a cigarette and would not lie down. He would not take any anesthetic. They sewed that finger back on. Bandaged it and put spatulas on either side, sort of a finger splint, and they put him in bed. I think they did give him a shot of something. I don't think he knew it, but by then he was a little in shock himself. But he smoked the cigarette while it was going on. . . . Then the next morning he was gone and a horse had disappeared. He'd stolen a horse in the night, got his clothes and rode off. We never saw him again.[28]

During the archaeological excavations, Navajo life in Chaco Canyon carried on as usual. In 1931 the students witnessed part of a Navajo healing ceremony. Marjorie described this ceremony:

There was an old man who was apparently very powerful from a religious point of view. I don't remember whether he was a singer or not, but anyway they made quite a to-do over him. The Navajos still had their big wagons with the canopies over them at that time. They had a big encampment down below Casa Rinconada. I think all the students learned a lot from an ethnographic point of view from those Indians there. Not all of us got to see them strip this little man down, but he had nothing on but a breechclout when they put him in this little sweat lodge that they had built with poles covered with sticks, dirt, and blankets with heated rocks inside. He had some disgusting-looking sores over his back and his front and on his skinny little legs. I remember the next morning we went to see how he was—this was before breakfast. They had taken the blankets off the front of the little sweat lodge and brought him out and other than little bits of charcoal there wasn't a sign of a sore on him.

Marjorie was intrigued by the Navajos and their cultural practices.

That was an experience that I enjoyed. I enjoyed how they got together. Some of the things I saw for the first time were pretty gruesome. I walked around one of these little arbors that the women had erected to do their cooking. They had a big goat upside down and they cut its throat just as I walked by. But they were nice. They invited us to some of their evening get-togethers. They did a little singing. They had fry bread. They served weak Arbuckle's Coffee with ashes from the fire in it. They never served it strong. The interesting thing was they could buy Arbuckle's Coffee in either blue cans or red cans in the trading post and the red cans would go like wildfire. They wouldn't touch the blue cans. They'd have to paint them red so that the Indians would buy them. The reason being they simply preferred the color red over blue.[29]

A Terrifying Exam in the Field

In the 1931 annual report of the School of American Research, Hewett reported that "candidates for the degree of Master of Arts, whose theses relate to the work of the region, are given their examinations by the graduate committee of the University in the field."[30] Marjorie was the second student to be given her master's oral exam while in the field school at Chaco Canyon.

One morning, Marjorie was called into one of the remaining stone buildings of the Wetherill complex that was being used as the excavation headquarters to take her exam that was administered by the graduate committee. Hewett and W. W. Postlethwaite were already at Chaco; Benjamin Haught, dean of the UNM graduate school, and Mamie Tanquist, of the Archaeology and Anthropology Department, came out specifically for Marjorie's exam.[31] Marjorie described the events that were taking place during her oral exam:

> *I was nervous when I went in naturally, but I began to relax and feel pretty well. We were doing the Southwest and the linguistic tribes and so on when Dr. Benjamin Haught said, "Maybe we'd better see what she knows about some of the other linguistic groups." So, we started in on the Northwest Coast and started coming back down into California and then sort of breezed into the Southwest again, and I thought,* Well here we go into Mexico and this will flunk me for sure. *Dr. Hewett pulled out his watch and said,* Time's going on, I think we've covered this pretty well and she obviously knows the field. *The thing I remember about Dr. Haught, who was Dean of Men and also head of the Psychology Department at the University of New Mexico, was that he felt that the Indians were mentally of a different cut from us. He was sure that the whites were more intelligent than the Indians. He told me to tell them why I thought the Indians were as intelligent as white people. And that came from a psychologist! I never will forget that. . . .*

I was kind of numb and I really didn't know if I was going to pass or not because the Navajos were having a sing for an old man who was completely covered with sores. . . . They had a devil chase because they were sure that was part of the trouble. The devil was in him in some way or another. Here came this screeching bunch of Navajos, the devil just going like the wind on one horse, and the rest of them with whips cracking and screeching all around the building and up and down the canyon while my oral exam was going on. Dr. Haught was not in a good mood anyway because he'd been held up by rain and had sat out in his car on the other side of Escavada Wash all night. The oral exam was at nine thirty the next morning. How I survived I don't know.[32]

Marjorie successfully passed her oral exams and completed her master's thesis on the acculturation of Sandia Pueblo in 1931.[33] Sandia Pueblo is located along the Rio Grande River north of Albuquerque and is considered to be one of the towns in the historic Tiguex Province. Marjorie felt that a study of Sandia Pueblo would be of interest to southwestern archaeology because there were still questions concerning the exact location of some of the old pueblos of the Tiguex Province—in particular, Sandia, Puaray, and Alameda.

Sandia Pueblo was a very conservative community, so Marjorie had to rely on traditional anthropological methods of data collection, including research among archived historical documents and available statistical information, as well as personal contacts and participant observation. Her goal was to bring about a better understanding of native peoples in general and the contributions they have made to society throughout history. She describes Spanish contact and then the influence of the United States government on culture change in Sandia Pueblo. Although they had been resistant to change in the past, by the end of World War I they had accepted government aid, "not because they understand and like it, but because they can no longer see the point of resistance."[34] Marjorie noted that the biggest influence was the establishment of a school in the Pueblo. Since she wrote her thesis there is no doubt that the acculturation process has succeeded in bringing about tremendous culture change among the Pueblos of New Mexico as well as Indian tribes across the nation. During the 1990s, Marjorie expressed her concerns about the negative impacts that Indian casinos were having on the Pueblos and other tribes in terms of culture change and the addictive nature of gambling in general.

Once she completed her master's degree at the University of New Mexico, Marjorie considered going on for her doctorate, but unfortunately this was hindered by Hewett and his convincing and forceful nature. She wanted to go to the University of Chicago or Columbia University because the University of New Mexico did not have a PhD program in archaeology or anthropology, and she still hoped to gain some experience at a more prestigious eastern university. She said:

> *I did consider going on for a PhD, but Dr. Hewett wanted me to go to the University of Southern California because he had just opened that department, but it wasn't a very good department.... What I really wanted to do was to go to Chicago and study with some of the people there. You see, Fred Egan, Paul Martin, George Quimby, and John Collier were there. I wanted then to go to Harvard or Vassar and to New York University.... And then go and maybe have a couple of turns in the field with Emil Haury who was then the big shot in southwestern archaeology at the University of Arizona. I wanted to do that more than anything, but Hewett wouldn't let me. He didn't think it was a good idea. He wanted me to go to Southern California. Later I talked to Dr. [Harry] Mera about it and he said, "If you are going to spend your life in a museum, I don't see that a PhD is really important." Now, I don't know whether he was right or not. Certainly, my salary wouldn't have been any better. I don't know that I have any real regrets about not getting a PhD, but in a way I was pretty close to it. I wish I had finished because I had taken some extra graduate courses and it wouldn't have been much of a problem to get a PhD.*[35]

After returning to the university at the end of the archaeological field season in 1931, Marjorie wrote "A Study of Architecture of the Chaco Canyon Indians, the Province of Tusayan, and the Indians of the Seven Cities of Cibola."[36] She stayed in Albuquerque and with her master's degree taught at UNM, and was a field supervisor at Chaco Canyon for several seasons from 1932 through 1937 and at other archaeological sites in New Mexico.

CHAPTER 4

Academia and Supervising Archaeological Excavations

1931-1936

> I think Lambert is best known for her work at Paa-ko, which
> exemplifies the particular kind of research for which she is
> known.
>
> —LINDA CORDELL[1]

After receiving a master's degree in anthropology, with a minor in history, Marjorie began her academic career at the University of New Mexico in the fall of 1931. At about the same time, the Laboratory of Anthropology (LAB) opened in Santa Fe despite years of opposition by Edgar Lee Hewett.[2] While some of her colleagues were settling into the LAB, as it has been referred to since it opened in 1927, Marjorie continued teaching anthropology at UNM, mentoring young archaeology students, and supervising archaeological projects.

The Beginning of a Career in Academia and the Tecolote Excavations

From 1931 to 1936 Marjorie taught anthropology classes at the University of New Mexico, was a field supervisor for the university's archaeological field school, and had status as a Research Associate at the School of American Research in Santa Fe. In 1932 she was hired as the instructor in charge of the archaeology field school at the Tecolote archaeological site (LA 296) for the New Mexico Normal University (now New Mexico Highlands University) in Las Vegas. The Tecolote site was located within a ten-acre parcel of land pur-

FIGURE 10 Marjorie Ferguson dressed in field clothes and boots standing in front of her rental guest house on Roberta Robey's property on Delgado Street, Santa Fe, in 1932. Courtesy of the Archives, Museum of Indian Arts & Culture, Lab of Anthropology. Marjorie Lambert Collection. Neg. No. 70.851.

chased by the Las Vegas Historical Society. The Las Vegas Museum served as the official repository for the material excavated at the site.

Marjorie's post in Las Vegas was clearly an extension of Hewett's influence. Don Fowler writes that "in 1897 Hewett met a prominent citizen and attorney of Las Vegas, New Mexico, Frank Springer, and the two became fast friends. Soon after, through Springer's influence, Hewett was appointed president of the newly created New Mexico Normal School . . . in Las Vegas. In addition to administrative duties, he taught anthropology and archaeology."[3]

While at his post in Las Vegas, Hewett traveled to Washington, D.C., where he met with several anthropologists and archaeologists and lobbied to create national cultural parks on the Pajarito Plateau and in Chaco Canyon. In 1898 he also helped form the Archeological Society of New Mexico. Hewett took advantage of his position at the Normal School to establish support and develop a network of patrons to support his fieldwork and to train students in Southwest archaeology. These activities, however, caused problems for him in Las Vegas.[4] He was well-liked by his students and faculty, but as Don Fowler points out, "local opinion makers disliked Hewett's unconventional teaching methods and his refusal to court them. His persistent efforts to get large tracts of public land set aside for national parks angered powerful ranchers and landowners."[5] This resulted in his contract not being renewed by the university regents for the 1903–4 academic year.[6] Regardless of Hewett's situation, Frank Springer continued to be his supporter, and it was Hewett's ongoing political connections that would take Marjorie to Las Vegas in the summer of 1932.

This was the first time that Marjorie was sent out in the field to supervise an archaeological excavation crew and to teach an anthropology class. It proved to be quite a learning experience for her. Marjorie recalled:

> *The president of New Mexico Normal University, a buddy of Hewett's, wanted to start a summer school course in anthropology that would last six weeks. Half-time for excavation and half-time to learn something about anthropology. . . . I selected my crew myself. I was convinced at the time, having never worked with Spanish Americans, as I did later, that Indians made the best helpers in the field. So, I got a small group of Indians together and they agreed to work for a pittance, of course, but it was a good experience for them.*
>
> *We excavated a few rooms in this little pueblo on the bank of Tecolote Creek. It had a nice kiva. We did not have very much of a range in pottery. It was apparently a very poor pueblo and much of it had already washed into the creek. That was one of the reasons the university had been asked to excavate it. Unfortunately, it was disappearing. We got some Chupadero black-on-white, a little bit of Santa Fe black-on-white and Tularosa black-on-white, and some very crude culinary ware, some of which was incised. The bones were never analyzed. The [Las Vegas] Museum didn't have the money to analyze them. I made a little sketch for El Palacio[7] and I did a paper on it. . . . Somehow throughout the years that got lost in the files of the museum or the university. . . . That was my first experience [running a field school].[8]*

Marjorie is referring to an unpublished report she wrote at the end of her summer at the New Mexico Normal University, "Report of Marjorie Ferguson, Research Fellow in Ethnology."[9] The report summarizes the two classes she taught and the three-week field school at Tecolote. She also discusses an ethological survey that she engaged her students in.

Marjorie noted in her report that she taught one course in archaeology and another in anthropology and then had about thirty-six students doing archaeological field work along with seven men she hired from Tesuque and San Ildefonso Pueblos. Three of these Pueblo men had been trained by Hewett during the archaeological survey and excavations at El Rito de los Frijoles in the summer of 1910. During the three weeks of excavation at the Tecolote site, the students and hired workers uncovered fifteen rooms,

FIGURE 11 Marjorie Ferguson (top left), instructor and supervisor of the Tecolote excavation (LA 296) in 1932 with her anthropology and archaeology students from New Mexico Normal University and field crew, including Rose and Joe Aguilar from Santo Domingo Pueblo. Courtesy of the Archives, Museum of Indian Arts & Culture, Lab of Anthropology. Marjorie Lambert Collection. Neg. No. 70.854.

one kiva, and one partial kiva. Marjorie concluded that Tecolote was closely related to Pecos, and she suggested that it could be older and was possibly abandoned during the first years of the occupation at Pecos.

In her 1933 published report in *El Palacio*, Marjorie revised her conclusions and suggested that the Tecolote site contained a mixture of Plains and Pueblo characteristics.[10] It was one of several sites located in the Las Vegas area, and Marjorie was convinced that there was additional evidence of Plains and Puebloan contact and exchange in the region. Unfortunately, she never had the opportunity to go back to Tecolote to continue this line of inquiry.

Marjorie would be delighted to know that her conclusions based on the evidence she found at these sites are being confirmed by anthropologists and archaeologists today. One example is the research focused on the ethnic shifting of the Apache and northern Tiwa in New Mexico. The work of Severin Fowles and B. Sunday Eiselt has focused on the Plains Apache groups coming to live in the Taos region and the northern Tiwa groups (Taos and Picuris) going to live on the Plains. They propose that during the early Spanish colonial period, "escape to the plains was part of the strategy adopted by the northern Tiwa to evade Spanish control." They go on to suggest that "such lateral lines between Pueblo and non-Pueblo groups during the colonial period appear to be extensions of deeper precolonial history in the region."[11] This aligns with what Marjorie observed in the Las Vegas area, which is located on the periphery of the plains.

Difficulties with Men

It was during the summer of 1932 in Las Vegas that Marjorie met George Tichy, a chiropractor and trained dental technician. Tichy was taking her class at New Mexico Normal University, and he immediately started courting her. The son of a prominent dentist, Tichy came from a good family, and after a two-year courtship, Marjorie married him in 1934. Unfortunately, shortly after they were married and living together, Marjorie discovered that George had a drinking problem and this was something that Marjorie had very little tolerance for. Having her own career outside of the home no doubt affected the marriage as well. Hewett was moving her around to different work locations, and she was not willing to make concessions in her career goals to follow the traditional role of a housewife. Even though the marriage would last almost sixteen years, Marjorie quickly realized that it was not a good match and she refused to have much to do with her husband.

This was the era before women retained their maiden names or used hyphenated names after marriage, so Marjorie used her married name, Tichy, both privately and professionally. She signed her work as Marjorie F. Tichy from 1934 to 1950. Even though Marjorie and George were separated, she decided to maintain her married status. She clearly thought this strategy through and believed this was the best way to approach her marriage and career at the time. Marjorie made this observation: *I kept my married name simply for protection. I thought in many cases it helped me in avoiding complications.*[12]

Throughout most of the years that Marjorie was married to George Tichy, she lived in Albuquerque and Santa Fe, and the only time she saw her husband was when he needed money. He would come to her since she had a steady job and a regular paycheck. It is a part of her life that she would prefer to forget, but it demonstrates the limited opportunities women had at the time given the stigma of divorce and where living alone as an independent single woman was frowned upon by society in general.

Given some of the verbal and physical abuse that Marjorie tolerated throughout her career, much of which came from her male colleagues, it makes one wonder what she would have endured had she been single. Interestingly, she never had problems with the Spanish American and Pueblo men that she supervised during her archaeological excavations. Instead, her difficulties were with the men in the museum and in the discipline in general, who clearly did not want to accept Marjorie as their intellectual equal. The harassment that she endured did not affect her career and reputation as much as it impacted Marjorie emotionally and personally. She never would have admitted to Hewett or any of her male colleagues that their comments, jokes, teasing, and actions toward her as a woman, and other women, whether intentional or not, were often derogatory, demeaning, and very hurtful. These were the days long before sexual harassment in the workplace became a recognized ethical and legal issue. Because she loved the work, she chose to ignore them and not make a scene. Until the 1980s, this was a tack that many women took as they worked hard to gain footing in male-dominated professional and academic arenas.

A New Deal for New Mexico Archaeology

Hewett took advantage of New Deal funding (1933–38) and a partnership with UNM to train students in archaeology. He selected three Ancestral Puebloan sites that had been abandoned in the late sixteenth and seventeenth centuries: Paa-ko, in the San Pedro Valley east of the Sandia Mountains, and Puaray and Kuaua, in the Rio Grande Valley near Bernalillo. Kuaua and Paa-ko were stabilized and preserved with the help of funding through the Works Progress Administration and were designated as New Mexico state monuments.[13] Nancy Lewis and Kay Hagan maintain that projects such as these "gave students valuable field experience and afforded young archaeologists an opportunity to assume positions of leadership. . . . Hewett's protégés soon surpassed their mentor in terms of technique and theory."[14]

Hewett reported that the School of American Research had sponsored the "excavation of two important ruins of the old Tiguex Province: Puaray, following the identification of Bandelier, and Kuaua, both towns of the Tiwa people which figure in the chronicles of the Coronado expedition."[15] In 1540

Francisco Vásquez de Coronado and his entourage had camped somewhere in the area of today's central Rio Grande valley in New Mexico.[16] Tiguex Province consisted of twelve pueblos along the banks of the river. The Tiwa peoples who occupied these pueblos had evacuated the Pueblo of Alcanfor (Coofor) on the west bank for Coronado's use.[17] Hewett launched this archaeological campaign in order to identify the campsite so that it could be part of the upcoming observances of the four hundredth anniversary of Coronado's *entrada* into New Mexico. After completing her work at the Tecolote site in Las Vegas, Hewett moved Marjorie on to archaeological projects at Puaray (LA 326) and Kuaua (LA 176).

The site referred to as Bandelier's Puaray was presumed to be located on the west bank of the Rio Grande River northwest of present-day Bernalillo. In her article on the little mission church, San Bartolome, Marjorie observed that the Spanish missionaries periodically tried to Christianize the Indians at Puaray, but finally in 1711 the mission was totally destroyed and Puaray was abandoned.[18] Puaray was described by Marjorie as being made up of "remnants of four compactly constructed buildings which surround a small plaza, containing a single kiva in the northwest corner. Each building extended well over three hundred feet in length. They were separated by small passageways which led to the exterior of the village as well as into the plaza."[19]

In 1936 Marjorie wrote of her concerns about making assumptions about the definite locations of Ancestral Puebloan sites in the Tiquex Province, in particular Alameda, Puaray, and Sandia. She felt that until the excavations were more advanced to include more sites and data matched to the historical records, the locations of some of the towns or pueblos visited by Coronado in 1540 were being named based on insufficient evidence. She surmised that more than likely the whole story of the Tiguex Province would never be entirely known because most of the tangible evidence of human occupation had been destroyed.[20] Marjorie repeated her concerns about the proper identity of Puaray in a subsequent report in 1939.[21]

Unlike the mystery of Puaray's exact location, Kuaua's identification was less problematic. Kuaua, also located on the west side of the Rio Grande River, is described by David Noble as "a superb archeological example of the Rio Grande pueblo. Constructed around A.D. 1300 of coursed adobe, it consisted of large roomblocks surrounding three spacious plazas with underground kivas. Like many prehistoric pueblos, Kuaua was a veritable fortress; its high, exterior, doorless walls serving as bulwarks from which to fend off potential attack. Entrance was gained only by narrow passageways."[22] The known descendants of Kuaua are the Tiwa-speaking people of Isleta and Sandia Pueblos.

The excavations at Puaray and Kuaua were carried out simultaneously and were supervised by Gordon Vivian and Marjorie Ferguson Tichy. They were assisted by a number of trained students working on small stipends under the classification of junior archaeologists. The list included Mary Arthur, Ele Baker, Lilla Barney, Wesley Bliss, William Chauvenet, Robert Coffin, Bertha Dutton, Annette Fossnock, J. W. Hendron, J. Charles Kelley, Alice Leinau, Elizabeth Long, Dorothy Luhrs, Don Mack, Gordon Page, and Jeffie Sharp Robinson. Marjorie was also in charge of the study of both the cultural and skeletal material from both excavations.[23]

Marjorie shared some of her experiences on the project: *We'd go two days a week to one [site] and three to the other and then switch. We had an old Cadillac that Hewett bought for us for seventy-five dollars and we all went out*

FIGURE 12 Aerial view of the Kuaua site, Coronado Historic Site, near Bernalillo, New Mexico, ca. 1946–47. Photo by the New Mexico Tourism Bureau. Courtesy of the Palace of the Governors Photo Archives (NMHM/DCA). Neg. No. HP.2007.20.467.

to the dig in that.[24] She acknowledged that the excavations at these sites were poorly done and that there was a lot of confusion and impropriety:

> *I think I would criticize that whole operation. Hewett had too many bosses. Vivian thought I was taking notes on certain things; I thought he was taking notes. The students were taking notes. The whole thing was a hodgepodge, and I wish it could have been better excavated. I remember there were sections of that site [Puaray] that had been burned and there were remains of these great big storage pots, quite large, several were two or three feet high. Not one bit of the corn was saved for analysis. Vivian was in charge and he didn't care. . . . I did keep all the notes having to do with pottery and pottery counting. I saw to that. We had a laboratory at the university. I kept all of that and I had a group of students who helped me. I also analyzed the pottery from Kuaua.*[25]

In November 1934, the Federal Emergency Relief Administration (FERA) approved funding to support the preparation, cleaning, recording, and storage of the cultural material coming to the university lab from the Puaray and Kuaua excavations.[26] Nine museum assistants including Dorothy Luhrs, Marian Hollenbach, Robert Lister, Annette Fossnock, J. Charles Kelley, Joe Toulouse, F. A. Campora, Shirley James, and Margaret Bliss were assigned under the FERA project to assist Marjorie in the laboratory at UNM. These students received training in museum and laboratory methods prior to working in the lab.[27]

Marjorie shares her thoughts on the excavations at Kuaua:

> *Both sites were extremely interesting. Apparently, Coronado did camp very close to what is Kuaua. . . . The significant thing about Kuaua is that it is the first report of an underground painted ceremonial chamber [in the Rio Grande Valley]. . . . I think there were seventy-five layers of plaster and I think about half of them did have ceremonies painted on them. I will credit Wesley Bliss who had come from CalTech as a student. Gordon Vivian and J. Charles Kelley helped with that too. Those boys, under Bliss's supervision, [removed the kiva mural layers]. . . . Three of them were in pretty good condition and were taken down to the University of New Mexico. . . . We never had a project of just stripping the walls, but we more or less worked on it when we could. We had one Indian boy [Paul Goodbear, Cheyenne] who was paid to make a set of small copies of everything on the walls and then we had one set of full-*

scale drawings. There are some interesting ceremonial scenes in that kiva. . . .
It was exciting.[28]

The recovery of the murals from Kiva III at Kuaua took two years. Three large walls were jacketed in plaster casts, removed from the site, and taken to the laboratory at the University of New Mexico. The removal process was led by Wesley Bliss, a graduate student in archaeology. There was a total of eighty-five adobe layers from three walls; seventeen of those layers contained painted images. The Bliss team of artists and archaeologists systematically documented the images through photography, notes describing the images, and colored pencil drawings to scale on graph paper. Each layer from the painted kiva walls was glued onto Masonite panels.

Seventy-seven of these Masonite panels were transferred to the Laboratory of Anthropology in Santa Fe in the early 1940s and have remained in the collection since. The Maxwell Museum at the University of New Mexico owns one of the panels, and several panels have been on exhibit at the visitor center at New Mexico's Coronado Historic Site (formerly Coronado State Monument) since it opened in 1940. The Museum of Indian Arts and Culture / Laboratory of Anthropology received funding from the Getty Foundation in 2006 to conduct a conservation survey of the murals and collaborated with surrounding Pueblos to develop a long-range plan for the conservation and preservation of these national treasures.

Excavations at Giusewa at Jemez Springs

Marjorie returned to the Jemez Mountains in 1936 to work at Giusewa. Citing information from Hammond and Rey, Michael Elliot reports that "the first Spanish contact with the people of the Jemez area occurred in 1540. Captain Francisco de Barrionuevo of Coronado's Expedition visited the area at that time. Castaneda, the chronicler of the Coronado Expedition, mentions seven 'Hemes' villages and three in the 'Aguas Calientes' area." Elliott concluded that "it is quite possible that these three villages were those that became known as Unshagi, Nanishagi, and Giusewa [*sic*]."[29] Marjorie had worked at Unshagi and Nanishagi previously and now Hewett sent her to do some excavation work at Giusewa.

When Marjorie arrived at Giusewa, she worked on one of the missions that had been established there historically. Elliott noted that the first priest

assigned to the Jemez people by Juan de Oñate after the Spanish reconquest was "Fray Alonzo de Lugo, whose work was apparently centered at
Giusewa Pueblo, now part of Jemez State Monument [renamed Jemez
Historic Site]. . . . There were . . . four missions established at one time or
another among the Jemez: San Jose de los Jemez (at Giusewa), San Diego de
la Conregacion (at Walatowa, present day Jemez Pueblo), burned in 1622,
San Diego del Monte (at Patokwa), and San Juan de los Jemez (the second
mission at Walatowa)."[30]

Marjorie described her time at Giusewa:

*The last site in the Jemez area that I worked at was San Jose de los Jemez, in
what is now called Jemez State Monument. Francis Elmore, Ele Baker, and I
think Wesley Hurt also excavated. We could excavate only part of it because
of the road that goes to Via Coeli [Monastery of the Servants of the Paraclete],
which belongs to the Catholics, and which served as a retreat for priests was
across the road. We weren't allowed to work there but there was a beautiful,
great big seventeenth-century mission church there, San José de los Jemez.
I was fascinated by that mission church. I thought it was wonderful and I
thought it was very good for all of us whether we were Catholics or Protestants
to begin to learn something about the mission period of the Southwest.*[31]

Marjorie recalled:

*At Giusewa [the ancient pueblo, Giusewatoa (LA 679)] . . . we cleared one of
the rooms, a specialized room . . . indicating Gallina influence. I also helped
collect some of the pottery. Joe Toulouse was the other one. He worked on the
monastery there. Joe did a very clean and neat job. . . . I studied the materials that came out of there. I analyzed the pottery. The title of my paper was
"Spanish Influences on the Pottery of San Jose de los Jemez and Giusewa."*[32]
*I brought in quite a lot of history of the Jemez Province and the number of
pueblos that had been gathered together. . . . I have always been in love with
that country up there. . . . It would be wonderful if those could still be studied.
We would find a lot of information.*

Marjorie always wanted to go back up to the Jemez Mountains to continue
her archaeological work, as she felt there was much more to be learned about
the ancient Pueblo people and the history of the area. But the opportunity

never availed itself and she never returned to work in one of the places that she loved.

The Excavations at Paa-ko

A late Ancestral Puebloan/early historic site nestled in the foothills of the Sandia Mountains not far from Albuquerque Paa-ko is a large, multiplaza pueblo. Dating from before 1300 CE, Paa-ko had two periods of occupation and was abandoned in the seventeenth century. In the 1936 annual report of the School of American Research, Hewett reported, "The excavation of Paako [sic], in the San Pedro valley east of the Sandia Mountains, lays bare an extension of the Tiwa culture of ancient Tano land, the great plain lying to the south of Santa Fe. The ruin, while riddled by the pot hunting of many years, is nevertheless proving to be a fruitful site. The thirty-acre tract surrounding the ruin has been acquired for the University of New Mexico. It has been fenced and a substantial field laboratory built."[33]

Excavations at Paa-ko were carried out in two separate field seasons as part of a Works Progress Administration–supported project. Albert Ely was the supervisor of the first field season from November 11, 1935, to September 11, 1936, and Marjorie supervised the excavations during the second season from September 11, 1936, to March 4, 1937.[34] Like several other archaeological projects in New Mexico at the time, this excavation was carried out jointly by the University of New Mexico, the School of American Research, and the Museum of New Mexico. As Linda Cordell notes, "part of the rationale for the work involved the potential to develop the site as a tourist center on the opposite side of Albuquerque from Kuaua."[35] Paa-ko was designated as a New Mexico Historic Site in 1938 and was opened to the public. The site became inactive around 1959. The site is owned and managed by the University of New Mexico.[36]

After returning from her work in the Jemez Springs area, Hewett asked Marjorie to take charge of the second season's excavation at Paa-ko. As the field supervisor, Marjorie reminisced about her experience working there.

I was teaching at the University of New Mexico and ran the archaeology lab at the same time. I used to take Hewett's night classes when he would come down from Santa Fe. Kuaua was still going on. [Gordon] Vivian was still working out there. Hewett and his driver came out to see me one day. I was out under the stadium. There was a storeroom there and I was out checking through

FIGURE 13 Marjorie Ferguson Tichy supervising excavations at Paa-ko, New Mexico, in 1936–1937. Courtesy of the Palace of the Governors Photo Archives (NMHM/DCA). Neg. No. 045384.

sacks of pottery. He called me out of there and he said, "I have a job for you. I want it to start in just two weeks. I've already put you on the payroll. . . . You're to take a crew of forty men. You can have some graduate students, those that want to earn a little money. I want you to take over the excavation at Paa-ko." I said that I thought that was supposed to be for Albert Ely. . . . He said he was transferring the man that was excavating the historic section down at Kuaua to do some stabilizing and he wanted me to take over the excavation at Paa-ko. He gave me full reign and said he knew I'd do a good job.

Hewett told me what the hours would be and what the length of the project would be. He said that we [UNM] had a lease on that site and that he felt that it was very important because there was a late occupation and an early occupation. He wanted me to take charge of it. He said I was to meet the truck at the university every morning during the week, five days a week, and I was to report on the site at eight every morning and work until four. . . . He told me what my salary would be. So we started in September.

The site was located on the east side of the Sandia Mountains, beyond San Antonito. Up through the Tijeras Canyon. Right on the slopes of the Sandias.

It was near the little mining town of San Pedro. [Nels] Nelson had given the name as the San Pedro Viejo and San Pedro was the little mining town. . . . I got J. Charles Kelley, a very dear friend; Ele Baker, who had excavated at the Alibates site and had experience; and Betty Murphy, who was a graduate student. I think she was majoring in social anthropology. They were the regulars and I had others off and on, but these were the three that I depended on. Especially, Betty, she was absolutely wonderful at cataloging. The university had built a little stone field house there. A little two-room place with a fireplace, and that's where we did our cataloging and where we got things ready to send to UNM. We kept our equipment, such as the paper sacks, shovels, picks, and things like that in there. My salary was $146 a month. . . . I wasn't told that I'd have to pay for sacks, glue, or rubber cement, whatever we needed. I wasn't told that I'd have to pay to have the shovels sharpened. But that didn't matter.

Once we got started I could see that there wasn't much in the historic section. In the meantime, I'd done everything I could to learn more about Paa-ko. I knew about it in a general way because I had made friends with Dr. Harry Mera. Dr. Mera told me that it had two occupations, a clearly historic occupation and then something really neat underneath. He wanted to get into the really neat stuff. I thought this wasn't going to be too bad, so I finished up the few rooms that Al Ely had started . . . and we moved over to the north side of the pueblo and to the early adobe section.

I had the nicest crew of men. I was told they wouldn't work for women and I was told that some of them were rebellious when they heard that a woman was going to be in charge. I think it was a rumor spread by Albert Ely to tell you the truth. I never had a bit of trouble. They were as nice to me as could be.

I had a good relationship with all the workmen. It was quite a mixed crew, mostly Spanish American. I had never worked with a Spanish American crew of laborers before. We had one African American, Dick Fowler. He was a wonderful old gentleman who found a burial that had a little clay pipe with it. We had one Scandinavian man who spoke very broken English. I don't know where he came from. The rest were from Albuquerque and the San Antonito area. They were a wonderful group of men. They couldn't have treated a woman boss any better. They were all perfect gentlemen and they treated me with just the utmost respect. I never gave them any orders. I have never believed in that. I have always asked people if they would help me. And I think that's the way to get along with people because that's the way I like to be treated. . . . Some of us had tears in our eyes when we had to close that excavation.[37]

The love and respect that Marjorie had for her workmen was mutual and reciprocated. The Christmas of 1936, in particular, was very special for her. She recalled what made it so.

I lived in an apartment in Albuquerque, and I was married to my first husband. . . . It was the day before Christmas, and early in the afternoon there was a tap on the door. There were three of my workmen there with a great big package. I guess it was about two feet long. They brought it in and they unwrapped it and said, "It is for you." And, as poor as they were, because they only got paid forty-eight dollars a month and many of them had five or six, if not ten, children. . . . In this package was a perfectly elaborate Christmas cake. It had white icing. It had all kinds of little red bells, all kinds of things that they'd added to it. One of them kissed me on the cheek and said, "Merry, merry Christmas to you." They were the boys from San Antonito.[38]

For the most part, these men had little or no experience and Marjorie had to train them.

I had to show them how a trowel was used. I also bought trowels for all of them, but I told them that either I would do most of the troweling, or Ele [Baker] or J. Charles [Kelley]. They got so they were very good and they knew just how far they were to go with the shovel. Of course, we had no backhoes then. That would have been a scandalous thing to do. They'd take the topmost layer off and they'd kind of tap the ground with the end of their trowels and then I'd tap. One of the interesting things I remember was . . . they were fascinated with me counting the layers of plaster on some of the walls. Some of the walls were beautifully plastered. . . . I would count the number of layers of plaster, figuring out that this may have had something to do with the length of time the room had been occupied.[39]

Marjorie had a theory about the rooms with painted plaster walls.

I don't know whether that would hold or not today. I remember that one of the specialized rooms or ceremonial rooms that was built right within the house block . . . had vestiges of painting. It had red ochre, and white and black and it appeared to have been done at the lower level of the room. It was very shallow at that end of the mound and probably most of it had been washed away. I think that indicated that some of those rooms were painted.

I did a little bit of excavation in the historic part of the site. There were three kivas there. They were discovered by Ele Baker and Dorothy Luhrs. They had excavated the larger of the three and they found that Nels C. Nelson had already excavated it and had filled it with his backfill. There were two nice little kivas, one in each corner of the plaza. I excavated one of them and that was my first personal sight of a foot drum. Then in the ventilator shaft, which I crawled into, I found a very nice, glazed cup. The handle had been broken but this was one of the further indications that this was a site that was occupied up to the Pueblo Revolt [of 1680].

All of the pottery from that section of the pueblo was from a later period. We had fifteen burials, as I remember, and we had all late historic material. One very nice thing that came out of that late section, and it was something that led me to believe that A. V. Kidder was correct, was a perfectly beautiful little ax, a miniature ax. . . . It was Kidder who had pointed out the fact that these were not necessarily ceremonial pieces, that these were probably used in warfare. You know, I think he was right because you could split a person's face or head open with that ax.

I decided that we weren't getting much more information from there. We had excavated about one half of the later part of the site. We did one of the small kivas and we knew where the big kiva was. So, I moved the whole project over to the extreme north side of the site, which turned out to be all adobe and very early. I was very excited because I started a trench down a little bit beyond the first mound. . . . My plan was to work it up to at least the top area of the site. We excavated rooms on either side. I carried on with this trench because that was where I was going to prove to myself that there was stratigraphy at the site. . . . So I started it and began to get a little bit of Kwahe'e black-on-white, Chupadero black-on-white, Santa Fe black-on-white, and Real black-on-white pottery. Lots of it down at the bottom. Then as I worked my way up toward the top layers I began to find the first smattering of Glaze A pottery, showing that this was a transitional site, a Santa Fe black-on-white site if you will, with Glaze A of the earliest glazewares.[40]

It seems to me that we excavated about 135 rooms. One of the interesting things, and I still don't know if this was actually true, but Earl Morris said that anytime you would find a flagstone floor in this part of the Southwest it would probably mean Mesa Verde influence. We started getting this toward the end of the rooms that were partly masonry with flagstone floors. We found a lot of detritus materials that had come from above, indicating that that part of the site was at least two stories.

There was a type of pottery called Galisteo black-on-white.... [Earl] Morris said that it was a clear indication of Mesa Verde influence because it was similar to Santa Fe black-on-white only it had a crackled surface. Most of the pottery did have a crackled surface. We found one whole bowl of that which I believe the University of New Mexico has now. We found some perfectly exciting ceremonial material in one corner of the plaza. I remember a great big slate spear point that must have been carried on a staff as a ceremonial piece. We found an altar stone that was a beautiful white stone with a big hole in the middle for two little ears of corn or possibly feathers, something like that.... There was also a broken cloud blower, if you want to use the term, which is a ceremonial type of pipe with incisions on it.

Below that area was a very interesting burial. In the early prehistoric period in this part of the Rio Grande you normally do not find elbow pipes, but here was an extended burial of an elderly male, as it turned out, with the first little clay elbow pipe that I have ever found. I thought that was a real find. There were all kinds of very interesting ceremonial materials there. We found more axes, a beautiful little amethyst fetish, and other materials which strongly indicated that it was a ceremonial or religious site. These are all in the collections at UNM.

The people living at Paa-ko did their farming across the San Pedro Wash. There were fields that had obviously been cultivated, but Hewett did not want the excavation to go on beyond the fence. The University had fenced the whole area off. So, I was not permitted to go over there. There were also petroglyphs in that area which we weren't allowed to record.

We had a very good and well-preserved group of burials at Paa-ko and Spencer Rogers did the analysis for me. It's in a separate publication from my Paa-ko monograph. His was right after mine.[41] But the disappointment is that he reported on only a few of them because they were really well preserved, and I think that you could get a wonderful study out of the whole series together and compare it with something like the Pecos Series.

This must have been a site that was closely related to perhaps some of the sites in the Galisteo Basin and maybe Pecos over to the east. I don't think people have always agreed with me on this. They want to know whether they were Tanoan or Keres. My feeling is that they were southern Tiwa, from all indications. They would have some relationship to the Puebloan descendants up north, in the Santa Fe area, but the interesting thing is that when Paa-ko was finally abandoned in the historic period, they may have been Keres. They may have moved over from Santo Domingo, so Santo Domingo has always felt certain ownership of that site. . . . I think that the later part of Paa-ko could have been Keresan and the earlier part Tanoan.[42]

Since the south and central portions of the site that had already been excavated were of stone masonry construction and considered to be of a much later date, this was quite an exciting discovery. However, Hewett did not share Marjorie's views about the site and her excavation techniques. As she recalled,

> *That was one of the things that, fond as I was of Hewett, I never could understand. I had quite an extensive stratigraphic test going on there, a great big trench from the lowest part of the site right up through the main part of the site, to determine when the building began and what was there. I had it all strung off and had my sections marked with stakes and I showed him what we were doing. Then I took him down to the field house and showed him what I was finding, which was so much earlier than the part he had designated in the main part of the site down below, and he said, "I still don't think there is any real stratigraphy in the Southwest." Of course he was a classicist and everything was so new and so raw. . . . He couldn't be bothered with anything like that. It was too tedious and not necessary to get the general picture. But how can you get the general picture without knowing where it started?*
>
> *Paa-ko is the first job I had where I was left absolutely alone to do what I wanted to do. It was up to me to decide [where to excavate] and also develop the procedures. I'm glad that I took so much time with that great long stratigraphic test trench. When Hewett came out and said, "You're wasting a lot of time. We aren't getting enough artifacts," I thought, well, I wasn't there to get artifacts. I was there to get information. But anyway, it gave me a chance to prove once and for all to myself how valuable simple stratigraphy is.*[43]

Marjorie and her crew excavated at Paa-ko until the late spring of 1937 when Marjorie's life would take a different direction professionally.

> *Hewett came out with his driver one day and he said, "I've made some changes in the Museum of New Mexico. I've arranged for you to take a position in the Museum of New Mexico and we'll have to close the excavation." Of course, I was heartbroken because I thought we should have gone on just a little bit further because I wanted to see what was going to happen. I never got to study the petroglyphs or run any trenches in what I think were the agricul-*

tural fields close by. Quite a lot of development has gone on in that area now so it's lost.[44]

> *It was a very interesting site and I learned a lot. After I came to the Museum of New Mexico I had some time to study some of the material. I had to borrow back from the university some of the material we excavated because we had to divide everything among the museum, SAR, and UNM. It was a three-way project. Hewett always had that going and it did not really work. That's why part of the skeletons haven't been studied. They were sent on to Spencer Rogers, who was the physical anthropologist at San Diego State.*

Marjorie was clearly disappointed that she was never able to go back to Paa-ko to continue her work there, but she did publish four reports on the excavations between 1937 and 1939.[45]

In a 1938 article in the *New Mexico Anthropologist* published by the Department of Anthropology at the University of New Mexico, Marjorie describes the kivas at Paa-ko and Kuaua and the different cultural materials recovered and analyzed from the excavations at these sites.[46] Even though Marjorie stressed the importance of reporting on the archaeological fieldwork, it was always a struggle for her to balance her work schedule with writing time. Marjorie noted that *the only papers that have come out of Kuaua are mine. I did that paper on the rectangular ceremonial rooms at Kuaua and Paa-ko, a comparison of it. I wrote on that little Spanish structure out on the point of Bandelier's Puaray. I like to finish an account of an excavation as soon as the fieldwork is done, but with Paa-ko there were years of interruptions before it was published in 1954.*[47] According to Linda Cordell, "Marjorie's published site report in 1954 presents both the archival research and detailed reporting of the archaeological work itself. Although there is nothing astounding or unusual about Paa-ko, the report achieves the level of excellence in descriptive reporting, synthesis of detail, and clarity that remains a model today."[48]

Is It Treasure Hunting or Science?

Marjorie had idolized Hewett and was thankful for all that he had done for her professionally, but she soon realized that she disagreed with many of Hewett's theories relating to the early human occupation in the Southwest as well as his methods of excavation and collections management. As

Marjorie recalled, *We had differences when it came to theory, stratigraphy, and classification. . . . He maintained that there were layers of civilization in Europe, but he never accepted the fact that there was stratigraphy in the New World—even though I would take him through the stratigraphic test I was running at Paa-ko.*[49] She was not the only one who disagreed with this premise or with Hewett's methodology. According to Malinda Elliott, "Hewett's critics in the later years objected to his methods of excavation, which had aroused [Alfred M.] Tozzer's opposition during the 1908 dig at El Rito de los Frijoles. Even his students and supporters agreed that he showed little interest in the increasingly technical and scientific aspects of archaeology, including such basic innovations as taking meticulous notes in the field and the use of stratigraphic methods of excavating and dating artifacts."[50] Some even accused him of treasure hunting.

At times Marjorie actually felt that she was in fact on treasure hunting trips for Hewett. She complained:

> *Every now and then, Hewett would get a bee in his bonnet and make us all go down to La Cienega. The School of American Research had a ninety-nine-year lease there and still does. Of course, they wanted to fill up the cases in the museums then. He said, "I want you and Ed [Ferdon] to go down there and start an excavation. We need more pots in the museum." Then we'd have to get Wayne Mauzy and Reginald Fisher to keep the thing from happening because there was no point in just going down there and looking for pottery. It's an interesting site. So that was always in the offing. I did do some work there with the Society later on. We excavated a few rooms to satisfy the Archaeological Society of New Mexico and give its members a little experience at La Cienega. I left all the potsherds washed and cleaned and everything in the files in the Laboratory of Anthropology.*[51]

Hewett's tendency to split up the excavated materials among different institutions created a quagmire in the later years that resulted in tensions and battles over ownership of the collections. According to Marjorie,

> *This is where Hewett made his big mistake. He had this idea that the Archaeological Institute, the Museum of New Mexico, the Archaeological Society of New Mexico, the University of New Mexico, and especially the School of American Research, all had a right to the pie. Sometimes before we got stuff*

studied he'd start dividing it up. He divided a lot of stuff from Cameron Creek, Three Circle, and Mogollon Village long before it came to the museum. He did that all the time. Stuff turned up in Toronto, Los Angeles, San Diego [and other places]. . . . He just gave it away before it could be studied and then he'd expect a report on it!

I hadn't quite finished with Paa-ko when he had Frank Hibben come up [from Albuquerque to Santa Fe] and start taking his share of the loot. I worked that out all right with Frank. . . . He returned a lot of stuff for me to study and after I got through with it I very nicely returned it to UNM. But that collection should have been kept together. I didn't care which unit, whether the university, the school, or the museum. But that's the way it was. . . . That's what Stanley Stubbs used to call the "Hewett Curse."[52]

A Chance Meeting

Before she went to work at Paa-ko, Hewett sent Marjorie to Santa Fe to work temporarily in the Museum of New Mexico.

I was down at the University of New Mexico and Dr. Hewett said that he wanted me to come up here [Santa Fe] to learn something about museums and collections and that I would work primarily with Paul Reiter. I was to learn all I could about museum exhibits and everything. Dr. Hewett had a secretary by the name of Carlotta Warfield, who was well known at that time in Santa Fe. Carlotta lived in Seton Village. There were all kinds of little houses out there. She lived in something that had been a boxcar and it was converted into a home, really quite a cleverly done interior of a boxcar. She gave a party one snowy afternoon. I can't remember how I got there. I must have gone with some of the museum people, perhaps Reginald and Grace Fisher.[53]

It was at this party that she met Everett Vey "Jack" Lambert, who became immediately smitten with her. *When he approached me he said, "Here is this little girl with great big eyes standing off in a corner." He said he thought I was absolutely wonderful.*[54] Shortly after the party, Jack started courting her while she was still working temporarily at the museum in Santa Fe.

[Jack] asked me to go on a picnic with him. To go on a picnic with a date doesn't seem like much, but to go with Jack Lambert was an experience. He

came in this cream-colored roadster, a very nice looking roadster. I don't know what make it was, probably a Chrysler or Chevrolet. And he had this great white western hat and he had on whipcord trousers and jacket and shirt that practically matched as a whole ensemble. He said, "Well, this is going to be a surprise. You told me that you've never been to Tsankawi and that you've never been to the Rito."[55] *It was the Rito de los Frijoles then. It was not Bandelier National Monument. So we went to Tsankawi and he had the chuck box with him. He gave me a few things to carry and we got up on top where the main site is. Of course, there was no Los Alamos [National Laboratory] then. There was nothing. We were the only people around for I guess maybe fifty or sixty miles. We had a delightful day just there on the ruins. He cooked one of his scrumptious lunches. He had canned soup that day [and] . . . some lamb chops. He always had a way of building a fire. He always dug a pit in the ground, a rectangular pit, always in a place where it would be nice and dry. He let me go help gather the wood, but he handled everything from then on. He spread out his tarp and that was the tablecloth and the cook area. . . . So that's where we had our first date and I can't think of any nicer date for a budding archaeologist to be taken on. That was real romance. And he was so nice and polite.*[56]

Born in Okarche, Oklahoma, in 1898, Jack Lambert was ten years older than Marjorie, who was in her late twenties at the time. He was working on the estate of Amelia Elizabeth White on Garcia Street in Santa Fe. Recalling her first date with Jack, Marjorie said, *I thought he was one of the most gentlemanly people I had ever known. He never made a pass or anything like that. He was just a friend. Then he really did start courting me and I remembered what my mother had said to both her daughters, "Don't ever get involved with an older man because they aren't up to any good." So, I just sort of cut it off.*[57]

When Marjorie moved to Santa Fe permanently in 1937, she left her life in academia for a career in museums, which would span the next thirty-two years. She loved her work, whether she was in the field doing archaeology or in the museum laboratory doing ceramic analysis; nevertheless, the one area that annoyed her throughout her career, both as an archaeologist and as a museum professional, was the inequity in her salary when compared to her male colleagues and being referred to as the handmaiden of the museum by Hewett. As a graduate student at Battleship Rock and Chaco Canyon, Marjorie quickly learned that her male colleagues resented having her around.

FIGURE 14 Jack Lambert at the White Estate on Garcia Street, Santa Fe, New Mexico, ca. 1932. Courtesy of the Palace of the Governors Photo Archives (NMHM/DCA). Neg. No. 007614.

When she completed her graduate studies and started teaching and working as an archaeological field supervisor, Marjorie recognized Hewett's double standards regarding her pay and the duties assigned to her.

In a 1985 interview with Jennifer Fox, Marjorie discussed how this double standard affected her.

I was hurt because Dr. Hewett was so good to me, and he thought the world of me—and he was sort of a father figure to all of us. It was like having your own father doing a dirty trick on you. When I got the Paa-ko job, for example, there had been a man ahead of me who hadn't done very good work for three months. I found out that he was getting almost two hundred dollars a month more than me. I found [this] out at a time when I was taking twenty-five dollars a month out of my own salary to have the shovels and picks sharpened. I paid for the photographs, too, out of my own salary.

This attitude would carry over to the Museum of New Mexico, where she would work from 1937 to 1969. Here Marjorie never made the same salary as her male colleagues, some of whom had less responsibility and expertise than she did. She also was not being recognized for the contributions she was making to the field of New Mexico archaeology.

Reflecting on Marjorie's work at Paa-ko, eminent southwestern archaeologist Linda Cordell writes, "Indeed, I think she is best known among southwestern archaeologists for being a meticulous and successful fieldworker."[58] As frustrating as her experiences were, Marjorie knew that her work was professionally done and that she played a role in how archaeological practices and methodology would be carried out going forward.

PART II

New Directions

CHAPTER 5

Museum Work in Santa Fe

1937-1946

> I loved doing exhibit work. I've liked interpretation. I think you
> can teach a lot of anthropology just through interpretation.
>
> —MARJORIE LAMBERT[1]

Shortly after Edgar Lee Hewett retired as head of the Anthropology Department at the University of New Mexico, he invited Marjorie to come to Santa
Fe to work for the Museum of New Mexico in June 1937. She accepted the
transfer and promotion without hesitation. Hewett was still the director of
the Museum of New Mexico and the School of American Research when
he told Marjorie that *he was going to trade Paul Reiter, who was curator of
archaeology at the Museum of New Mexico, to UNM because he wanted me
to come up to Santa Fe and work for him. . . . I went in first at a preparator's
salary and then almost immediately became curator of archaeology.*[2] This
was an abrupt staff change and it no doubt caused some hard feelings as this
was more than likely viewed as a demotion by Reiter, especially since his
mentors and male colleagues were primarily tied to the museum in Santa Fe.

Marjorie was thrilled to be moving to Santa Fe permanently and was excited about her new position at the Museum of New Mexico (MNM). She
was assigned an office at the Palace of the Governors that had previously
been occupied by the renowned linguist and ethnologist John Peabody Harrington. She described her initial reactions when she learned about some
of the activities that had taken place in some of the offices there in the past:

> When I came to work at the museum my first office was in the Palace of
> the Governors and it was in that big room in the northwest corner of the
> patio. That's where Kenneth Chapman said J. P. Harrington lived, cooked,
> ate, and slept, and that he kept his notes all over the floor so you couldn't
> step anywhere. "It was a regular pigsty in there," he said. But anyway, it was

FIGURE 15 Marjorie Ferguson, while serving on the faculty at the University of New Mexico, 1932. Courtesy of Geoffrey Ferguson.

very romantic to me to know that this great linguist had lived there and that some of Hewett's first students had had quarters there. I think that people like [Sylvanus] Morley, [Alfred V.] Kidder, and [Frederick Webb] Hodge, among others, had offices there.[3]

As excited as she was, it didn't take long, however, for Marjorie to realize that she did not have equal status with her male colleagues and that the gender inequality within the patriarchal hierarchy in the museum was not unlike the university. She was one of several women who struggled to make a career in both the museum and the academy.

An Opportunity or a Trap?

In the early twentieth century, museums provided career opportunities outside of academe for many women anthropologists and archaeologists. In some instances, women were preferred over their male peers due to the ascribed gender roles of the time. Hewett, who hired both Marjorie and Bertha Dutton as curators in the Museum of New Mexico, once told Marjorie, "I approve of lady curators, because they are such good housekeepers."[4] Marjorie resented these types of comments and said:

I don't think that Hewett thought he was being chauvinistic when he would make remarks like this. He liked female curators when it came to collections because they had been trained as housekeepers by their mothers and, therefore, they were so much better at it than men. He meant it as a compliment, but what he was really saying is that we were housekeepers. I remember him coming up to some of the big shots at one of the receptions at the annual board meeting of the School of American Research and the Museum of New Mexico, where he introduced me by saying, "This little girl is my best curator; she has cleaned up the Art Museum basement." . . . I was so appalled.[5]

This type of behavior by males in powerful museum positions supports Parezo and Hardin's point that while "the realm of the muses enabled women to have meaningful work in anthropology, . . . it was, simultaneously, a trap that marginalized women by identifying them with undervalued, albeit necessary, labor—i.e., housework, primary and secondary education—and with traditional stereotypes of women as behind-the-scenes assistants."[6] Nonetheless, Marjorie often claimed, *I liked classification. I never minded washing potsherds. I think you learn a lot through washing potsherds. All the menial tasks that befell me were really part of my education and my development. I always got along very well with the public so the public relations part of it never bothered me. I got so I didn't even mind lecturing. In fact, it was even sort of fun.*[7]

In her capacity as preparator and then as curator of archaeology, Marjorie was responsible for the anthropology collections, which had been moved from the Art Museum to the basement of the Hall of Ethnology in the Palace of the Governors.[8] She would later be assigned responsibility for the history collections as well. In addition to her work in collections management, she interpreted and installed numerous exhibitions, and provided public lectures and museum tours for visitors and school groups.

During the Great Depression, when Marjorie received her training and began her career as an anthropologist, Parezo and Hardin note that "university professorships became almost nonexistent for everyone, women who wanted to work in anthropology, were drawn to and hired by museums. This was partly because they were willing to accept less pay, to work in western rather than eastern museums and in small rather than large institutions."[9] Throughout their dedicated years with the Museum of New Mexico, neither Marjorie nor Bertha Dutton, who was the curator of ethnology, earned as much as their male colleagues, and it was obvious to both of them. Marjorie felt that the rationale for this salary differential was unfair. She recalled:

Every now and then the paper would publish salaries of the top people in the museum and you'd find out someone whose job you were partly doing was getting more money. . . . I know two men I worked with were getting $100 to $150 more than I was and I was doing exactly the same work with the same title. And you know what the excuse was? "Well, we're the head of our families and you're not." . . . They thought they were giving us a break by having us in the profession. They didn't come right out and say it, but I'm sure that's what it was. And their attitude was, if she wants to have everything, why doesn't she go and find a man with money and marry him?[10]

Much to her disappointment, Marjorie also soon realized that working in a museum did not provide much free time for research or fieldwork. She was frustrated and pointed out:

When I went into the museum, and I'm sure Bertha was told the same thing because she came in at the same time, we were told that we would spend half our time at curatorial work and the rest would be research, whatever we wanted to do. It never did work out that way. The duties that I had to perform just took all my time. They didn't have a docent program then, so I was expected to spend part of my time taking school groups through [the museum]. The men on the staff wouldn't do it so it was left to the women on the staff. . . . I felt again that it was part of my job to teach. I also felt it was part of my job to go out and give lectures to service clubs and so on. You have to prepare for those things. If you are invited, you are expected to perform. It was good publicity for the museum. I might as well be honest about it; it helps you too. It makes you better known professionally.[11]

From the beginning of the creation of the School of American Research and the Museum of New Mexico, Hewett was constantly battling to keep both under his directorship, thus in his control. Occasionally this surfaces as one reads the Annual Reports of the SAR. During the late 1930s and early 1940s, Marjorie was listed as staff under both the Museum of New Mexico and the School of American Research. While working for the museum she was consistently listed as curator of archaeology under the SAR staff listing. In 1941 the SAR annual report has her listed as curator of archaeology under the museum and as a research associate at the SAR. Hewett often listed his staff under both institutions while each maintained separate missions and governance as mandated by the New Mexico State Legislature. There are other inconsistencies in the SAR's Annual Reports. At various times the staff provided their own information, and at other times they provided information to Hewett, who then wrote about their activities.

As the curator of archaeology, Marjorie cataloged and cared for the archaeology and history collections; designed, built, and interpreted numerous exhibits; gave lectures and arranged for guest speakers; was on call to see about excavations being carried out for new buildings and roads when archaeological evidence began to surface; and kept up with public relations for the museum through public tours and popular articles in journals, newspapers, and *El Palacio*. She provided many services to the public in the form of volunteerism and membership in several cultural, historical, and arts organizations, and gave lectures to different groups and assisted researchers with collections and archaeological research. The period between 1937 and

1946 was a time for Marjorie to gain experience in all the "realms of the muses" as well as navigate her way through numerous roadblocks set up to hinder her progress professionally. She was able to overcome the periodic setbacks and continued to build a successful career as a museum curator while maintaining her professional status as a southwestern archaeologist.

The Museum's Handmaiden

Marjorie, like several other women in museum curatorial positions, always felt that part of her responsibilities included record keeping and the care of the collections, which often involved "housekeeping" duties. The men on the staff, however, were never found with a broom or dust mop in their hands cleaning the basement where the collections were stored. Early on, Marjorie devoted a great deal of time thoroughly cleaning and fumigating the Palace of the Governors and parts of the Art Gallery, while paying special attention to the archaeology collections housed throughout the different buildings. In addition to the physical care of the collections, Marjorie also focused on improving the record-keeping process. She spent a good deal of time reorganizing the storage space so that the artifacts and their associated reports would be protected from fire and theft. She also developed a records management system to make them more manageable and accessible.[12] It should also be pointed out that the collections Marjorie was overseeing had a mixed bag of ownership by the school, the museum, and the New Mexico Historical Society so record keeping was not only necessary, it was essential. She was applying collections management best practices long before museum professionals were trained in this and other areas of collections care.

Marjorie also carried out her other curatorial work, which included the documentation, cataloging, and repairing of the archaeological and historical collections so they could be placed on exhibit. She was especially concerned that "every archaeological object shown in the Governors' Palace has been properly recorded."[13] Marjorie's goal was "to make laboratory and storage facilities in the Art Gallery as adequate as those in the Hall of Ethnology, when conditions and finances permit." And she wrote that "in the meantime, waterproofing and replastering the vault and storage closet where rare textiles, skin paintings and other historical items of a perishable nature are kept, has just been completed. A temporary dust proof alcove for historical storage specimens has also been prepared."[14]

FIGURE 16 The Hall of Archaeology exhibit at the Palace of the Governors about the time that Marjorie started her new curatorial position, ca. 1940. Photo by Wyatt Davis. Courtesy of the Palace of the Governors Photo Archives (NMHM/DCA). Neg. No. 001449.

After making numerous improvements in the collection storage area over the summer, Marjorie pointed out, "With these tasks almost completed, the curator hopes to proceed soon with the repair of historical specimens and to a program of research and writing."[15] After five years as a curator, Marjorie was still trying to find the time to continue her archaeological research and write up the projects she had already worked on. Nevertheless, Marjorie and Bertha were able to occasionally get out of the museum to visit archaeological sites.

Educating the Public Through Interpretation

In addition to her collections management duties, Marjorie also had responsibility for changing the archaeology and history exhibitions. It was noted in a 1981 article in the *Santa Fean* magazine that "Marge set up the Museum's

FIGURE 17 Marjorie and some of her colleagues visiting the ancient Alibates Flint Quarries outside Amarillo, Texas, ca. 1935. Left to right: Hulda R. Hobbs, Jean Cady, Marjorie Tichy (Lambert), and Bertha Dutton. Courtesy of the Archives, Museum of Indian Arts & Culture, Lab of Anthropology. Bertha P. Dutton Collection.

exhibits in the Hall of the Modern Indian in a building behind the Palace of the Governors. In the Palace her archaeological exhibits were on Early Man in the Southwest, Pueblo III which lasted from about A.D. 1050 until the end of the 13th century, and Pueblo IV from then on until historic times."[16] Marjorie noted that in 1938, *There were only two units of the Museum of New Mexico then. There was the Art Museum and the Palace of the Governors. Hewett had already been dickering for a Hall of the Modern Indian. It was called the Hall of Ethnology then. Bertha [Dutton] was curator of ethnology, and I was curator of archaeology. Those were the first really good displays we had of modern Indian life in that building.*[17]

The following year, Marjorie worked on nine special exhibitions. The photographic exhibits in the Puye and Rito de los Frijoles rooms were cleaned and bordered or framed. Two large oils of the Missions of Jemez and Pecos were hung in the Pecos Room. She also worked on exhibitions that were sent outside of the museum. This was a series of exhibitions on weapons, jewelry, fetishes, pottery, bone, and stone tools that were sent to branch museums through the Museum of New Mexico Extension Project.[18] Marjorie prepared an exhibition of materials from Kuaua, Bandelier's Puaray, and Paa-ko, along with site photographs for the Works Progress Administration authorities in Washington, DC. She also prepared and sent an exhibition to the San Francisco World's Fair that illustrated the pottery restoration work that she was doing.[19]

When Hewett reassigned the history collections to Marjorie in 1941, there was also a change in the way in which these collections were to be interpreted going forward. For Marjorie, this required an almost complete reinterpretation of the exhibitions currently on view in the museum. The intended goal was to integrate archaeology and history so that the museum visitor would come away with the understanding that these two subjects were interrelated in the Southwest. The interpretive strategy for these new exhibitions was reported in the 1941 SAR Annual Report. "The installation will present the earliest cultures that have been firmly established and pro-ceed with chronological developments as nearly as can be, through all the stages down to the Spanish occupation. Here southwestern archaeology, his-tory, and ethnology blend to such an extent that no attempt should be made to separate them. The historical collections accumulated during the past half-century by the New Mexico Historical Society are probably the best of their kind in existence. These will be installed as far as possible by periods, and will aim to illustrate the domestic, economic, and ecclesiastical phases of New Mexico history."[20]

Marjorie reinstalled several exhibitions at the Palace of the Governors in 1942. The Spanish Colonial and Mexican Period Rooms were entirely renovated with the addition of two dioramas, three table models of New Mexico missions added to the Mission Room exhibits, and changes were made in the Ecclesiastical and Historical Rooms. Based on staff observations and some sample testing, these new exhibits appealed to visitors who were spending more time in these exhibitions and were studying the displays and the labels.[21]

Changes were also made to the archaeological exhibits. The former Chaco Room, which was now called the San Juan Drainage Room, was completely remodeled. One of the features was a reproduction of the benches and niches of the great kiva at Chetro Ketl, where the famous jewelry finds were made by the SAR and UNM in 1931. Marjorie, who was there when the niche was opened, recreated this in the exhibit and displayed the turquoise and shell necklaces in a setting similar to the one in which they were originally discovered. Marjorie also had two table models created that depicted Tyuonyi, a typical great house pueblo of the Rio Grande, and a Mogollon village scene. These were displayed in the Hall of Archaeology. She also installed new exhibitions in the Rito de los Frijoles, Puye, and Pecos rooms. According to Marjorie, these changes had drawn great interest from the public.[22] These new exhibit installations were quite an improvement over the static cases full of artifacts that she found when she started in her position as curator of archaeology. Her new form of interpretation and storytelling was not only engaging for the visitors, but it also educated the public about New Mexico's deep and continuous history. She published a short description of the new installation, in the Early Spanish Colonial and Mexican Period Rooms as well as the Hall of Archaeology at the Palace of the Governors, in *El Palacio*.[23]

Marjorie was almost finished with the reinstallation of the exhibitions at the Palace of the Governors in early 1943. The wall cases in the Hall of Archaeology had been installed and improvements in the Mimbres-Chihuahua Room were completed. She designed the space by painting the wall and casework with a turquoise background using pottery motifs painted in a light gray as spatial dividers. She used earth tones on other exhibit cases holding sculptural works and basketry. In one exhibit case holding Mimbres pottery, she used terraced risers to create a Southwest pueblo architectural effect. These colors and exhibition techniques continue to be popular in Southwest museums today.

Service men and their families were among the visitors who came to the museum, and Marjorie observed that the new exhibits had become a source of pleasure for many servicemen stationed in New Mexico.[24] For Marjorie, the museum provided an outlet for teaching through her interpretive exhibits along with the guided public tours she often provided.

Finding Time to Write

In addition to her curatorial responsibilities and new exhibit installations, Marjorie wrote articles for both scholarly and public audiences. Shortly after taking her position at the museum, she published an article in 1938 on the kivas of Paa-ko and Kuaua and their comparison to kivas in areas outside of the Rio Grande Valley.[25] She also did a great deal of writing for the newspaper. *I was always being called on for articles on this and that. I never kept a copy of the stuff, so I can't tell you what it was all about. It was mostly about lectures we were going to have. Public announcements to lure people into the excitement, and the mysteries, of the Southwest.*[26] Although she didn't mind writing, she often said, *I would rather do the research. Again, it's fieldwork versus the lab work. I think writing is hard in a way. It either flows very readily or else I sit and stare at a page for half a day and it won't come.*[27]

In 1939 Marjorie carved out some time to write a summary of the excavations at Bandelier's Puaray, more commonly known as Santiago Pueblo today. She describes a large pueblo of 450 ground-floor rooms built of adobe along with a description of some of the artifacts recovered.[28] She also wrote a short popular article on Paa-ko for *New Mexico Magazine*. Being very descriptive, it no doubt appealed to the layman as much as the avocational archaeologist.[29]

In line with her goal to educate the public about archaeology, Marjorie wrote another popular article for *New Mexico Magazine* in 1940. This time she focused on the role of the professional archaeologist in excavating, collecting, and preserving the artifacts from a site. She also provides details on how artifacts are preserved and cataloged once they reach the museum, thus providing a glimpse into what goes on behind the scenes in the care and preservation of museum collections.[30] That same year, Marjorie wrote sections on Kuaua, Puaray, and Paa-ko in *Landmarks of New Mexico*, published by Edgar L. Hewett and Wayne L. Mauzy.[31] As noted in the SAR's 1941 Annual Report, Marjorie was also "given the assignment of writing the section on ceramics in the next forthcoming number of the Handbook Series, the Archaeological History of the Rio Grande Valley."[32]

Marjorie always wanted to compile a complete bibliography on New Mexico archaeology, and throughout 1944 she continued her research on this project. She also contributed one lead article in *El Palacio*, "Taakaa, Pueblo Indian Dwarf."[33] She reviewed books by Mischa Titiev and Leo Simmons, and an article on archaeological nomenclature by T. A. Richards, along with writing numerous short news items for *El Palacio*.[34]

While working in the collections, Marjorie wrote short articles about some of the more interesting pieces that she discovered, and in 1945 she penned one of her popular articles in *El Palacio* on the distribution of early elbow pipes.[35] At this point in her career, Marjorie found it more fruitful to write short, well-researched articles for the Museum of New Mexico's membership publication *El Palacio*, which served a popular audience while keeping content detailed enough to appeal to scholars. Crossover writing such as this is difficult to achieve but Marjorie mastered it.

Sneaking in a Little Archaeological Fieldwork

Even though Marjorie was not engaged in active fieldwork in the late 1930s to early 1940s, she made numerous weekend trips to investigate archaeological sites that had been discovered and reported to the museum, that were under excavation or reconstruction by the museum, or had been reported as having been vandalized. She also visited sites that had not been explored or reported on, with the idea of planning archaeological work in the future. While on these trips she made notes, took photographs, and collected samples of sherds.[36]

In her 1946 summary of archaeological work done by the SAR and MNM, Marjorie reported on work that had recently been carried out at Pecos Pueblo. Today located within Pecos National Historical Park, Pecos Pueblo is located approximately twenty-five miles southeast of Santa Fe. As populations along the Rio Grande expanded into the upper Pecos Valley to form small, scattered settlements between 800 and 1100 CE, farming groups eventually consolidated and Pecos Pueblo was founded around 1300 CE. Pecos grew to nearly seven hundred rooms arranged in a quadrangle of multistoried community houses around a large central plaza. It was one of the first North American villages to feel the impact of European contact as early as 1540. The Pecos mission established by the Spanish monks of the Franciscan Order was destroyed during the Pueblo Revolt of 1680 but was rebuilt following the reconquest of 1692.[37] In 1788 the population of Pecos Pueblo was devastated by a smallpox epidemic, and by the mid-1830s the population had declined to only twenty-seven individuals, who abandoned their homes and traveled to Jemez Pueblo, where their descendants continue to reside today.

Marjorie reported that "in 1938–40, stabilization of the mission and monastery ruins of Pecos was done, mainly under Bill Witkind; and excavation of the South House was conducted in 1939 under J.W. Hendron and members of the Museum staff."[38] John M. Corbett was also listed as a field supervisor at the site. Although not recognized for the work she did there, Marjorie also worked at Pecos during this time period. As she recalled,

I've done a lot of work at Pecos. . . . You don't get any of that in the literature at all. There were some miscellaneous papers. J. W. Hendron was sent out [in 1938] to do some work there, and he came in and talked to me. We were very good friends. In fact, I used to date him. He was a nice guy. J. W. said, "You know, I don't want to be messing around with something Kidder did. I'd just as soon do my restoration. That's what Hewett wants. You think I could get around the church?" I said, "Well, do whatever needs to be done. He wants stabilization. Let him see you're doing some stabilization." He built the little house. It's supposed to be close to the visitor's center and it's about the size of a little outhouse. Then he excavated a kiva connected with the South House. He found out that it had been excavated by Kidder, and it had a stake down inside that said, "Finished on such-and-such a date." So we laughed about that.

Then the next person that was sent out there to work on the monastery and the church was Bill Witkind [in 1939]. He was doing the monastery rooms and a lot of good work in the church . . . then he was called up by the army during World War II. . . . One of the things that I was left to do for a couple of weeks when he was gone was to excavate around what was left of the altar. That's the one time that I backed off from a job. It turned out that recent people in the valley there, probably too poor to afford anything in the cemetery, had been burying their dead there. I remember there was a little girl. Probably she would have been about seven or eight. She had dark brown curls and a hair ribbon. I went to Hewett and I said, "I just don't think we should be doing this. I think we should just cover this up." So he gave orders to close that up. I guess they are still there and I hope they are.[39]

I worked over [Bill Witkind's] field material as much as I could and left it on file at the museum. . . . One of the pieces of knowledge concerning what went on here in the Rio Grande Valley is at the South House at Pecos. Because it is in that mound that you are going to find material that will close the gap between the Pueblo Indian Rebellion (1680), or around 1700 A.D. to about 1820 to 1830. Why do you find a gap there in the collections? Why do you find it elsewhere? The pottery is there. You've got Ogapoge Polychrome. You've got Puname Polychrome. You've got the whole works, and that's the one part of Pecos that has not been studied. It adjoins the big church. . . . These were the people who were living there in the last days of the Pueblo. There is some perfectly wonderful material there. That is where Bill Witkind found that little humpbacked stone figure. It's in the museum collection.[40]

Bruce Ellis and Stanley Stubbs were excavating that little church that a lot of people don't know about at Pecos, way outside of the ruin. It's the first one that was built by Fray Luis [de Escalona] when he first came there [around 1542].[41] He probably planned to live there. He was living in the Pueblo, but he probably planned to live there while he was doing his greater work. Bruce Ellis and Stanley Stubbs had become interested in small "lost churches" and Stanley later did a paper for El Palacio *on that little church. They came to me about three or four weeks before my birthday, which is in June, and they said, "We're going to give you a birthday present. For a birthday present we're going to invite you to spend some time with us on the excavation in the little lost church. Would you like to come?" And so we all went out together, no workmen or anything, just the three of us. They wanted to outline the foundation, which incidentally was beautiful masonry and still very good. No adobe. Nothing had been built over it. Some sort of tragedy had happened I guess by that time.*

One was digging on one side and one was digging on the other. I had my trowel and everything there and I said, "Well, what do you want me to do?" And they said, "Oh, you can just sit around and watch us." I said, "How about doing that little anteroom? It's small and I won't be in your way." They kind of looked at each other and said, "She can do that. Let's let her have it." Well, first thing I began finding was that there was something that felt very exciting below. I didn't say a thing. I kept on going. Finally, with my whiskbroom, I began to see these adobe blocks that had been made. They looked as though they had been made yesterday. They were stacked ready to start the church. It was going to be a little adobe church. But the interesting thing about them was that little goats had walked across some of them while they were still damp and there were little footprints. This was the first evidence of goats being tethered there at Pecos. So, I exposed my site without saying anything and Bruce Ellis said, "Well, I'll be damned." So, we had our lunch, and they had a little cake for me with a candle. . . . I had a wonderful time with them, and I think they were glad I was there too. They didn't want to bring any of those adobes into the museum, but I insisted because I thought it was so important to have on record some of the earliest adobes that we knew of that had been made and that there had been livestock there. Of course, it was at Pecos that some of the Indians had been making little figurines of horses.[42]

It was during this time at Pecos that Marjorie started to develop a theory related to the early use of anthropomorphic figures for religious and ceremonial purposes in Pueblo life. She reported on the little humpbacked stone figure found by Bill Witkind at Pecos in a 1957 *El Palacio* article. After a discussion of the strong evidence toward a "definite Mexican antecedent for this and perhaps many other Southwestern stone anthropomorphs including the Fire God related deities, and perhaps the Humpbacked Flute Player," Marjorie argued for a southwestern origin for this figure and observed that "it may be that in a remote period of Southwestern prehistory there were only one or two recognized deities, and that the pantheon increased as the Pueblo culture became more complex. The God of Fire and the Humpbacked Flute Player could very well be the oldest in concept among the Southwestern archeological supernaturals. It is also important to remember that stone anthropomorphs are still in use in a number of pueblos. Their magical powers are still recognized, particularly with reference to rainfall, and crops and human fertility."[43]

By 1943 Marjorie was becoming very concerned that she was not going to get into the field to conduct her own archaeological project, such as the ones that were being carried out at Pecos by her male colleagues. As her concerns grew about being stuck in the museum, Marjorie started to question whether she made the right decision or not. Even though she often said that she loved working in the museum, her heart was not completely there and she always had the strong desire to do archaeological fieldwork and yearned to have a project of her own again. The war no doubt had an impact on the work being done, but there was New Deal funding available and Marjorie could have been assigned a project if Hewett wanted to give one to her. Although she probably would never admit it, she was starting to feel trapped in the museum doing "women's work."

As World War II escalated, Marjorie's travels to archaeological sites and state and national monuments were curtailed. Nevertheless, being the creative and curious young woman that she was, she managed to squeeze in a couple of field trips to some of the surrounding Indian pueblos and New Mexico State Monuments, as well as archaeological sites near Santa Fe in 1944.[44] She also attended the annual Feast Day at Zia Pueblo that summer, one of her favorite things to do. She reported on this feast day in *El Palacio*.[45]

Marjorie did conduct a "small amount of field work at the ancient Pueblo site of Yuque-Yunque, where the first Hispanic settlement in New Mexico was made."[46] As Nancy Fox suggests, "In 1944, combining archaeological with historical investigation, [Marjorie's] search for Oñate's capitol, San Gabriel, led to excavation at the ruins of Yuque-Yunque near San Juan [Pueblo]."[47] Nevertheless, when Hewett sent her out to excavate the area by Ohkay Owingeh Pueblo (formerly San Juan Pueblo), Marjorie had a particularly frightening field experience. Even though she was excited by the prospect of actually doing some archaeological fieldwork, it was not a good time to be in the field alone and Marjorie tried to convince Hewett that given the circumstances it was not the time to do such a project. She pointed out that

> Hewett was old, there's no doubt about it, and I don't think he was thinking clearly. He said, "I want you to go up and dig a few rooms at Yuque-Yunque. Not in San Gabriel but at Yuque-Yunque." I said, "It's wartime. I don't think we could get a crew together." He said, "Well you can find a couple or three Indians in San Juan that will help you." There was no sense in it at all.[48] I had an awfully hard time trying to convince him that it wasn't the thing to do, that we didn't have the budget, that we wouldn't be able to get the proper equipment, the number of men and so on, but he insisted on my going. That was when I stayed in that horrible old hotel which has since been torn down and had that awful experience on All Souls Day.[49]

Marjorie recalled the frightening conditions that she had to work under: *I stayed in a ratty old hotel in Riverside. It was kind of on the outskirts of Espanola. There were some very drunk men in the room next to me that were on some kind of a road project or something, and they were drunk every night. The door to my room kept popping. The only thing that really gave me any security was the fact that I had two Scottish Terriers with me and they're fighters. They were very protective toward me.*[50]

In addition to being concerned for her safety at the hotel at night, Marjorie also had to deal with a dangerous situation at the site and while traveling across Ohkay Owingeh Pueblo lands. As she recalled,

> The man who was my chief excavator was a very strange person. He believed in witches, and he told me that he felt witches were around. I think it was because Halloween [October 31] and All Souls Day [November 2] were coming. He brought to work one day a gun with notches on it. He said, "This is for the witches that I have killed. Every time you see an owl that means that a witch is watching you. I've been hearing witches around here at night." I almost got the feeling that he thought maybe I was one in some way or another. Most of the

FIGURE 18 Marjorie with one of her Scottish terriers, Sandy, in front of her rented guest house on Delgado Street in Santa Fe, ca. 1932. Courtesy of the Archives, Museum of Indian Arts & Culture, Lab of Anthropology. Neg. No. 70.852.

time I was there alone with him and his wife. We could not get workmen. She would help me push the wheelbarrow, and he and I would do the excavation.[51]

An old Indian who was helping us said that it was All Souls Day and the Indians were going to cross where we were digging with baskets of stuff and they had candles with them. He lived in a little village up above San Juan Pueblo, and I took him home that night. On the way that ratty old car I had died and here were those Indians going across to these hills just beyond us with their baskets of food. It was dark. The old man said that he'd go for help because he didn't know how to fix the car. He never did come back. Then an Indian on horseback came back and I thought, Well, this is it. Something's going to happen to me. I'm close to a sacred area. *He said, "You just stay here. I'll go back to the Pueblo and I'll try to find a mechanic for you." I couldn't believe it. This was about two in the morning. Hours later, another Indian came by in an old rattle-trap truck and said, "Well, I found a fuel pump. That's what's wrong with your car." This was around 5 o'clock in the morning, and he replaced the fuel pump in the car. I had $15 with me. That's all I had. I signed an IOU and told him about the Museum of New Mexico and Dr. Hewett and he trusted me. I went back to Espanola and I got my things out of that old hotel room with the drunks next door and I came back to Santa Fe. I think that's the only scary thing that's ever happened to me. It was All Souls night of all times. I should not have been sent out there anyway. But you know, you couldn't complain to Hewett. Woman or not. It would have been worse if I had complained. . . . I turned in my notes to Hewett and I said, "That's it." Oh, and the business manager, Wayne Mauzy, complained about the bill. My bill for the three weeks for the room was fifteen dollars and I would fix my own lunch, maybe just bread and cheese or milk and coffee, and then eat in that cheap little old restaurant. I was afraid to leave my room most of the time because of the drunk men. Overall, I got very little out of it. It was a waste of time and a waste of money and it should never have been done. . . . It was the only really bad experience I think that I've ever had. It really was a frightening experience.*[52]

Marjorie reported on this fieldwork in the SAR's 1944 Annual Report:

The curator spent the week of October thirtieth to November fourth at Yuque-Yunque, where investigations and a small amount of excavation were carried out. This is said to have been the site of the first capital of New Mexico, named San Gabriel by Don Juan de Oñate, the founder in 1598.[53] It is, therefore, of extreme importance, both archaeologically and historically. . . . The most important point to be made here is the necessity of preserving what remains of this site, so that further cultivation and various inroads on the mounds will not destroy what may reveal an important historical secret.[54]

Much of the site had already been destroyed by an adobe-making operation. To prevent any further destruction to the site, Marjorie recommended that it be marked off until further investigation could be made that would "settle the important historical and archeological question of the site of the first capital of New Mexico."[55]

In a 1944 *El Palacio* article, Marjorie wrote that

> While no definite conclusions can be made from so little work, a few pertinent deductions can be made at this point regarding the site. Careful examination of the entire vicinity, as well as the excavation, seemed to verify that this is the Yuque-Yunque of history and tradition. The site consisted of one, or more, large communal type, adobe dwellings of one or more stories. It is regrettable that no actual proof of the site being San Gabriel as well could be gotten at the time of this investigation, but appearances on the surface surrounding the Indian dwellings to the west and southwest of the mound, where actual tests were made, reveal remnants of what may well have been a late 16th, or early 17th century settlement.[56]

In September 1946 Marjorie's deepest fear that Yuque-Yunque would be destroyed came to pass when she was informed by a nearby resident that large-scale adobe-making operations were in progress. Two days later, Marjorie and others paid a visit to the site to find that a bulldozer was being used and that less than half of the only remaining mound of any size was left. She found that a considerable number of rooms were destroyed, including all of those excavated by her in 1944. This was heartbreaking for Marjorie, especially when she had raised these concerns both vocally as well as in her 1944 *El Palacio* article.

Subsequently, a letter was sent to the United Pueblos Agency in Albuquerque concerning the destruction of the site and a representative was sent to investigate this. He met with the governor of Ohkay Owingeh Pueblo, who in fact owned the land on which the site was located. The governor's explanation was that the Pueblo people did not know that they were causing any harm and that in the future they would contact the museum before doing any cultivation or heavy digging in the vicinity of the site. This didn't stop all activities at the site, but it did minimize further destruction somewhat.[57]

At this point, they salvaged what they could and brought the artifacts back to the museum for analysis and curation. One important find was a badly corroded mass of metal, which appeared to be chain mail.[58] Marjorie also provided a report on her work at Yuque-Yunque in the *New Mexico Histor-*

ical Review, where she discusses the discovery of a piece of metal that was thought to be a fragment of the San Gabriel bell. Originally discovered by Stephen Trujillo, a member of Ohkay Owingeh Pueblo, Marjorie and others wanted to believe that this could be from the first capital of New Mexico. Nevertheless, it was felt that more research needed to be done and that a search for bells dating to the 1600s would be beneficial for comparative purposes.[59] A second opinion in the 1950s concluded that the fragment was too small to have been a mission bell and that it may have been a mortar for grinding spices or medicinal materials.[60]

Florence Hawley Ellis later led a summer archaeological field school at San Gabriel del Yunque from 1959 to 1962. They found the first capital established by Oñate exactly where Marjorie had been working in 1944. Ellis concluded:

> In its first stage, Yunque was a long-lasting and successful pueblo. In its second stage, as San Gabriel del Yunque, it was in large part not reconstructed but revised to alleviate some of the Spaniards' discomfort at living under conditions to which they and their ancestors had not been accustomed. San Gabriel was the second [European] settlement in what is now the United States. Here we have a different story from that of San Marcos and we also have much more of the physical remnants than were preserved in Florida. What is left should be saved, a symbol of cultural heritage for three peoples: Pueblo, Spanish, and Anglo.[61]

This certainly closed the chapter on the mystery of whether this was in fact the first Spanish settlement in New Mexico. It was through Marjorie's efforts that the site was protected long enough for Ellis and her students to carry out their full-scale excavation.

Added Responsibilities

Beginning in 1942 Marjorie was also given the responsibility for managing all of the lectures for the museum, the SAR, and the Archaeological and Historical Societies of New Mexico. She selected the speakers, entertained them, did all the publicity, and often ran the slide projector in St. Francis Auditorium in the Art Museum where the lectures were held. Marjorie also traveled around the state giving lectures at branch museums and to different organizations.

In her position as curator of archaeology, Marjorie was also assigned duties relating to the Archaeological Society of New Mexico. She reported that she was appointed secretary and ex-officio trustee of the Santa Fe chapter of the Archaeological Society of New Mexico on July 28, 1943.[62] She recalled how this new assignment came about:

One afternoon when I was classifying bone pins from Paa'ko, the excavation I did on the east side of the Sandia Mountains, I got a call from Edgar Lee Hewett's office. Sitting with him in his office was the Assistant Director, Reginald Fisher, and Hewett said, "We've been going over the bylaws of the Archeological Society of New Mexico and it says in the bylaws that the curator of archaeology of the School and the Museum of New Mexico, is to be the secretary of the Archaeological Society of New Mexico. So, we are hereby notifying you of your duties. I want you to read the bylaws carefully and abide by them." He said that one of the things would be that I should probably confer with Mr. Walters over at the bank because he was president of the Historical Society and he said the two work closely together. This is the way it worked. It was obvious to me, even as naïve and as young as I was at that time, that the Museum of New Mexico had total control over the Archaeological Society of New Mexico. The president of the Board of Managers of the museum was to be the president of the Archaeological Society. The curator of archaeology was to be the secretary. The assistant director of the museum would be the State Archaeologist, and that would be Reginald Fisher. The overall boss would be the director of the museum, Edgar Lee Hewett.[63]

As secretary of the Archaeological Society of New Mexico Marjorie was responsible for organizing the society's lectures on top of all her museum responsibilities, something she was not too happy about. She also had to record the minutes of the society's board meetings. Serving as secretary of the society added an extra burden to what was already a demanding work schedule.

Marjorie served in this position until 1959, and even though she enjoyed it for the most part, it also gave her plenty of headaches. During this time, they held meetings four times a year and Marjorie noted that she

would read the minutes of the last one and then we would get to talking about what my additional duties would be. Mr. Walters told me that as long as I was getting speakers and sending out notices of meetings why couldn't I do this for the Historical Society too. I was very young. . . . They told me what to do and I had to do it. This is what I did. I selected the speakers of the Archaeological Institute of America. I selected the speakers for the Archaeological Society, the Historical Society, and the School of American Research. I was responsible for seeing that they were entertained. Sometimes there was no money at all and I had to pay for their dinner. Someone had to entertain them. Sometimes there wasn't anyone available to run slides for their talks so I had to do it. But I did meet some very interesting people and in time I think I brought some very good speakers to Santa Fe. Watson Smith talked on the Awatovi kiva murals. Paul Martin talked about his work at Point of Pines. Poor Joe Ben Wheat. The night he was to talk on his early man research in Colorado, we had a heavy snowstorm. My husband [Jack Lambert] and I and the Lippencotts [Sallie and Bill], and Joe Ben turned up! That was one of the disasters. But, I think it was too much work to put on one person, because I was supposed to be doing archaeological work and had to get my publications out too.[64]

In addition to her other tasks, Marjorie also answered calls to monitor excavations at construction sites or to remove human burials. At the time neither the Museum of New Mexico nor the School of American Research had a contract archaeology program so Marjorie was the one who would get the calls. She never knew when a call would come in. One day she recalled, *I got a call, this was from Morley's office, saying that I had to go over where they were excavating for a new building near the state capitol. It was an extremely interesting burial, but you should have seen my dress. I was to give a talk in the La Fonda Hotel. [The burial] looked like an old, old woman . . . with a beautiful corrugated jar. But that's what salvage archaeology was then. I was it.*[65]

In addition to her duties as secretary of the Archaeological Society of New Mexico, Marjorie provided numerous lectures and programs in her role as a curator for the museum. She did two radio lectures on KVSF about the place of archaeology and history in telling the story of "man" in the Southwest in August and September 1944. She focused on public outreach and provided a lecture on southwestern archaeology to seventh-grade students under the auspices of the Altrusa Service Club of Santa Fe. She also provided numerous tours of the museum to special interest groups. On June 15, 1944, Marjorie traveled to New Mexico Highlands University in Las Vegas to give a lecture on the Archaeology of the Frontier Pueblos to a group of students.

As time went on, Marjorie grew resentful of the fact that she had to do all the "secretarial" work in addition to everything she was responsible for and was frustrated that none of her male peers would assist her. She kept this bottled up inside and said, *I never argued. I just did it. Somehow, I got my work done. I don't know how I did it all. And I had to write all the newspaper publicity too.*[66] After fourteen years, Marjorie resigned as secretary of the Archaeological Society of New Mexico. She claimed, *I finally caught on and had the nerve to say, "I'm not going to do it anymore and you're going to have to get someone to run the slide projector; you're going to have to get some additional help."*[67]

Volunteer Service During the War

Despite her busy days at the museum and many evenings setting up lectures and entertaining guest speakers, Marjorie found time to volunteer. She wrote that she had "devoted many evenings throughout the year to duties and activities of the Red Cross Motor Corps and assisted in transporting patients and nurses to and from Bruns Army Hospital." She also acted as a guide "taking service men to San Ildefonso and archeological sites on the Pajarito Plateau. Time and services were also given to the Red Cross War Fund Drive and to similar activities."[68]

Marjorie remembered this time period as one of those unique experiences that many women gained during the war. *I became captain of the women's Red Cross unit here in Santa Fe, and if there's anyone who knew less about an exhaust manifold or how to turn on the ignition and keep it going it was me. I knew less about machinery than anything else. We had an instructor, Jimmy Wheeler was his name. . . . He gave us courses in different parts of the automobile. Our final test was to go out somewhere in the country and he'd do something to the car that would keep it from running and you had to fix it and come back.*[69]

During her training, she was put to the test. For her final test, Marjorie reminisced:

It was on Hyde Park Road where he [the instructor] left me and he had done something to the fuel pump. I was very proud of myself. Of course, you couldn't do that to a car now, they're too complicated, but I could lift up the hood of my car and kind of check things out, make sure that the wiring was all there. I knew that something had been done to the fuel pump and that's how I got by with that. . . . I don't know how I ever passed, but I did. Then we were taken to one of the buildings out at Bruns Hospital and we took Red Cross first aid.

That I really enjoyed and had a lot of fun. . . . We worked quite a bit with the
patients out at the hospital.[70]

One of the activities that Marjorie was involved in was taking the ambu-
latory service men out to the pueblos to see ceremonial dances. She soon
found out, however, how ingrained the negative stereotypes were among
people from other parts of the country. She noted that *some of them would*
say, "So this is the twentieth century? So these are American Indians?" . . .
Their background had nothing pertaining to Indians other than the so-called
Squaw or Me heap big Chief. Tomahawk type of thing. Cigar store Indians
and all that sort of thing. They didn't realize that this was religion . . . and
they couldn't get over the hospitality. The way the [Pueblo people] would just
invite the service boys right into their homes and feed them. . . . Some of them
had never tasted red chile and fry bread, things of that sort.[71]

In 1944 the museum took over the War History Service at the request of
the Governor of New Mexico. It had done this during World War I and, given
past experience, this project would take a number of years and staff time.
As World War II continued to impact the country, Hewett reported that "in
spite of adverse conditions brought on by the war, the School has been able
to function on approximately its normal program, though forced to operate
on a reduced budget."[72] Marjorie also continued to volunteer an average of
four hours per week with the Red Cross Home Service and the Motor Corps
activities, as well as giving time to work on the War Fund Drive and other
community activities as she had done the previous year.

Involvement in the New Mexico Association on Indian Affairs

Marjorie reminisced about the war years and recalled:

> *During World War II, whenever a group of young men had been checked*
> *through the post office where their final papers were given and they were on*
> *their way to wherever they were going to be processed, boot camp or whatever,*
> *they would march them from the post office around the plaza and then get on*
> *a bus to go to Lamy to get on the train.*
>
> *I remember one morning rather early, about eight o'clock, before the mu-*
> *seum was really open, I heard talk out on the plaza so I ran out to see what*
> *was going on. . . . There was the usual group of Spanish American lads com-*

*ing from Taos and that part of New Mexico and there was a large group of
Jicarilla Apache youths that had been gathered together. . . . They had long,
shiny, beautiful black hair. Some of them had braids; others had it growing
long. Some of them were still wearing moccasins. And here they went along,
marching. . . . I knew they had had very little schooling and that it would be a
very scary experience for them. They looked frightened. They looked like cattle
that were being rounded up.*

Witnessing the young men going off to fight a war in a foreign country
was difficult for Marjorie. *It sounds ridiculous, but one of the things was they'd
never come back as Indians. . . . The other thing that upset me was I knew that
a lot of them wouldn't be coming back at all.*[73]
Marjorie was part of a group of Santa Feans who were concerned about
the welfare of the Indian soldiers returning home.

*It was Margretta Dietrich's idea that we do something for these poor lonesome
boys that would be dumped off a bus and maybe be here for several days.
There was no place for them to go. No bathroom or anything of that sort. So,
we rented a little place on the corner of Washington and Palace. It used to
be a filling station. We had it turned into a little coffee and donut place. We
hired a local woman to be the hostess of the place and she was very good with
the Indians. The place was open every day from noon until twelve o'clock at
night. There was a place in there where they could sit and talk with one another. They could talk with tourists if they came by. Sometimes some of them
would have family friends coming through Santa Fe and they would stop in
to see them. There was a little desk and chair and they could write letters and
so on. They got to be very close to all of us. They would write to us during their
times away. . . . They were seventeen- and eighteen-year-old Indian boys from
pueblos as far away as Hopi. . . . They wrote to all of us and I think it was a
real service and I really enjoyed being with them. I felt they were part of my
life there during the war years.*[74]

It was during this time period that Marjorie became more involved with
a group of local Santa Feans who supported the Pueblo people, and Indian
people in general, both politically and economically. In 1944 Marjorie took
a more active role in the activities of the New Mexico Association on Indian
Affairs (NMAIA).[75] The NMAIA was formed in 1921 by a group of Santa Fe

writers and artists to fight against the Bursam Bill that would make it easy for non-Indian settlers to obtain Indian lands. As word spread that Pueblo lands were threatened, people from throughout the Southwest came together to protest the bill. The Bursam Bill failed in the House of Representatives after a last-minute appeal. The NMAIA was also concerned with Indian rights such as religious freedom, and economic and health improvements for Native peoples. Margretta Dietrich was one of the central figures in the NMAIA and was a mover and shaker on the Indian Fair Committee. Dietrich continued to work on the Indian Fair and Indian Market through the 1950s.

Even though Marjorie always had an interest in the welfare of the Pueblo people she met and worked with, she did not become actively involved in the NMAIA until one day when Margretta Dietrich approached her at the museum and said,

> *"We are having trouble. The Indians are very much disturbed about all of this talk of building dams on the Rio Grande. I have been told by Dorothy [Stewart, Margretta's sister] and people I know that you are very much interested in Indians and that you know a lot about the Indians." I said, "Oh, I am. I would love to help with anything that would help the Indians." Apparently, this was when the construction of the Cochiti Dam was under discussion and several of the Pueblo people were upset about it. They knew their farmland was going. They knew they [the U.S. government] were doing it for Los Alamos [the Manhattan Project] and not really for them. So, we raised the money and they raised some money too, and we sent a delegation of Indians—this was sponsored by the New Mexico Association on Indian Affairs with Margretta Dietrich as instigator—to Washington, D.C. When we put them on the train at Lamy, I called out, "Don't get mad and scalp anybody!" They said, "Well we're mad. We'll scalp them if we feel like it." One young Indian boy, I remember it just broke my heart, opened his suitcase and all he had in it was an apple and a pair of socks. They were so poor. Anyway, that was my initial involvement, and we worked on that and tried to help them, writing letters and so on.*[76]

The Santa Fe Indian Market

When Marjorie first moved to Santa Fe, Pueblo artists were selling their arts and crafts under the portal at the Palace of the Governors on Saturdays, much like they do today seven days a week. Marjorie remembers:

There would be Indians from all over with nice things spread out. . . . There was a mini-market going on all summer long under the portal of the Palace of the Governors. There would be Tesuque people selling bread, and they made beautiful micaceous culinary pottery. Some of them were big jars with an effigy lid, and I never see those anymore. But there would be the Tesuque regularly.[77]

There were people from San Ildefonso. Sometimes Maria's [Martinez] sister or one of her relatives would be there with lovely San Ildefonso black-ware . . . and redware. There would be people from San Juan, and I'm speaking both annual Indian Markets and sometimes during the war years under the portal. But I don't see that kind of pottery anymore. They did a redware, and I think Geronima [Cruz Montoya] told me that it was either her aunt or her mother who made this type of pottery. It was incised redware, and they would rub micaceous clay into the incisions so that it would sparkle. That you don't see anymore. They also did a nice sort of polychrome ware, redware basically but with some polychrome colors.

One of the things that I think is a shame that you don't see any more unless it's on special consignment would be the beautiful Cochiti pottery that came in regularly. Lorencita Herrera was one of my dearest friends and she was one of them. Some of her sisters and one of her aunts would come in with the pottery in bas relief. There would be little lizards. Sometimes there would be birds and so on. Sort of in the tradition of some of the old Zuni water symbols. What I would call a prayer meal bowl with little pieces of feathers. . . . Once in a great while, but especially for the markets, would be the whole Trinidad [Medina] family from Zia. Trinidad was the famous one, the old lady that made this beautiful pottery with the red and orange designs always with the rainbow. Some people think that the bird that is so familiar on both Acoma and Zuni pottery has also probably been borrowed from the Indians of the eastern pueblos. I'm not sure about that, but anyway, the parrot as they call it.

Marjorie was often called upon to judge the entries at the Santa Fe Indian Market:

Kenneth Chapman and Harry Mera had asked me to judge with them and later on I had to judge with other people when they were out of the picture. Richard Spivey and I judged quite a bit together. Sallie Wagner judged one year. . . . Many of my friends came from there. The Shuplas did. I knew Kenneth and Helen Shupla when they were just a young married couple living

out in the Pueblo. Kenneth was the farmer at the old Indian School and Helen
used to bake the first pottery she ever made. She certainly was not a very good
potter then. She baked her pottery in the oven. . . . I knew Geronima. . . . I
knew some of the younger Cochiti who are now gone. . . . Jose Rey Toledo and
his group of Indian friends were all studio painters. I knew practically all of
those studio painters.[78]

The Santa Fe Indian Market was and continues to be quite an event in
north-central New Mexico. According to Marjorie, the earlier annual markets were incredible:

Then the people from Taos and Picuris would come in with a mass of pottery.
You wouldn't believe the bean pots you could buy then. You could buy great
big jars of micaceous culinary ware. I used to experiment with the pottery
after I bought it. It never dawned on me that it would become so very precious.
I know that you can boil water in it. You can make stews in it. Some of the best
pottery that was ever made was made by the Picuris ladies. Now it is some-
thing if you can find someone who will make one on special order. . . . For the
big markets, the Acoma would come in. There would be people from Laguna.
Really the only difference between Laguna and Acoma pottery as far as I could
tell at that time anyway, was the tempering. The Tesuque did occasionally
bring . . . those so-called Rain God figures that were sold along the railroad
track in Lamy and Albuquerque. I never really cared for them particularly. As
far as effigy figures of the Cochiti, I think that became popular later.[79]

The End of an Era

Marjorie spent much of 1946 installing three major exhibitions: one featuring Ecuadorian archaeological, ethnological, and photographic materials
collected by Edwin N. Ferdon Jr;[80] one commemorating the seventy-fifth anniversary of the First National Bank of Santa Fe;[81] and another on the Steven
Watts Kearny Centennial. She also started writing the material section of her
report on Paa-ko. She continued to take short field trips to archaeological
sites and spent time preparing programs and meetings for the Archaeological and Historical Societies of New Mexico.[82]

Suddenly, at the end of the year, one era ended and a new one began. After
suffering a stroke and additional complications, Edgar Lee Hewett died on

the morning of December 31, 1946.[83] Hewett left a large group of admirers as well as adversaries in his wake. Malinda Elliott described his legacy:

> For his staff and students, Hewett bridged the gap between the Victorian way of life and the dawning twentieth century. . . . While his staff may have been youthful and boisterous at times, Hewett maintained an air of dignified reserve that elicited either admiration or irritation. . . . For many who worked with him, he was a difficult and dogmatic personality. Yet others saw him as a source of inspiration and support. Certainly he was complex enough to have been both loved and intensely hated by those around him. . . . Some of Hewett's staff recalled that he seemed to regard them as his children, perhaps because the Hewetts had no children of their own. In a sense, the staff of the School and the Museum were Hewett's family, the entire focus of his immense energy and drive.[84]

Marjorie certainly had her criticisms of Hewett but she also admired him and she will always give him credit for introducing her to southwestern archaeology and New Mexico. The 1940s would close out with major changes at the museum and the SAR.

CHAPTER 6

A New Boss and New Experiences

1947-1949

> Attending the Pecos Conference was part of the Southwest. . . . It was part of my life here.
>
> —MARJORIE LAMBERT[1]

As the curator of archaeology, Marjorie's favorite projects were conducting excavations, doing the analysis and interpretation of the collections of materials retrieved from the archaeological sites, and then developing exhibits based on the results. She maintained:

One of the joys of stratigraphy, especially when you see the lenses of earth and you've got your profile and you can see in a rather superficial way while you're in the field what's coming out—you know you shouldn't be making up theories beforehand. Instead, you begin to see a picture. It's very exciting to take that material after it's cleaned and washed and interpret what you've found. Especially, if it works out the way you thought it might work out, it's great! That's just one example of interpretation.

If you take data from excavations and research of your own and of other people and you're trying to work out an exhibit, which I always did, to tell the story of man in the Southwest from the Ice Age on up to the present. Because there are so few artifacts in some instances, especially the Pleistocene, there's just a few bones and a few chipped projectile points to tell the whole story of that vast period. It's very exciting and very rewarding to me. . . . I have done some Territorial, military type things, for the Historical Society, but most of my interpretative work has been with Indian cultures.[2]

As she continued her curatorial duties, Marjorie was given travel opportunities under the new director of the SAR and MNM that opened up a new
interpretive model for Southwest archaeology that she would continue to
pursue throughout her career and is used by archaeologists today.

A New Boss and New Opportunities

Upon Hewett's death, Dr. Sylvanus Griswold Morley was appointed by the
School's Board of Managers to succeed Hewett as director of the Museum
of New Mexico and the School of American Research beginning in 1947.
Famous for his knowledge of Mayan hieroglyphics, Morley explored the
jungles of the Yucatán, Guatemala, Honduras, and Mexico for decades. He
returned from the Yucatán to assume his directorship. Based on his long association with the Carnegie Institution, Morley intended to use their organi-
zational structure as a model for restructuring the school and the museum.[3]

While Morley was settling into his new position, Marjorie continued
her usual duties around the museum. Her primary concern turned to the
preservation and welfare of the collections. She was well aware of what
was required for collections storage and reported that "at this time a plea is
again made for bettering our storage facilities for archaeological and historical specimens. The space allotted to these collections in the Art Museum
basement has become totally inadequate, even actually harmful, for many
objects. Only one small vault can be considered averagely usable; walls in
two other storage rooms are damp, with plaster falling on pottery and other
objects. There is a constant battle against mice, silverfish, and dust. Much
of this space could be better utilized if certain walls were moisture proofed.
Dust-proof specimen cabinets are badly needed."[4] She was clearly frustrated
that the care of the collections was not a priority for the museum's administration, a condition that can be found in some twenty-first-century museums
that are dealing with expanding collections, inadequate storage facilities,
lack of staffing, and reduced budgets.

Throughout the year Marjorie presented lectures at Highlands University,
to a study group at Seton Village, on the radio, and to school groups, clubs,
and special parties at the museum.[5] She would continue to provide public
lectures and museum tours throughout her career. She also fit in a few field
trips with Agnes Sims and Dorothy Stewart to examine petroglyph sites in

the Upper Rio Grande and Santa Fe vicinity, many of which had not been previously reported. She took trips out to old Oraibi on the Hopi Mesas in Arizona. She found some time to continue writing articles, book reviews, and news items for *El Palacio*, but her Paa-ko report continued to be delayed due to her museum duties and the additional responsibilities as the secretary and board member of the New Mexico Association on Indian Affairs (NMAIA) and as secretary for the Archaeological Society of New Mexico.[6]

Adventures South of the Border

Marjorie had already established a good relationship with Morley beginning with her early Colorado College and UNM student days, so it was a fairly smooth transition for her to work for him. For decades, Morley spent half his time in the Yucatán and Guatemala excavating Mayan sites and studying the hieroglyphs on the stelae. The other half of the year he worked out of an office at the Palace of the Governors. There he would share his findings and adventures with Marjorie and other staff as he worked on his reports for the Carnegie Institution.

Toward the end of 1947, Marjorie completed an exhibit installation based on Morley's work in the Yucatán and Guatemala for the museum. It had been a rough year of endless tasks at the museum and the Laboratory of Anthropology. She was feeling discouraged that she was not finding time to complete some of her writing projects and was not able to get into the field to do any archaeology. Sensing Marjorie's frustration,

> *Morley told me I needed a complete break, that I needed to get away from everything. He said, "I'm going to send you south for a little bit of experience. Some rest and relaxation." He sent me to Wayne [Mauzy] to get some money. I think the whole thing was about $400. That was quite a bit of money then.*[7]
>
> *Morley said I had to go with someone else. He didn't think it was a good idea for a woman to travel alone in Mexico. I told him I wasn't afraid, that I could get along all right. He told me he was going to send Martha M. Walker with me. . . . We stayed in Merida to begin with. Morley got us a place to stay in an old, I guess you would call it a pensión [hostelry], if it was that much even. We called it the Gamboa. It was an awful place. It was not clean, and the sheets smelled sour and the mosquitoes were all over and there was a cat having kittens under the dining room table and so on. But it was a wonderful*

experience because Morley took us out to a great many of the sites that the Carnegie Institution had been connected with. We had a wonderful trip out in some of the villages on the way to Uxmal. We went to Uxmal and we saw one of the stelae that Morley had never been able to decipher because it was so worn. . . . Then we went with Morley to Chichen Itza and there we stayed with Doña Isabela instead of one of the tourist places. They had nice tourist places there. The Mayan children were just adorable. There was this one little boy who adopted me and I think he wanted me to take him home. He was just loving me all the time. I had such a good time there. When we got through doing all the ruins in the vicinity Morley also told us where to walk to go down one of the Mayan causeways. You could still walk God knows how far into the jungle on those. They kept them pretty well cleared and they were still used.[8]

Sometimes Marjorie's independent spirit got her into interesting and sometimes dangerous situations. She tells of one particular adventure while she was in the Yucatán. One day after visiting one of the archaeological sites, Marjorie had an errand to run and here she tells the story of one of her forays out on her own:

When we got back to town and before we went out again, I had some things that I was supposed to mail at the post office. I had a package of film, and I also had some letters to send to some people in the museum, particularly because I'd been asked to. Martha said her feet hurt. She didn't want to go with me. . . . Of course she didn't speak any Spanish at all and mine . . . wasn't the best. So I left her and she went back to the Gamboa, and I inquired around the streets the best I could. I went into an awful old bar by mistake. I got out of there in a hurry I can tell you. They gave me general directions, and I went into this building that looked like a public building. It was a great big pink building. I can't forget that. It seemed very quiet in there, except for noise coming from upstairs. Suddenly this little guy who was very husky looking and very scarred came down the stairs and said he was glad to see me. He shook my hands and he took hold of me and pulled me up the stairs. I got into this room with all these guys like him around and pinned to the walls were ears and parts of bulls, the tail, and different things. I got into a meeting of the National Bullfighters Association. Their regional meeting. They thought I had come on purpose to be with them. And I didn't know how to get out of it. They were nice enough and they kept giving me these things that they were eating.

I don't know what it was. It may have been some kind of dope. It smelled kind of like copal but it wasn't. But they were chewing on it. So, I did it too. Finally, I told them that I was a senora, not a senorita, and that mi amiga [my friend] was waiting. They walked me all the way back to the Gamboa in a procession. Bullfighters! I still don't quite know what happened or who they thought I really was.[9]

After visiting Chichen Itza and Uxmal in the Yucatán, Marjorie went on to Guatemala to observe an excavation at the pre-Columbian Mayan site of Zaculeu, located in the highlands outside of Huehuetenango. Zaculeu was the capital of the Postclassic Mam Kingdom. The site sits on a hilltop with steep ravines on three sides and was occupied for more than 10,000 years until its defeat by the Spanish in 1525. It was there that she met Richard Woodbury, which grew into a lifelong friendship. *Dick was on that excavation. It was the United Fruit Company excavation. They wanted me to stay [and work for them] but the museum would not release me.*[10] Marjorie sent a telegram to the museum requesting to stay and work with Woodbury and John Demmick, but she was told to return to Santa Fe.

While still in Guatemala, Marjorie visited other areas.

One of the places we stayed in addition to Huehuetenango was Antigua, which is still a delightful place I understand. And also Lake Atitlan, which is beautiful. We took a boat to all the pueblos that are scattered along the shore. We stayed in one of the villages down along the shore where the markets were held called Panajachel and there was a little pensión and restaurant. We had lunch there. We had been up the mountain to San Antonio Palopó that morning and Martha was feeling a little better because she'd gotten some good pictures in the little market. She went out in the market in Panajachel to take more pictures.

I was sitting at the table having a rum and Coca-Cola. Suddenly I looked out on the veranda and here were three very shiny new jeeps, the army type. They probably got them fresh out of army surplus from the United States. These good-looking officers of the Guatemalan army started getting out and coming in. They were across the room, and they were drinking beer. Finally, one of them came over to me and he bowed very formally, clicked his heels together, and holding his hat in a certain way he asked me if I would play a game of ping-pong with him. I had never played ping-pong in my life. I didn't know what to say. I thought it would be the rudest thing possible to say no. I said, "No estoy bueno." He took me by the hand, and we went over and we played ping-pong. It was a disaster. I was a disaster more than anyone. I found out later that he was the ping-pong champion of Guatemala! He was just charming, and they all took my picture and then they looked at their watches and said they had to leave. They were all half inebriated. I was very careful. I had just my little Cuba Libre and that's all. But imagine me playing ping-pong with the champion of Guatemala.[11]

Marjorie had fond memories of her travels in Guatemala, especially Antigua.

All those little pensións and places where we stayed in Guatemala, each family or each person living in one of those was given a house boy and those little boys would come in and draw your bath for you and get the fire started in the fireplace and even offer to dry you off. The delight for me was the monkey. There were two monkeys that I fell in love with. They were white spider monkeys. One was Chita and the other was Panchita. Little Chita was the one that fell in love with me. She would come down from the tree and get on my shoulders and pat my ears and look into my eyes with her tail wrapped around her like an old black snake. Half the time she'd be eating an avocado and get this green stuff all over me. I wanted to get her a present because she was such a sweet little thing. We walked all over the markets. The only thing I could find was a child's little play mirror. I brought it home and I called, "Chita, Chita." She came down and I gave it to her. She looked in the mirror and then she looked around. She couldn't figure it out. Every time she'd see herself in the mirror she'd smile. I don't know if she ever got the idea or not. She took it up in the tree with her. There were also some wonderful parrots, macaws, and so on. We even saw the Quetzal bird.[12]

Marjorie enjoyed her experience so much that she planned to return to Antigua the following year. *I was going to go with the Petits to stay in Antigua the following winter, but Gordon was too sick. They rented a very nice home there on a long-term basis that had servants to wait on them.*[13] Even though Marjorie's interest in Mesoamerica would continue, she would not be able to travel there again any time soon.

Connections Between the Southwest and Mesoamerica

It was during her travels in Yucatán and Guatemala that Marjorie started seeing the early connections between the Southwest and Mesoamerica, which she based on the evidence of cultural exchange found in the archaeological record. Her interests extended into Mesoamerica because of the similarities in ceremonies, pottery designs, and iconography. She observed: *The plumed Avanyu dance, for example, among the Tewas is really an outgrowth of the Quetzalcoatl cult. You can't be interested in the Mimbres phase of the Mogollon without seeing a very strong connection between Mesoamerica and the Southwest—in the pottery designs, for example, and in some of the Hohokam material. It's archaeology coming alive again. Some of the masked ceremonies of the Indians and then the comparison between "Earth Mother" of the Southwest and the "Goddess of Filth," which means Dirt or Corn Mother, in Mesoamerica—there are very strong similarities.*[14]

Marjorie was convinced of other connections between the Southwest and Mexico, especially in terms of the work of one of her colleagues, Charles Di Peso. She noted, *I always had the feeling that with all the work that Charlie Di Peso had been doing at Casas Grandes that probably many of the traits that we associate with the Toltecs and the Valley of Mexico probably came up not only by way of El Paso but also through the southwestern part of New Mexico and Hidalgo County. I still think that there are a lot of early man sites down there as well as historic sites that could be related to what Di Peso called the Medio Period of Casas Grandes because some people undoubtedly came up into this part of the Southwest and also to Zuni.*[15]

Marjorie argued that the influence was from south to north and that many of the ideas and materials stayed and became part of the Pueblo cultural milieu. She posited:

> *We know that these trade relations were very important, and I think one thing we don't take into account is the fact that when traders were going back and forth they didn't have any beasts of burden. They were walking. I think it's regrettable that the Piro villages were destroyed and abandoned early on because the Piro were the first Indians that the Conquistadors saw. They did describe what they saw, but suddenly all the Piro were gone. I think that a lot of them moved to what is Gran Quivira or Las Humanas and the sites of Abó and Tompiro. On the other hand, I think a lot came up from Mexico.*

I often wondered if the eagle sacrifice . . . of the Hopi and the Jemez people wasn't the northern manifestation of human sacrifice. The Mayans, Toltecs, and Aztecs did have human sacrifice, and you see it depicted in Classic Mimbres pottery. Macaws came in from Mexico and are depicted on the pottery. Macaws were ceremonially buried. There was a macaw burial not too many years ago up at San Juan Pueblo [Ohkay Owingeh] . . . and things like that I am sure came from Mexico. You don't hear much about it anymore, if at all, and that is the plumed Avanyu dance. I don't know whether any of the other Tewas performed that. I don't know whether the Keres performed it. I did see it performed at San Ildefonso. That definitely is Mexican influence.[16]

Not everyone agreed with Marjorie and there was some resistance to the idea of influence coming from Mexico. She pointed out that at the time, *I don't think Hewett liked to see too much of it. Then there was the excavation work of Charlie Di Peso at Casas Grandes. I think he did some very important work. But again, did those influences come from Casas Grandes as people who believe in the theory say, or did it come directly on its own up through the Jornada branch of the Mogollon into the Rio Grande Valley?*[17] Even though Marjorie was seeing these connections primarily through trade networks, she would no doubt be excited about our recent understanding of the migration and movement of people across the landscape over millennia.[18]

Back at the Museum

As much as Marjorie was interested in pursuing her interest in the Southwest-Mesoamerican connections, her museum work kept her occupied for the rest of 1947. Morley spearheaded the merger of the Laboratory of Anthropology with the Museum of New Mexico in 1947, which added more responsibilities to Marjorie's already busy schedule. In 1948 more than five thousand pots were moved from the Art Gallery basement to the pottery storage room in the Hall of Ethnology basement. Other parts of the collections were moved to the LAB, including the original Kuaua murals, a large lot of duplicate pecked and ground stone implements, and the Museum of New Mexico sherd file, which was to eventually be incorporated into the more functional LAB sherd library. The metal shelving belonging to the Archaeology Department was also moved in order to house the pottery sent from the Museum's Ethnology Department. Even with the move of some of

FIGURE 19 Unidentified couple in the Pueblo pottery collections area when the public was allowed to go into the basement of the Laboratory of Anthropology, ca. 1948. Photo by Robert H. Martin. Courtesy of the Palace of the Governors Photo Archives (NMHM/DCA). Neg. No. 041215.

the collections more storage space was needed, and Marjorie advocated for additional study and storage space in the Palace of the Governors for the Historical Society collections, which were inadequately housed at the time.[19]

In May 1948 Marjorie opened an exhibition at the Palace of the Governors featuring Florence Dibell Bartlett's Collection of Rio Grande Valley

Colonial Art. Bartlett was a Chicago heiress and folk art collector who is best known for founding the Museum of International Folk Art, which opened in Santa Fe, New Mexico, in 1953. Marjorie wrote one short article in *El Palacio* about the opening of the exhibition and another longer article about the Florence Dibell Bartlett collection. Overall the exhibition received wide interest from the public.[20] She also published several book reviews and contributed numerous news items to *El Palacio*. Progress was also being made on the pottery section of her report on the Paa-ko excavation.[21]

To network with her colleagues and to stay abreast of current trends in the profession, Marjorie attended the Southwest and Rocky Mountain Division of the American Association for the Advancement of Science meetings in Las Vegas, New Mexico, and the Southwestern Archaeological Conference at the University of Arizona Field Camp in Archaeology at Point of Pines, Arizona. She also made time to visit historic and archaeological points of interest throughout the state and attended Indian feast days and ceremonies.[22]

Marjorie continued to be involved in the activities of the New Mexico Association on Indian Affairs as a board member and serving on the program committee. She also served as a judge at the annual Indian Market, which was held during the Santa Fe Fiesta.[23] Her secretarial duties for the Archaeological Society of New Mexico were heavy, along with setting up program meetings that were held on average every two months.

The Indian Arts Fund

Given Marjorie's interest in Indian art and her relationship with Kenneth Chapman and H. P. Mera, it is not surprising that she would become involved in the Indian Arts Fund (IAF) for many years. The IAF was active in supporting local Pueblo Indian artists by both purchasing and promoting their arts. It was well-known in Santa Fe for its efforts to preserve and promote the arts of the local Native Americans.

Originally called the Pueblo Pottery Fund, the collection was founded by Kenneth Chapman, H. P. Mera, Elizabeth Shepley Sergeant, and Wesley Bradfield in 1922. In 1925 the important work of collecting the finest examples of historic and contemporary Indian art continued under a new name, the Indian Arts Fund, and membership increased to include "Mary Austin, Andrew Dasburg, Alfred Kidder, Sylvanus Morley, Amelia Elizabeth White, Charles Springer, Mabel Dodge Luhan and numerous other luminaries."[24]

When Marjorie joined the IAF, membership also included Frank Mera, J. F. Collins, Mrs. Gerald Cassidy, Margretta Dietrich, Cornelia Thompson, Mabel Morrow, Arthur Seligman, and Stanley Stubbs.[25]

The IAF collection, which had been housed in the basement of the Art Museum and Palace of the Governors, was eventually moved to the Laboratory of Anthropology.[26] According to Marjorie, *The museum owned a collection of pottery. They had a pretty good one, but nothing could rival the Indian Arts Fund collection. . . . It wasn't just pottery. It was the textiles and the jewelry. Miss Amelia Elizabeth White brought in some perfectly gorgeous old pueblo jewelry that she had. The problem with us [the IAF] was that we had no money. We had dues. We had annual dues of two dollars apiece, and you can see how much you can buy with that. We depended on people donating things.*[27]

Marjorie knew the members of the IAF very well and had many anecdotal stories about several of them. She recounted one about Amelia Elizabeth White.

I think that people think of Miss A. E. White as being primarily a patroness of the arts and you might say fine arts because she was related to so many big organizations like the Metropolitan [Museum of Art] and what not in the East. It was Miss White's interest in Indian art, southwestern Pueblo Indian art, that eventually brought her to Santa Fe. She loved the country here, she and her sister [Martha Root White] both. A lot of people have forgotten this, but she took the first traveling exhibit of American Indian art to Europe. She didn't live here when she did that. She did it through her New York colleagues.[28]

As Marjorie became more involved in the IAF, the members also got to know her very well and appreciated her interest and breadth of knowledge about the Southwest and the pueblos. Her involvement with the IAF became even more important as time went on.

I got a call one night in my little apartment from Sylvanus Griswold Morley. Morley was still very much involved with the Laboratory of Anthropology. Up to that time I had an office in the Palace of the Governors. He called me at night, and I thought that was rather peculiar. He said, "We've had a big row in the Indian Arts Fund. We have to have a new trustee. The only one that they all would agree on is you." I said, "I'm curator of archaeology. There are other staff members that are more in line in ethnography and so on, why me?" He said, "They want you. You will be indoctrinated at our next meeting." From then on, I met all the people. Many of them were original members of the Indian Arts Fund. . . . Stanley Stubbs was curator of the [IAF] collection then. That's when I began to learn something about pottery dating from about 1820 to about 1942 or thereabouts.[29]

Marjorie became a trustee for the Indian Arts Fund in 1948. This also meant other changes for her. She recalled:

At the same time I got an office given to me for research at the Laboratory of Anthropology. Ed Ferdon had an office out there too. He had nothing to do with the Indian Arts Fund, though. But Stanley Stubbs certainly did. We did get a secretary to help us do the cataloging and the initial work of bringing something in. We had a committee and we would either reject or accept something. Generally, we accepted though. I remember coming in a bit after that—I think it was about 1954—when Sally Lewis, Hugo Rodack's wife . . . went to work for Eric Douglas [at the Denver Art Museum]. She did some of the initial cataloging. I didn't have to do that. All I had to do was to be part of the fund and then too I had to do some of the secretarial work. Later Nancy Fox was made a member of the Board of the Indian Arts Fund and she was very helpful to us. But always it was the lack of money. Mrs. Thomas Wood Stevenson had been working on the Mary Austin collection of unpublished manuscripts and so on, which she had willed to the Indian Arts Fund with the hope that it would bring us money someday. What really set us on our feet was that we—after much wrangling and arguing at meetings and so on—it came about that the Huntington Library would buy the collection of unpublished Mary Austin papers for $30,000. That was a fortune then and that gave us a nice little nest egg to buy things at the Indian Market and to get things that we really wanted for the collection that heretofore we could not collect.[30]

There was a lot of wrangling and so on, but a lot of fun too. We would talk about our aspirations for the future and so on. Unfortunately, the Indian Arts Fund collection eventually became involved in state and local politics. A group of people wanted to take the collection out of its private status and throw it in with everything that the museum had, just make one collection. In the fifties, there was a big row over that. Even the governor got involved.

It's funny, but the governor called up I guess it was Al Packard who was the chairperson and asked, "What is going on in that outfit?" And Fabian Chavez was another one that called. They didn't want to have trouble about any of this. They wanted the collection to stay the way it was. I remember little Miss White, who was so tiny and petite and so feminine, she spoke up and said, "We don't have to have our collection in the Laboratory of Anthropology. I've got my kennels down on my property. We can turn those kennels into collections storage, with a little bit of revitalization." She turned to John Gaw Meem . . . [and] they started right then making plans for a building. . . . And that is why it [Indian Arts Research Center] is down there in the School of American Research—because at the time the Laboratory of Anthropology and the Board of the Indian Arts Fund were one and the same. When the split came in September 1947, the state wanted the Lab of Anthropology as part of the Museum of New Mexico system, but it didn't want any private collections belonging to either the LAB or the Indian Arts Fund. . . . We just operated on a shoestring and of course Stanley Stubbs's death in the 1950s during all this furor was just a heartbreak to all of us. That almost killed the organization. Just that whole situation. It's all ironed out and working fine now. The Indian Arts Fund is now part of the School of American Research. The Board is the same as the one that managed the Laboratory of Anthropology, so instead of the Indian Arts Fund of Santa Fe, it became the Indian Arts Fund of the School of American Research. It may last a long time. I think it will.[31]

Marjorie served as a trustee of the Indian Arts Fund for thirty years from 1948 to 1978. She served as the secretary from 1948 to 1949 and was elected chair from 1949 to 1950. Some might question how Marjorie, as a state employee in the Museum of New Mexico, could be made a trustee of a private organization, such as the Indian Arts Fund and the School of American Research. It was a different time, and as Marjorie points out, *It is simply because from the very beginning, years and years ago when I was still a graduate student down at UNM, Hewett made me a research fellow and member of the School of American Research. Same with Ed Ferdon and Bertha Dutton, and there were others too as time went on. I have always been very proud of that connection, and it's served me well throughout the years.*[32]

In 1972, the Indian Arts Fund dissolved as a corporate entity and donated its collection to the School of American Research. According to Malinda Elliott, "By entrusting its collections to the School, the IAF recognized the integrity and commitment of the School's management in caring for these works of Indian art. IAF collectors had assembled a superb, definitive collection of mainly historic, southwestern Native American art, and with its acquisition the School assumed the responsibility of developing a well-conceived program for the collection's conservation and use."[33] It was also a way to protect the collection from the state, which the members of the IAF felt would sell the pieces.

Marjorie always felt a special attachment to the IAF collection housed in the Indian Arts Research Center at the SAR. She enjoyed being able to see the IAF collection throughout the years. *I love to go in the building. As long as I have known that collection, every time I go in there I see something that I haven't seen before. It's just one of the, I think, one of the really exciting parts of the history of Santa Fe and the School of American Research.*[34] The IAF collection continues to be researched and cared for at the SAR's Indian Arts Research Center.

The End of a Difficult Decade

Sylvanus G. Morley passed away unexpectedly on September 2, 1948, and the Honorable Boaz W. Long was appointed director of the Museum of New Mexico and the School of American Research. The following year the financial outlook was not much improved. As her work continued at the museum, Marjorie dedicated much of the year to cataloging, preservation, and related routine museum duties while answering queries about the collections and requests for use of the study collections. In the school's 1949 annual report, Marjorie pointed out that budget restrictions made it impossible to send out the study collections and to accommodate all of the requests for school tours and special parties. She once again voiced her concerns about the lack of adequate storage space for the growing archaeological and Historical Society collections. She specifically noted that "the situation has steadily become worse over the past few years as gifts have been coming in."[35]

In the same SAR Annual Report, Marjorie wrote that she had been invited to Chicago by the Atchison, Topeka, and Santa Fe Railroad to install a Spanish Colonial exhibit at the Chicago Railroad Fair in June. She took advantage of being in a big Midwest city to study exhibition techniques in some of the leading museums located there.[36] She came back with many fresh new ideas and assessed the current exhibition situation at the Museum of New Mexico.

Unfortunately, most of her time was focused on gallery maintenance and repair, and very little exhibition work was done that year. Marjorie expressed her concerns about the archaeology exhibitions and noted:

> This building [Palace of the Governors] continues to draw more visitors than any other in the plant; yet it remains in the poorest condition. Specifically, new floors are needed, calcimining [of the walls] should be continued, and all lighting should be improved. Furthermore, the picture of southwestern archaeology has changed so completely in the past ten or fifteen years that many of the permanent installations have become obsolete. It is my recommendation that consideration be given to re-installing one or two of the exhibition halls each year, until the desired improvement has been made. So far, the only changes made in the past year have been minor.[37]

Clearly Marjorie was concerned about keeping the exhibitions up to date as well as educating the public about the importance of archaeology to our understanding of the human past in the Southwest, as well as keeping the museum relevant to the profession.

Marjorie participated in the planning of the annual Pecos Archaeological Conference hosted by the Museum of New Mexico in Santa Fe on August 22–24, 1949.[38] The annual Pecos Conferences offered Marjorie another occasion to meet and interact with her colleagues. For several southwestern archaeologists, the Pecos Conference, which continues today, was an opportunity to get together at the end of the summer field season to discuss what was done that year and what new discoveries were made and to debate possible theoretical changes. The Pecos Conferences were held at different places throughout the Southwest. They were informal, as most participants were just coming out of the field and there was an atmosphere of excitement as new directions in southwestern archaeology unfolded. Marjorie pointed out:

> *The Pecos Conference has a niche that is unlike any other in the United States as far as I know because of the camaraderie and the camping out and the people that influenced us and so on. I would not have had the opportunity to have a personal relationship probably with people like Ted [E. B.] Sayles, for example. Ted was a wonderful person and he became one of my close friends. I became very much interested in his early work, defining where the Mogollon and the Hohokam came from. Then Emil Haury, of course, was a towering*

figure. . . . Then people like Joe Ben Wheat . . . J. Charles Kelley, and the Woodburys [Richard and Nathalie], H. Marie Wormington, one of my favorite people. Florence [Hawley Ellis] would always be there and sometimes Bruce [Ellis] with her. We had such wonderful times at all of them. I liked the ones the best that were held in someone's [field] camp. To have them at the University of New Mexico as we did, or the University of Arizona, it was nice . . . to be at these different southwestern universities and colleges, but out in the [field] camp was it! And the best was at Pecos [National Historic Park], of course.[39]

Marjorie recalled a memorable Pecos Conference when

J. O. [John Otis] Brew was much in evidence. . . . He came to one of the Pecos Conferences. There was going to be a confrontation between [Emil] Haury and J. O. Brew over the Mogollon.[40] *You know, right to the end, I don't think J. O. really accepted the Mogollon. He would just argue and argue and argue.*

FIGURE 20 Shelby Tisdale and Marjorie Lambert at the 1987 Pecos Conference held at Pecos National Historical Park, site of the first Pecos Conference convened by A. V. Kidder sixty years earlier. Courtesy of the Arizona State Museum, University of Arizona. Helga Teiwes, photographer. Neg. No. 67970.

It was really heated at that time, but I remember all of us participating in that and throwing in our own ideas now and then. Of course, I think that Haury, with his defining the Mogollon the way he did, his Three Circle and his Mogollon Village, changed that whole part of my life. I think that's where I had my first real run-in with E. L. Hewett. He wouldn't accept it either. He said, "Well if you are so smart, show me anything that proves that the Mogollon exists and that it isn't part of the Puebloan culture." I had my copy of the American Anthropologist *right there and some of Haury's first papers came out in that.*[41]

Neither Marjorie nor anyone else was able to convince Hewett that the Mogollon existed as an ancient culture in the Southwest.

For anyone who has attended a Pecos Conference, there are always several memorable moments. *The most delightful ones that I remember were the ones when A. V. Kidder [attended]. . . . One year we gave him a little silver trowel.* For Marjorie, *attending the Pecos Conference was part of the Southwest. . . . It was part of my life here. It is my hope that the Pecos Conference will go on as long as there is anthropology in the Southwest. The relationships that form out of these conferences are lifelong relationships.*[42]

Participation at the National Level

Marjorie felt it was important to be in touch with archaeologists on a national level. She kept up with the newest trends in the field by reading journals and articles published by the profession's organizations.

I think it was about 1949 that I officially joined the Society [for American Archaeology], but I always read the journal when it came in and I read right back to the beginning of the SAA. Some of the early papers I recall, one would be of Dr. Mera's, who helped in a roundabout way of founding the SAA. I felt that I would be better in my job if I could get more involved on a national level. I realized that I was becoming too regional, basically the prehistory of the Rio Grande and environs, and I wanted to be broadened out a little bit, so I asked permission to go to the national meetings and they did give me a stipend to go. . . . Anthropology is a sort of brotherhood and sisterhood. I think that those contacts I made with other people who were doing different things was educational for me. . . . I was involved with several panels at different meetings and so on. I guess as far as the society is concerned, I think it was one of my favorite organizations the whole time I was a professional.[43]

While visiting museums in the host cities for professional conferences and meetings, Marjorie met several colleagues and she especially enjoyed participating in and was stimulated by this intellectual exchange. Even though she didn't receive much support from her home museum colleagues, she often found her research and opinions were more readily accepted by her colleagues outside of the Museum of New Mexico. She met many of her colleagues—for example, Paul Martin, Gene Weltfish, W. Duncan Strong—and many other icons in anthropology at the SAA meetings and when visiting museums in Chicago and New York. She was convinced that without these professional contacts and stimulating conversations at the meetings and in other museums she *would have been maybe sort of provincial, the way some of the people I worked with were. They didn't care. As long as they had a job in the Museum of New Mexico and got their paychecks and got to go to Indian dances, I don't think they cared.*[44] Marjorie chose to involve herself in the Society for American Archaeology, even though she felt that her male colleagues at the museum were not in support of her efforts. For example, she assumed that *because they didn't present papers, they didn't think I should either. They didn't tell me I couldn't, but they frowned on it.*[45]

Marjorie kept up with her writing as much as possible and submitted a paper titled "A Comparison of Paa-ko Clay Artifacts Other than Pottery with Similar Material from Pecos" to the Southwestern Division of the American Association for the Advancement of Science meeting at Alpine, Texas, in May. This paper, along with several other articles and book reviews, was published in *El Palacio*. One of her ongoing major concerns was the completion of the Paa-ko report, and she continued to work on it. She also hired Patricia Ferdon to do the pottery drawings that were to be incorporated into the report. Based on her assessment, the report was about two-thirds complete.[46]

These past two years were clearly a time of growth and expansion for Marjorie both professionally and personally. With Hewett no longer in control of her activities, she was able to start seeing the limitations of her museum work, and through her networking with others in the profession outside of the Southwest, she was realizing that her work and ideas were valued more by others outside of New Mexico. This was quite a shift for her, and her life would change tremendously as the 1950s begin to unfold.

CHAPTER 7

Home, Hearth, and a Good Marriage

1950

> Her professional career and her personal life were enhanced by a good marriage.
>
> —LINDA CORDELL[1]

As you may recall from an earlier chapter, Marjorie met Jack Lambert when she attended a party near Santa Fe while she was working temporarily at the Museum of New Mexico in 1937. After a picnic date at Tsankawi, an ancestral site located in a detached section of Bandelier National Monument near the town of Los Alamos, Marjorie said, *I sort of forgot about him. Then he came down to the University of New Mexico, this man, and he found out which one of the dormitories I was in, and he asked me to go out to dinner with him. I couldn't go. Well, that sort of ended that.*[2]

Several years later, Jack happened to catch a glimpse of Marjorie and realized that he was still smitten with her after all this time, so he inquired as to her marital status. As Marjorie tells it, *[Jack] saw me in a grocery store in 1949. Of course, he was divorced at that time. He said he didn't know whether he should approach me or not, so he went over to the Art Museum and asked Hester Jones, an old friend of his, about my marital status and she said she imagined I was available.* When Jack contacted her again, Marjorie recalled, *I just vaguely remembered this very charming older man. He was very tall. He said that he remembered this little girl standing in the corner, my eyes absolutely bugging out at the singing and the behavior of those people. They were drinking Brandy Alexanders. It was a potent drink, and they were all drinking that stuff and playing the guitar and singing.*[3] *So that's how the whole*

*thing got started. . . . He started courting me and we courted a year and then
we married in October of 1950.*[4]

An Interesting Man, This E. V. "Jack" Lambert

Jack was a nickname that stayed with Everett Vey Lambert for most of his
life. Marjorie noted that *he was called Jack before he came to New Mexico.
When he was in Wyoming and Utah, he got the name Jack because there
were so many things he could do. He could build houses or round up horses or
whatever. A Jack-of-all-trades.*[5]

In describing Jack, Marjorie pointed out:

*There's an interesting story about Jack and his career in the Southwest. You
might say that he's almost totally self-educated. His family were Mormons
from Illinois. They moved first to Iowa and then to Oklahoma. [Born in 1898]
Jack's childhood home was Okarche, Oklahoma. I was always kind of fascinated by the fact that he said his father had an opera house and a livery
stable. He grew up there and he always wanted to be a frontiersman, and the
family, all the Mormon relatives, laughed at this little boy who wanted that.
He was always around horses. He would go out camping by himself and so on.
And one day when he was fourteen years old, he took off on his horse and he
never went back. He went up into Wyoming and he worked for two bachelors
that were very well educated. He was a horse wrangler for them. He would
go to town, Cody, Wyoming, and get books from the library. The [bachelors]
would give him the titles of the books and he would come home and they
would study geography and mathematics.*[6]

Eventually Jack would move on.

*Having been a wrangler for some time, he heard about a job coming up in
Cisco, Utah [now a ghost town]. It was getting very cold, and the two old
men were not sure they wanted to go on with this horse enterprise anyway,
so Jack and another boy took off on their horses and they went to Cisco. They
had twenty-five cents between them, along with their horses, saddles, and
blankets. They went into a little grocery store and bought some pancake syrup
and some pancake flour and some work gloves. There was this man who came*

in with a string necktie and a very nice suit, a very pompous sort of man. He said, "Do you know where I could hire a couple of good men?" And Jack, being very tall for his age, spoke up and said, "Right here." And they were hired to build that bridge over the Green River between Cisco and Moab. After that adventure, he came to Santa Fe and he was sitting in the plaza when a man came up to him and said, "Are you Jack Lambert?" He said, "Yes I am." The man said, "Well, I've heard about you. I understand you're a fine man with horses and I understand you get along well with people. How would you like to go into the dude ranch business with me?"[7]

The man was Richard LeRoy (Roy) Pfäffle, who was introduced to a young cowboy named Jack Lambert in front of the Capital Pharmacy near the Santa Fe Plaza in the spring of 1918. At the time Jack was twenty years old and had just arrived in Santa Fe. Roy and his wife, Carol, were setting up the new Bishop's Ranch, later named Bishop's Lodge, and learning that Jack was a seasoned cowboy they hired him to work for them. Roy and Carol had only been married a short time, and this was a new adventure for them and they knew they were going to need some help to get the ranch up and running. Jack accepted and this began a twelve-year partnership. Roy and Jack took the Bishop's Ranch guests on trips to the Four Corners region by auto and horseback. They visited Canyon de Chelly, Chaco Canyon, and Mesa Verde, as well as Indian dances.[8]

Jack told Marjorie that *they opened their first dude ranch at Bishop's Ranch. They didn't like the place. It was owned by two wealthy men from New York who wanted to make it into some sort of fancy place and that wasn't their idea of a dude ranch, so they went up to Alcalde and they bought this old ranch and some of the property around it.*[9] Frances O. Wilson, a Santa Fe attorney, negotiated the purchase of 34,000 acres that had historic and decrepit buildings near Alcalde, New Mexico. Bordering Ohkay Owingeh Pueblo and the eastern bank of the Rio Grande, it was a spectacular location for a guest ranch. The Pfäffles named their guest ranch San Gabriel, which paid homage to San Gabriel del Yunque, the first Spanish settlement that Marjorie had worked at during World War II. Jack was the ranch manager.[10]

Lois, Roy's teenage sister, lived with them at Bishop's Ranch. She was a typical teenager and "frequently left the ranch in Tesuque to horseback ride with friends and go to the movies in Santa Fe. Lois especially liked to do anything in the company of Jack Lambert, who, although only three years her senior, was not considered a proper suitor, at least by Gaga [her mother], Roy and even Carol."[11]

The Pfäffles sent Lois back East in hopes of continuing her education and possibly meeting a more suitable young man for a husband. Her sister-in-law, Carol, was especially opposed to Lois marrying a cowboy. Nevertheless, when Lois graduated from St. Mary's in the spring of 1921, she returned to New Mexico and San Gabriel Ranch. According to Lesley Poling-Kempes, when Lois arrived, "Jack Lambert was waiting exactly where she had left him—on the train station platform in Lamy, New Mexico. Jack still had eyes for Lois. Lois was nearly twenty-one, and, after seeing a bit of the modern world, knew what she liked and whom she loved, and several weeks later on June 23, Lois married her favorite cowboy, E.V. 'Jack' Lambert."[12] Lois and Jack had a daughter they named Louise.

Jack was able to make a pretty good living on the ranch and taking "dudes" on trips throughout the Southwest. Marjorie noted that Jack

took a lot of early anthropologists on their first field trips. He took Elsie Clews Parsons and Mary Cabot Wheelwright, and Florence Dibell Bartlett, who gave us the Folk Art Museum here in Santa Fe, just to name a few.[13] The dudes that came were absolutely fascinating and the most important ones are still well known in Santa Fe history and in museum circles and in anthropology. Jack took Mary Cabot Wheelwright on her first trips into the Navajo country and he introduced her to the Indians that she worked with later. He said she was the best dude he ever had that way. Later on in life she became known as a very cranky old tyrant. He just wouldn't believe it because she was so nice and such a good sport. Quite often they'd be in a sandstorm and be delayed and she'd never complain if she had nothing but just a tin cup of water at night. He said sometimes that's all they could do because they couldn't even build a fire, the sand would be blowing so hard. But he said she was an excellent dude.[14]

Fed up with Roy Pfäffles's drinking and gambling, Jack decided to cut his ties with San Gabriel Ranch and moved his family to Santa Fe. The Lamberts managed a little restaurant in Sena Plaza that was owned by the White sisters.[15] Amelia Elizabeth White and Martha Root White formed the De Vargas Development Corporation in 1924 for the purpose of acquiring and developing land. Jack worked on several of their development projects. He took the White sisters on several trips across the Southwest, including one

FIGURE 21 Jack Lambert and Mary Cabot Wheelwright near Soap Creek, Arizona, 1927. Courtesy of the Wheelwright Museum of the American Indian.

trip to Rainbow Bridge in Utah in the late 1920s that was captured on film.[16] In addition to being their tour guide, he helped build most of the buildings on their estate on Garcia Street throughout the years.

By now the Lambert marriage was in trouble and Jack and Lois were divorced in 1929. Lois took Louise and moved to New York while Jack continued to work full-time for the White sisters. Jack often took the White sisters on visits to the Rio Grande Pueblos. As Marjorie noted,

The White sisters liked to go to Indian dances. They liked to go out to the Indian pueblos and they liked horseback riding, so in addition to [being the estate manager] Jack was the perfect person to take them. He was a marvelous camp cook. He loved to cook. So, they went on many trips. I remember one of the stories he told. They were going to go to San Felipe to a corn dance. I think it was May 1st. Of course, you didn't have the crowds then that you have now. They set up a little camp beforehand because Miss White always liked to have Jack cook for her. She told me once that he made the best cream of potato soup that was ever made. She said it could not be matched anywhere in Europe or anyplace she'd ever been. He always had lamb chops. She liked lamb chops. Of course, then they had canned peas. I can't imagine anything worse, having been in archaeology camps with nothing but canned peas and canned corn.

Those were his staples. And then they'd have canned apple sauce and then they'd go to the Indian dance . . . you could ride horseback from San Felipe to Santa Fe and not have any problems with traffic at all. When he used to take Mary Wheelwright on trips out to Navajo country, they didn't have to open a gate. They just went over open country.[17]

According to Stark and Rayne, "Jack was a friend to the Whites from the time they established themselves in Santa Fe to the end of Elizabeth's life, serving as their estate manager, and builder."[18] Marjorie told Nancy Fox that *Jack started building with William Penhallow Henderson, they called him Willie Henderson, the estate for the White sisters [that they called El Delirio] on Garcia Street in 1927–28.* Jack was officially hired to be the estate manager in 1929. *Martha didn't last very long. She died of cancer in 1937 and the animal shelter was given [to the City of Santa Fe in 1939] by Elizabeth White in memory of them [both] because they loved dogs. They had Afghans, Irish Wolfhounds, and Scottish Terriers. That's where Jack got his first Scottish Terrier. The dog cemetery is still up on the property.*[19]

Marjorie always talked about what a gentleman Jack was, and she always lit up when describing him.

Jack was a perfectly charming man. He was certainly very definitely the last of the old western gentlemen. I asked him once where he got his wonderful manners, and he said, "I couldn't stand my father. He wasn't worth anything. But my mother was a perfect lady. She taught me my manners. She taught me how to be polite to ladies." I know in all the years we were married we would eat in the kitchen at night because both of us had been working. He'd always hold my chair for me. He was like that. Miss White admired his manners too. He liked to do special things for Miss Elizabeth, and they liked to visit with each other. They were just good friends.[20]

The Courting Years

In a 1981 *Santa Fean Magazine* article, Marjorie is quoted as saying:

When Jack was courting me, I lived in one of Mrs. McComb's historic chicken houses. He had a cream-colored roadster, and he'd drive me to picnics on the Pajarito (Plateau) where he took his dudes. He always looked so wonderful in his crisp, spotless khaki clothes, his big Stetson and his polished boots! He'd cook roasting ears, steak and coffee for us, and through all the years he's taken me all over the Southwest, even to the Cody water tower where he woke up after his clash with apricot brandy. . . . We went with everyone else in town to the Marangs' Saturday Nights for years, and I always think of their house as the "West Bank" of the Acequia Madre. Alfred played his violin and Dorothy and John Sloan played the piano.[21]

During their courtship, Jack had a well-paying steady job in Santa Fe managing the large estate owned by Amelia Elizabeth White. Marjorie recalled visiting Jack at the estate while he was courting her. *When Jack was estate manager for the White sisters he lived on the property, in what is now the Seminar House [at the SAR]. That was Jack's home. Of course, it wasn't as big then because it didn't have as many bedrooms, but that's where he lived. Quite often when he was courting me he would take me there and fix a dinner for me and his brother, Gordon. Gordon lived with him for a while there.*[22]

Marjorie compared Jack with her good friend and colleague, archaeologist Watson Smith.

He and Jack are the same age, and I think they belonged to a generation of natural-born gentlemen that look at women as being equals. They seem to be few and far between. My husband [always thought that] we are superior to men. I never knew a man who thought that except him. He just [thought] that we have better stuff and that we're just better human types. He treated all women as though they were ladies. I've never seen Jack say anything derogatory about women or be chauvinistic in that respect. He [was] chauvinistic, but just a little bit. He [didn't] think we should go places unescorted and that sort of thing. He [was] gentlemanly chauvinistic.[23]

Despite her distrust of men after her disastrous marriage to George Tichy and her relationship with several of her male colleagues at the museum, Jack finally won Marjorie's heart. Jack knew the only way he could ask Marjorie to marry him was to break George Tichy's financial dependence on Marjorie. Jack was finally able to convince Tichy to divorce Marjorie. Their marriage was dissolved in February 1949. Jack had secretly paid Tichy a lump sum of money to stay away from Marjorie for good. It was not until many years later that Jack told Marjorie about this.

Nancy Fox wrote that "her marriage in October 1950, to Jack (E. V.) Lambert proved a union of kindred spirits. Jack, who came West in his youth and whose experiences as a cowboy provide a fund of anecdotes in their own right, shared wholeheartedly her enthusiasm for the Southwest, its landscape, peoples, and traditions."[24] Marjorie was forty-two and Jack was fifty-two at the time. After she and Jack were married, Marjorie dropped the Tichy from her name, and all of her subsequent reports and publications were signed Marjorie F. Lambert.

A Good Marriage

When Marjorie and Jack first got married, they lived in a small house off Canyon Road. Jack's brother Gordon was still living in the house they shared on the estate and Elden Butler, his main horse wrangler, was living in the corral house. *We lived in what is known as the Compound Restaurant now. There were little houses there, and I had been living in one of the very attractive little adobe houses and so we lived there. Then Miss White wanted us to move up on the property so we moved into the corral house.*[25]

In 1951 the Lamberts moved to the corral house just up the hill and across the street from the main White estate "El Delirio" on Garcia Street. Jack had built the corral house and box stalls there for the estate's horses. Eventually the little kitchen was added on to it. Jack's horse wrangler *Eldon [Butler] lived up there. It was never meant to be a residence because part of it was a hay room, part of it was for horse trappings and things of that sort, but Eldon lived in what is the little kitchen. There was a little bathroom and then a little closet there. They used to have some wild parties up there on Saturday nights and Eldon would get out his six shooter, or else Jack would, and they would scare the girls by shooting at the vigas. And that's where all those bullet holes came from.*[26]

When the Lamberts moved into the corral house, *Jack had done some renovation and things there and had some of the workmen help him. Eldon was gone by then. They didn't have any horses then. Sadly enough, we never had any horses. We used the box stalls just for storage. That was a very happy time. We had a good life. We loved that little place. We had the best view of Mt. Taylor and the Pajarito and the Sangre de Cristos.*[27]

The Lambert's corral house was on Garcia Street where it joins with Camino Corrales.

When Jack and I lived up there, there were no other houses anywhere. We could sit out there at night and we could see the stars and the moon. There was no pavement, no traffic to speak of. It was a dirt road and we did not like it when they paved it, but when traffic started coming we knew what it would be like to have dust all over everything all the time. So the paving came later and it was very hard on Miss White and the estate because she had to pay the bill from the beginning of Garcia Street straight up to the Camino [Lejo] and part of the Old Pecos Trail. Jack said the way they figured this was that if you could own the land then you could pay for the paving. It didn't seem right because other people were living there then and they owned property too. But she had to pay for it.[28]

They were a social couple and enjoyed what Santa Fe had to offer in entertainment.

Jack would take me to the Thursday night dinner dances at La Fonda, which was the only nice place to go then. We had a little theater group here then. He would take me to those little plays. Sometimes we'd go down to the new Canton Cafe for Chinese food. But mostly we would take trips out and around. I learned so much about the country. I liked going to Indian dances, particularly the Tewa dances, because he had hired so many of those people to work up at the ranch. He'd say, "Well we're going up to Santa Clara tomorrow. I want to get you some new moccasins." We just had a wonderful outdoor, nature-loving relationship.[29]

Jack didn't like Mexico very much, so any trips Marjorie took with him were usually brief. On the other hand, she and Sallie Wagner would head down to Guaymas now and then where they would take boat trips and walk the beaches. *Now I guess the beaches are gone. But we would spend the whole day from early morning until it began to get dark just collecting shells for the Indians. We brought boxes of shells home.*[30]
Marjorie kept a few shells for herself and gave most of what she collected to her Pueblo friends.

The San Ildefonso redid their bandoliers with the shells that we brought. Then I sent some out to the Laguna and told them to see that some of the Acoma got some. Sallie took some down to the Cochiti. . . . Jose Rey Toledo was work-

ing for the Indian Service and he was stationed at Laguna. That's one of the reasons why I sent this big box of shells, because I knew how important they were and that he would see that the right people got them. He wrote the most interesting letter back to me about how in the olden days they would go down to the Pacific coast, as he called it, to collect and trade for shells and what they'd take with them and how long the journey would take. And even later when they had a burro that could help them carry stuff. They did the whole thing on foot.[31]

While Marjorie worked at the Laboratory of Anthropology, the Lamberts entertained fellow employees and others working in the Santa Fe museums.

We had a lot of people from the museum who would stop by on their way home from work. It got to be kind of a little sanctuary. Staff from the Museum of International Folk Art [MOIFA] would stop by after it opened, such as E. Boyd, who was the first curator of Spanish Colonial Art at MOIFA. Before she came I had to take care of that collection too, among other things. I had to restore the broken pieces and everything. I knew E. Boyd pretty well as I worked with her in the Spanish Colonial Arts Society. She was a character, but she certainly knew her stuff and she was certainly interesting. She put in a very good exhibit there at the Folk Art Museum. She turned the main gallery into what looked like little Spanish American placitas. She had a little adobe house built. She had a little chapel. Of course, she showed all the artifacts from the collection. It made a perfectly wonderful exhibit. I would say that was E. Boyd's crowning achievement in the museum. Otherwise, she didn't come to work very often.[32]

Even though they had a small house, the Lamberts liked to entertain and often held big parties.

We had a nice party for Chap [Kenneth Chapman] on his eightieth birthday. We had it at the corral house. I had a cake made and I had borrowed, out of the collections, some bone toothpicks. We had olives and pickles and little sausages on those. The cake had pot sherds all over it, mostly Powhoge Polychrome because he'd been working on that in San Ildefonso. I had made Jack's punch recipe, which was a very innocent-looking punch, but you really knew it if you had a glass and a half. We invited friends that Chap and his wife Kate had in the Atalaya Garden Club and so on. There was Margretta

Dietrich there and Miss Conkey and the Oteros. It was a wonderful party and everyone had such a good time. Then we used to have parties with some of the LAB people there and some of the people we knew around town, some of Jack's friends like Rex Arrowsmith and so on. We used to roll up the Navajo rugs on Christmas and drink hot buttered rums. That was Jack's favorite drink for cold weather. He was a master at making hot buttered rums. And we'd all dance and have the best time.[33]

Their circle of friends was wide and extended beyond the MNM, SAR, and the White estate. They were acquainted with several of the artists and writers that Santa Fe was so famous for. Oftentimes the Lamberts would be invited to join Miss White's parties:

The [Gustave] Baumanns would be there and William Dean Howells. Bill Howells, the anthropologist, was Miss White's nephew. He and his wife, Muriel, would be there. By the way, Bill and Muriel were taken on their honeymoon by Jack Lambert. He took them out to Navajo country. Muriel said she would never forget that trip.

Miss White had wonderful parties in what's now the Board Room [at the SAR]. That's where she spent most of her time. That was her living room. There would be various artists there. She would have these little gatherings in the late afternoon which were delightful. Sometimes at night there would be chamber music and she would play the harpsichord or Dick Stark would. She would invite people for high tea, I guess you'd call it, in the room downstairs, which is now the office of the president of the SAR. It was the library for many years when the place was a home. She [entertained] celebrities from all over, lots of people from New York and the East.[34]

Marjorie and Jack were especially fond of the well-known photographer Laura Gilpin.

Laura was one of our closest friends. She would come up to the corral house. In fact, she had Christmas Eve with us once. We knew Laura very well. We would be at her house or she'd be at ours. She and Jack could talk about the Navajo by the hour. I thought Jack and Laura were just real simpatico. We had wonderful friends. They were the art and music people. Jack never approved of the opera, though. He said it was going to ruin Santa Fe and change it, and he

FIGURE 22 Jack Lambert at the door to the corral house on Garcia Street in 1976. Photo by Marian Love. Courtesy of the State Archives of New Mexico. Collection Photo 0119–0126; Marjorie F. Lambert Photograph Collection. Image No. 26132.

was right. The old Santa Fe disappeared shortly thereafter. It was a nice time to have the life that we did have then, and I'm glad that we did.[35]

Jack continued to work for Amelia Elizabeth White until he retired in 1969. Before Amelia Elizabeth White passed away she officially gave the corral house and property to Jack. *Miss White gave that place to Jack. She said, "I had hoped that Bill and Muriel would come here summers and stay there,*

but they never wanted to come so, Jack, I want you to have it." So that's how
we happened to have the corral property.[36]

The Lambert's corral house, including the box stalls, now belongs to the
School for Advanced Research, and both have been remodeled to house the
School's resident fellows and scholars. Marjorie took great pride in that.

> *It is now preserved as part of the school. When Doug [Schwartz] came to see*
> *us and said he wanted the school to have it, we were more than willing to*
> *consider it. I think that was about twelve or thirteen years ago [1978–79]. I*
> *was very touched that the main corral house is now the Jack Lambert House*
> *and then my little plaque [Marjorie Lambert House] is on the remodeled box*
> *stalls. I think it's kind of fitting that my name is over where the box stalls were*
> *because I loved to hear Jack talk about the animals that had been there.*[37]

Wonderful stories are attached to everything that the Lamberts had in
their home. As Marjorie reminisced, this particular story came to mind.
[Jack] kept talking about Valentine's Day. He said, "I know you don't like boxes
of candy and stuff like that. You just wait." When I got home there was a wagon
he found someplace. It was in very good condition when he brought it home,
but some kids got into it once when we weren't there and they kind of tore the
seat up. But I'm glad the old wagon is still there. I've had offers to sell that
thing several times, but it belongs there.[38]

Marjorie was convinced that

> *the reason why Jack and I got along was because we weren't in the same pro-*
> *fession but we were both very much interested in the outdoors and the Indians*
> *and Indian artifacts. He liked nice silver and he liked to get blankets and*
> *things. My husband and I amassed a nice collection of Indian art, pottery, and*
> *so on. He laughs when I say we don't have any Indian pottery or rugs anymore.*
> *Most of them are on loan to the SAR. We spent a lot of time camping and going*
> *to Indian sites and exploring the Southwest. All the time we were married we*
> *had a very good relationship.*[39]

Marjorie repeated on numerous occasions that Jack

> *was one of the greatest men I have ever known and he was my best friend for*
> *years and I still miss him. I know a lot of people have asked me why I didn't*

FIGURE 23 Marjorie and Jack with Helen Cordero (Cochiti Pueblo), who is known for her clay storyteller figures at an exhibit opening at the Wheelwright Museum, ca. 1988. Photo by Rain Parrish. Courtesy of the Archives, Museum of Indian Arts & Culture, Lab of Anthropology. Neg. No. 70.872.

marry an anthropologist. They said, "You shouldn't have married him. You should have married one of us." This was Wat Smith and people like that. . . . They just don't know a thing about it. You have to bear in mind that Jack was raised in a large part with Indians. He had been associated with them. He knew the Chumash Indians in California. He knew the Shoshone very well. They were great horsemen, he said. He knew the Bitterroot Indians. He knew all the Pueblo Indians. He knew the Navajos. And he loved being with them. What more could a girl ask for? We didn't compete with each other. He liked antique guns. He liked trading. That's where I got all my wonderful jewelry. I used to have a wonderful collection of Indian jewelry. Jack got all of that for me.[40]

When Marjorie married Jack, he had already been married four times and he only had one child, a daughter. Marjorie gained a stepdaughter who became one of her best friends. *He had a wonderful daughter named Louise Rosser. She was married to Walter Rosser. They were in Heath, Ohio, and then they moved to another part of Ohio. Louise was one of my best friends and I was her best friend. I liked her very much. She was tall and looked very much like her dad. She was born in Alcalde and died before her dad of a horrible cancer. She was a very nice person.*[41]

In the mid-1980s Marjorie's eyesight was getting worse and Jack could no longer hear and his balance was getting worse. After a couple of falls in their home, where Marjorie had difficulty getting him up, it was decided to move Jack to La Residencia Nursing Center in Santa Fe, where he could receive the type of care he needed. Marjorie moved from their home to an apartment located on a hill across the highway from the Santa Fe National Cemetery, and the SAR took over the Lambert home and property. Friends would take Marjorie to see Jack and take them to events and museum openings. As her eyesight continued to deteriorate, Marjorie moved to an assisted living apartment at El Castillo. For the first couple of years, she could walk downtown with friends and visit the museums and shops on the Santa Fe plaza.

E. V. "Jack" Lambert passed away on January 23, 1991, at the age of ninety-three. He was often referred to as the last living cowboy. He was a part of Santa Fe's history and will be remembered for all that he added to what was a colorful, exciting, and vibrant time.

The marriage between Marjorie and Jack was a wonderful blend of a young female intellectual with the rawness of the life of a "real" cowboy. After a disappointing first marriage, her second marriage to Jack proved to be very different. He was a supportive and loving husband who respected Marjorie's independence and shared her many interests in New Mexico archaeology and the diverse cultures of the Southwest. Neither Marjorie nor Jack led the standard mainstream American life. Instead, they followed their hearts and dreams and shared a sense of adventure, a deep love for the New Mexico landscape, and a curiosity and fascination for the Native Americans who have dwelled in the Southwest for millennia. They were happily married for forty-one years, and their marriage was a true partnership in every sense of the term. In fact, they shared so many interests that work imitated life for both of them. Their marriage, their work, and their social activities blended into one.

CHAPTER 8

Professional and Community Engagement

1950s

> I think one of my important contributions was those very good
> exhibits I did over a fifteen-year period in the museum.
>
> —MARJORIE LAMBERT[1]

While being courted by Jack in 1950, Marjorie's duties as curator of archaeology at the Museum of New Mexico continued much as they had before in terms of dealing with the ongoing problems with inadequate collections storage and the exhibition updates and installations. As the chair of the Indian Arts Fund, Marjorie installed a special exhibition of the IAF collections in the Palace of the Governors and held a special open house for the public in February. She was assisted by Laura Gilpin and other members of the IAF Board.

In May, Marjorie and Bertha Dutton attended the joint meetings of the Central States Branch of the American Anthropological Association and the Society for American Archaeology held at the University of Oklahoma in Norman. In August, Marjorie paid a visit to the Fine Arts Center and the Colorado College Museum in Colorado Springs.

In addition to her duties as secretary of the New Mexico Archaeological Society, Marjorie continued to be very active in the New Mexico Association on Indian Affairs, raising funds to support the annual Fiesta Indian Market and Indian dances. As she had done in previous years, she served as a judge of the Pueblo pottery entries at the Indian Market. Toward the end of the year she was invited to catalog and evaluate the extensive Casas Grandes collection at the El Paso International Museum. While there she also cataloged its southwestern material.[2]

In May of 1951, some of Marjorie's concerns for the preservation and safety of the collections were finally addressed. A new storage area for historical materials in the Art Museum basement was complete. As she stated in the SAR Annual Report that year, "After years of an almost hopeless situation, we now have new cupboards for artifacts, a costume closet, and sword and gun racks, all of which should be adequate for a number of years to come. Space has also been supplied in other parts of the same building for historical furniture of various kinds."[3] Many improvements were also made in the public spaces of the Palace of the Governors, including the cleaning of the ceilings and vigas and the painting of the walls and woodwork throughout. During the refurbishment process, some of the exhibits were improved upon as well.

Continuing her participation at the national level, Marjorie attended the joint meeting of the Society for American Archaeology and the Central States Branch of the American Anthropological Association at Northwestern University in Evanston, Illinois. While there she visited the collections and exhibits at the Chicago Natural History Museum (now the Field Museum of Natural History). In September she and Jack made a four-thousand-mile trip through Mexico. While in Mexico City, Marjorie met with the director of the National Museum of Anthropology and History, Dr. Daniel R. de la Borollo, to discuss the possible exchange of cultural material between the museums.[4]

Marjorie continued her community service and her work with the IAF, the Archaeological Society of New Mexico, and the NMAIA. She made some headway on her backlog of archaeological reports and wrote that "the last section of the report on the excavation at Paa-ko is being written, and the text should be ready for printing in 1952."[5] She contributed articles to the *Biennial Report of the Historical Society of New Mexico, El Palacio*, and the newspaper under her new married name, Marjorie F. Lambert.

In the spring of 1952 Marjorie completed the installation of the Manderfield-Otero Sala in the Palace of the Governors. In 1949, the Historical Society and museum received the largest single gift in their combined histories to date. Mrs. Josefita Manderfield de Otero (1874–1951) donated a large costume collection, historical materials, and the contents of the family drawing room. Josefita, the daughter of William R. Manderfield, founder of the *Santa Fe New Mexican*, was married to Eduardo Otero. They lived in the Luna-Otero Mansion in Los Lunas, New Mexico. Marjorie spent three years cataloging the collection and preparing it for display. As she pointed

FIGURE 24 Manderfield-Otero Sala, an example of a nineteenth-century drawing room in the Palace of the Governors, ca. 1955. Photo by the New Mexico Tourism Bureau. Courtesy of the Palace of the Governors Photo Archives (NMHM/DCA). New Mexico Magazine Collection. Neg. No. HP.2007.20.540.

out, "The Sala is based on furnishings of the family home . . . and on related costumes."[6]

Throughout the year, Marjorie kept busy representing the museum and the Archaeological Society of New Mexico at the annual meeting of the Society for American Archaeology at Ohio State University in Columbus. While in Ohio she visited some of the archaeological sites, and she noted how different they were from what is found in the Southwest. In April the Indian Arts Fund held a special reception in honor of Mary Jane Colter, the well-known architect and designer for the Fred Harvey Company. Shortly after this, Marjorie completed her term as chair of the Indian Arts Fund Board. She continued to serve on this board and on the boards of the New Mexico Association on Indian Affairs and the Spanish Colonial Arts Society.[7]

Marjorie finally completed a draft of her Paa-ko monograph, and it was in the hands of reviewers. Dr. Spencer Rogers had also completed the skeletal study. One important article penned by Marjorie that appeared in *El Palacio* that year was "Oldest Armor in the United States Discovered at San Gabriel del Yunque." In order to authenticate a potential Spanish helmet, Marjorie consulted a number of researchers and specialists, including Harold Peterson of the National Park Service in Washington, D.C., Stephen Grancsay of the Metropolitan Museum in New York, and Rutherford J. Gettens of the Freer Gallery of Art in Washington, D.C. According to Marjorie, "They all verified that this helmet [was] the oldest piece of European armor ever found in the continental United States."[8] This article would be rewritten and published in the journal *Archaeology* in 1953.[9]

In 1953 and 1954 Marjorie carried out her curatorial duties as in previous years. According to Nancy Fox, "She was indefatigable in building and enhancing the museum's collections. It was due to her efforts that the School of American Research, in 1954, purchased from the widow of A.M. Thompson of Deming an unparalleled collection of Mimbres pottery and artifacts."[10] Marjorie also found time to participate in national and regional conferences. In 1955 Marjorie was put in charge of the Palace of the Governors while still serving as a research associate of the SAR and curator of archaeology for the Museum of New Mexico.[11] She continued to be in charge of the Palace until 1964.

In the mid-1950s Marjorie was finally able to improve the lighting and upgrade the wiring in the Palace of the Governors and the library. These improvements were twofold: to alleviate any fire danger from the old wiring and to improve the lighting in the exhibition galleries. She continued to make improvements on the exhibitions at the Palace of the Governors and on August 6, 1955, opened a major exhibition in the westernmost gallery, "Early Man in the Southwest." She provides a detailed description of the exhibition in an *El Palacio* article.[12] She reported that the exhibit focused on "the leading ice age cultures of the southwestern part of the United States, which existed between 7,000 to 20,000 years ago." These were "graphically illustrated by attractive case displays, colorful maps, diagrams and charts." The exhibit opened in time for the annual Pecos Conference, held in mid-August at the Palace of the Governors.

This exhibition was indirectly influenced by the discovery of ancient human skull fragments on a ranch near Midland, Texas. Fred Wendorf was contacted in 1953 by Keith Glasscock, an avocational archaeologist who had found some skull fragments on the Sharbauer Ranch. The "Midland Skull,"

FIGURE 25 (Left to right) Marjorie Lambert, Bertha Dutton, and Florence Hawley Ellis in the Gila Pueblo Laboratory during the Pecos Conference held in Globe, Arizona, in 1954. Courtesy of the Palace of the Governors Photo Archives (NMHM/DCA). Neg. No. 013143.

dating to the Pleistocene, proved to be the oldest human remains found in North America at the time. The skull became the centerpiece of the exhibition and attracted a large number of visitors. The skull was loaned to the Palace of the Governors by Keith Glasscock for a period of ten years.[13]

The Paa-ko monograph was finally published as "Paa-ko, Archaeological Chronicle of an Indian Village in North Central New Mexico" (parts I–V), *School of American Research Monograph*, no. 19. The monograph also included "The Physical Type of the Paa-ko Population" (part VI) by Spencer Rogers. It came off the press and was available in January 1955. Marjorie continued to publish articles in *El Palacio*, which included an obituary on one of Hewett's longtime associates who also had an influence on her early college education and archaeology career, William W. Postlethwaite.[14] She also wrote a paper about the clay and stone figurines in the Thompson collection and had two additional studies in process.[15]

As in previous years, Marjorie continued to be active in professional organizations at the national level and attended the SAA annual meeting held at the University of Indiana, Bloomington, in the spring, and in November she traveled to Boston to attend the American Anthropological Association's annual meeting. While in Boston she visited museums and historic landmarks both there and in Cambridge. She and Jack also traveled throughout New Mexico to various archaeological sites and pueblos. Their travels enhanced both her professional and personal relationships with the people that she and Jack knew.[16]

New Bylaws for the Archaeological Society of New Mexico

Probably one of the biggest events of 1955 for Marjorie was the changing of the bylaws of the Archaeological Society of New Mexico. She was still serving as secretary, and there was a big change in the Board of Trustees. At the society's annual board meeting four new trustees, Norris Bradbury, W. J. Keller, Charlie Steen, and V. F. Tannich were elected to join the board. Upon the resignation of Daniel T. Kelly, president, and Ruth L. Alexander, vice president, who had served in these positions for many years, the society's members elected Norris Bradbury as president, W. J. Keller as vice president, Albert G. Ely as treasurer, and Marjorie as secretary. During the meeting, Norris Bradbury requested that a committee made up of Charlie Steen, W. J. Keller, and Marjorie revise the society's bylaws.[17]

The organization of the Archaeological Society of New Mexico had remained the same since its inception until Marjorie and Charlie Steen started working on the proposed changes. Marjorie expressed her concerns that she would lose her job if she proposed any changes to the bylaws, but Steen made it clear that the recommended changes would come through him and the National Park Service. They would leave Marjorie out of it, except for the planning. As Marjorie tells it, *We worked and worked, and we worked and we got this state society really going the way it is today. It is the Archaeological Society of New Mexico. It started with Al Schroeder coming into the picture—people like that. We started getting these publications; the Collected Papers started. We had very good relationships with the amateurs of the little local chapters around the state. All were very helpful. We would have twenty-five to forty-five at our meetings.*[18]

Even though it was a lot of responsibility and work to keep track of the society's business, there were advantages as well. As Marjorie recalled, *I met some very interesting people throughout the state. As a result, I managed to bring in some very interesting collections. People got interested [in heritage*

preservation] and they started giving things to the museum, mostly archae-
ological stuff, so it wasn't bad. It had its good points. But I didn't think one
person should be handling it who had so many other duties to perform.[19] In
other words, Marjorie was still handling everything without any offers of
assistance from the other archaeologists on the museum staff.

The committee worked on the new bylaws throughout the year. Marjorie
always supported the organization, and she has never been recognized for
her role as secretary historically nor for her input in its transformation to a
higher level of professionalism in the state of New Mexico. In a 1997 interview she said, *It's a good organization today and I played my part in devel-*
oping it. Dear Charlie Steen died not too long ago. He really backed me up
every bit of the way and he stuck by me thick and thin. He went to the director
several times. I got the bylaws changed so the secretary position was part of
the State instead of just an adjunct of the Museum of New Mexico. It should
not have been just the Museum of New Mexico.[20]

The amendments to the bylaws of the Archaeological Society of New
Mexico were approved by the Society's Board on October 6, 1955. These
were published in the November issue of *El Palacio*.[21] According to the
amended bylaws, the organization's secretary was considered a member of
the Executive Committee of the Board and was to be elected at the same
time as the president, vice president, and treasurer. The secretary position
was no longer the de facto responsibility of the curator of archaeology of the
Museum of New Mexico.

An Exhibit on the Mimbres

In 1956 Marjorie continued to be listed as both an associate and the curator
of archaeology in the annual report of the School of American Research.
She reported that she had opened a major exhibition, "The Mogollon Mimbres Culture of the Southwest," featuring the Alex M. Thompson Mimbres
collection from Luna County that had been purchased by an anonymous
friend of the School of American Research in 1954. It was such an extensive
collection that it took over a year to process. This Mimbres collection was
added to the other Mogollon materials from the Three Circle Ruin excavation and a Highway Salvage Archaeology project in the Reserve area to
complete the exhibition.[22] Marjorie wrote an article about some of the clay
and stone figurines in the Thompson collection for *El Palacio*.[23] She later

wrote an article for *El Palacio*, where she provides a detailed description of this Mimbres exhibition that opened to the public on September 5, 1956.[24] In this article Marjorie advocated for scientific work to be carried out in Luna, Doña Ana, and Hidalgo Counties in the southern part of the state, as well as northern Mexico. She concluded that the figurines, even though randomly collected by an avocational archaeologist in the Deming area, were significant in adding information about late Mimbres Period settlements in southwestern New Mexico.

During this time period, there was an increase in highway salvage archaeology projects throughout New Mexico. Fred Wendorf and Stewart Peckham ran the salvage archaeology program out of the Laboratory of Anthropology. Marjorie assisted them in preparing the first in a series of exhibits to be installed in the new State Highway Building in Santa Fe. She also installed special interest archaeological displays from time to time in the vestibule at the Palace of the Governors and at the Laboratory of Anthropology.

Excavation of a Historic Well at the Palace of the Governors

While Marjorie was in her first office in the Palace of the Governors, she became interested in its history, especially the well in the patio area. Her interest piqued while learning about the work of Jesse L. Nusbaum, who did the restoration on the Palace of the Governors. She claimed:

Dr. [Frederick Webb] Hodge was a historian, and he told me more about the history of the Palace of the Governors than I ever learned at the University of New Mexico or through my reading. One of the things that Hodge told me, which has always bothered me very much, was that when Jesse (Nusbaum) was given orders [by Hewett] to get the place in shape so that it could be opened in 1909, they used wagons and horse teams to clean out the debris and so on. There were all kinds of potsherds and majolica ware, all kinds of imported china, and so on mixed in with the debris from some of the walls that had rotted that he was cleaning out to restore. All that was taken over to a dump. One of the things Hodge said when he was there for one of the board meetings—he was on the Board of the School of American Research and the Museum of New Mexico, and they had a joint meeting every year. He said that the most important structure in the patio of the Palace of the Governors was the big well at the east end of the Palace. Years ago, after talking to him, I did some research in the archives, and I feel very certain that was the well that De Vargas had built after the Rebellion [Pueblo Revolt of 1680] because the water supply had been cut off. . . . I think it was in 1707 that it is said that the well was four varas wide and forty varas deep. Well, that's a pretty deep well.[25]

The reason I was interested in the well was that I had been reading some of the reports by people like John L. Cotter, who had excavated wells in the east, some of them within fortifications and so on.[26] *I went to the director of the museum, the Honorable Boaz Long, and I told him what Hodge had said. He said he wouldn't let me excavate the well. I asked why not, and he said he didn't want any Texas tourists falling into it and suing us. I said we could arrange to keep it safe, but I was never allowed to excavate that well. I asked if I could excavate the smaller well and he said he didn't think we had any money for it. I said I could raise the money for it. He asked how much money I thought I'd need. I said I needed enough money to build some scaffolding and I wanted to borrow Roy Ghent and Bernie Valdez to help me. So, I was allowed to do that little well in the southwest corner of the patio.*[27]

Marjorie and her crew, which consisted of Roy Ghent, Bernie Valdez, and Sallie Wagner, began excavating Well I (LA 4451) on May 9, 1956. As Marjorie recalled, the actual excavation of the well

wasn't difficult at all. We arranged a pulley and a bucket and a crank with a rope on it, and we started by filling the bucket and then putting the stuff in the wheelbarrow. It was a neat excavation in a way because I had other duties going on at the same time. I would come to my office dressed nicely for the day and then put on an apron and jacket and go out and check on what was coming out of the well. Sallie Wagner would come in now and then, and she would help look at potsherds. But Roy and Bernie did most of the digging inside [the well]. I felt confident and I was proud of myself because people who looked at our scaffolding asked, "Who designed this? It is very well done." I was the one who designed that. But it turned out to be a very interesting little well. It was cobble lined, but it was only seventeen-and-a-half-feet deep. We were getting water at sixteen feet. We found a broken glass inkwell. I guess one of the scribes of the Territorial Period [threw it in the well]. The Hall of Archaeology used to be the United States Post Office, so it could have been someone from there. There was a surveyor's office in there too and some of the Fort Marcy people who were still hanging around.[28]

Marjorie briefly described the well excavation in an *El Palacio* article in 1956 and a more extensive article in 1981.[29]

In addition to the *El Palacio* articles on the Mimbres collection and the well excavation, Marjorie penned two additional articles. One featured a "Rare Glaze I-Yellow Potsherd from San Cristóbal" and the other "A Prehistoric Stone Elbow Pipe from the Taos Area." Marjorie and Charlie Steen compiled the *News Letters* of the Archaeological Society. She also prepared a five-year plan for the Department of Archaeology and the Palace of the Governors for the museum director, the Honorable Boaz Long.[30]

An important meeting took place in 1956 that would have an impact on Marjorie's work and her contributions to southwestern New Mexico archaeology. She recalled that one day

> *John Gaw Meem, who was president of the School of American Research, called the research staff together. Of course, we had lost Stanley Stubbs by then. Fred Wendorff was director of the LAB. Ed Ferdon was assistant director of the Arizona State Museum. He called us together—that included anyone associated with the School of American Research, Bertha Dutton and Bruce Ellis, any of us doing any kind of research. He wanted us to work on some projects for the school. He said the School of American Research had acquired its reputation on the basis of its fieldwork and its field training program up in the Jemez Mountains and the Pajarito Plateau, and he wanted to bring it back to its former glory.*[31]

He asked the research associates to submit project proposals to the SAR for consideration.

Marjorie didn't waste any time submitting proposals for projects that she had been thinking about for quite some time:

> *I submitted two programs that I thought would be interesting and worthwhile. One was an archaeological survey and excavation of important structures in Santa Fe. In other words, do a complete history of Santa Fe and environs. That would have been valuable because during the Pueblo Revolt, Indians moved into the Palace of the Governors. It would have made a wonderful study. That was one idea. The other one was to point out relationships that I felt existed between Mexico, the country south of us, and the Southwest. I pointed out different areas where I thought traits come into the Southwest. One was*

FIGURE 26 Marjorie Lambert supervising Roy Ghent and Bernie Valdez during the excavation and reconstruction of the well in the patio of the Palace of the Governors, May 1956. Photo by Arthur Taylor. Courtesy of
the Palace of the Governors Photo Archives (NMHM/DCA). Neg. No. 006821.

through the Mogollon and the other one was in Arizona where the Hohokam
were. One of them I thought would go back to the Ice Age. I mentioned those
big playas down in the areas of Lordsburg, Luna County, and Hidalgo County,
and I based that on the fact that extinct bison remains had been found down
in that area plus broken Folsom points.[32]

Marjorie took some time in 1957 to visit ancient sites in Hidalgo and Luna
counties. This no doubt was an area she seriously wanted to investigate, and
she was hoping the SAR would eventually support it. So, she headed south
and spent some time with friends and toured the area. She also collected a
sample of pottery sherds from the surface and took photographic records of
the sites she was visiting.[33] As Marjorie recalled,

I had made friends with a lot of people in Luna County, not only in Silver
City, but also Deming. One of our friends and one of my mentors was V. F.

Tannich, the manager of the Victorio Land and Cattle Company. He took us on preliminary surveys all through that country and helped us make a map of the sites that I thought would be important. So, I submitted that study. I submitted a preliminary study [to the SAR] that I said would be a survey of caves and possibly an excavation of one or two of them in Hidalgo County, having already been taken to some of the cave sites. There were also some very interesting Apache remains down there. Their little forked hogans and things like that.[34]

In 1958 Marjorie completed the reinstallation of the Hall of Archaeology in the largest gallery in the Palace of the Governors in preparation for the Fiftieth Anniversary Celebration of the SAR and the MNM that was scheduled for 1959. She also installed exhibitions in the Laboratory of Anthropology, a textile exhibit at the Museum of International Folk Art, and prepared the exhibition "Man, the Hunter" to travel around the state.

In addition to her regular duties installing new exhibitions and the heavy demands made upon her time by program-arranging, guided tours, education, and other public relations activities, she also prepared an illustrated catalog for the Mimbres-Mogollon exhibit, which was still awaiting printing. She continued her collection of data for a paper she was writing on ancient stone effigies and other ceremonial material and contributed time to the UNM-Museum course in museum technology held in the spring. From June through September, she served as program chair and field supervisor for the Santa Fe Archaeological Society, which conducted Sunday excavations at Pueblo Wells just outside of the city. Interested in getting the local youth involved in archaeology, Marjorie helped sponsor the newly formed Santa Fe Junior Archaeological Society.[35]

A Change in the Relationship Between the SAR and MNM

In 1958 consultant Mitchell Wilder was hired by the executive committee of the SAR's Board of Managers to examine the relationship between the School of American Research and the Museum of New Mexico and "the combined institution's program and potentials."[36] In his report, Wilder questioned the "legality of a policy in which the head of a public institution, the Museum, was appointed by the board of a private institution, the School." He noted that even though this arrangement had been established by the terri-

FIGURE 27 Marjorie Lambert conducting a tour in the Spanish Colonial chapel in the Palace of the Governors, ca. 1960. Photo by Charles Herbert. Courtesy of the Palace of the Governors Photo Archives (NMHM/DCA). Neg. No. 001616.

torial legislature in 1909 it appeared to be in conflict with the New Mexico constitution.[37]

This report prompted Alexander V. Wasson, a member of the SAR's Board of Managers and president of the MNM's Board of Regents, to ask Frank Zinn, New Mexico's attorney general, for an opinion. Zinn replied in a letter dated January 20, 1959, that in his view the current arrangement indeed was unconstitutional.[38] In response, the New Mexico state legislature passed Senate Bill 147, which officially ended the fifty-year-old arrangement between the SAR and the MNM. It was signed into law by Governor John Burroughs on April 2, 1959. The MNM's Board of Regents would now consist of seven members appointed by the governor, and the director would be selected by the board and his/her salary paid by the state.[39] The SAR, which had depended on state funding through the museum to pay staff and cover some of its operating costs, now faced an uncertain future both financially and programmatically.

The severing of the formal connection between the MNM and the SAR brought into focus the ownership of the co-mingled collections, which became an area of contention between both institutions. This was the beginning of a long period of negotiations starting in the early 1960s. First the trustees of the Indian Arts Fund transferred ownership of their collections to the SAR. The staff of the anthropology division was given the task of determining ownership of the remainder of the collection. Beginning in 1960 Nancy Fox and Albert Ely, representing the MNM, and Betty Toulouse, representing the SAR, began the ten-year inventory of the collections. Collections belonging to the SAR were placed on long-term loan to the MNM.[40]

The SAR also lost most of its staff, who, even though listed in the annual reports, were in reality MNM staff and had been paid by the state. This meant changes for Marjorie and other staff in terms of their relationship with the SAR, as well as changes in titles and responsibilities. As curator of archaeology, Marjorie's work continued as before and she "installed a series of displays at the Palace of the Governors which received widespread acclaim for their fresh and visually exciting approach to the presentation of Southwestern prehistory."[41] She continued to do the same with the exhibitions she worked on with Stanley Stubbs at the Laboratory of Anthropology.

A 1962 article in the *Santa Fe Scene* encapsulated Marjorie's career up to the end of the 1950s:

> Her major fields of interest are in the prehistory of the Southwest and Central America and their relationships, in Southwestern ethnology and history, North American archaeology and education through museum exhibits and interpretation of the research materials. With the assistance of Mrs. Mary Spencer, during the past five and one half years Mrs. Lambert has reinstalled nearly all of the anthropology exhibits housed in the Palace of the Governors; installed one history exhibit; an Indian musical instruments show at the Laboratory of Anthropology; three major exhibits in the Hall of Ethnology; and collaborated on the traveling exhibit "Man, the Hunter," for the Folk Art Museum. The aim of the exhibit program is to tell the public the story of man in the Southwest from the Ice Age to the present day.[42]

Marjorie observed that *none of them [exhibits] are there now, but people from all over the country said they were the best. . . . These were professionals that said that. Not only the school groups, but these were professionals from other museums. Maybe they were good. At least I thought that they told the story, and I liked assembling the material and I liked working with the material and telling the story and then working with an artist who could bring it to life for me in a way that I wouldn't have been able to do.*[43]

As the 1950s came to a close, the next decade would prove to be both challenging and rewarding.

CHAPTER 9

From the Caves of Hidalgo County to Retirement

1960s

> We did a survey there and we excavated two caves. We did
> Pinnacle. We did some testing in Buffalo and then in U-Bar.
>
> —MARJORIE LAMBERT[1]

Marjorie was now working full-time out of her office at the Laboratory of Anthropology. In 1961 she was made the curator of anthropology and exhibits for the Museum of New Mexico. In 1963 her position was changed to curator of the research division, and she continued to be in charge of the Palace of the Governors until 1964. Throughout the 1960s, Marjorie continued to install anthropological exhibits focused on up-to-date interpretations of archaeology in the Palace of the Governors in downtown Santa Fe.[2] Even with all of her additional administrative and curatorial duties, Marjorie was able to do a little archaeological fieldwork in the early 1960s.

Decisions made in the late 1950s regarding the split between the School of American Research and the Museum of New Mexico became the focus of the members of the School's Board of Managers as to what direction it should take in terms of its future identity. It was decided that its reputation was based on field research and scholarly publications. According to SAR historian Malinda Elliott, "During the early 1960s, in a scaled-down way the School continued its tradition of sponsoring archaeological surveys and excavations. For example, excavations in Hidalgo County resulted in discoveries of prehistoric archaeological sites in dozens of caves and in the 1965 publication of a *Survey and Excavation of Caves in Hidalgo County, New Mexico* by former Hewett student and staff member Marjorie F. Lambert and co-author J. Richard Ambler."[3] For Marjorie, the opportunity to be engaged in archaeological fieldwork again was a dream come true.

The Caves of Hidalgo County

In her report to the SAR's Board of Managers in 1959, Marjorie recommended that the School sponsor an archaeological survey of Hidalgo County in the southwestern corner of New Mexico. It was an area that was little known in terms of its archaeological and scientific value, even though it was being extensively pot hunted. There was a large number of collectors interested in the Mimbres pottery from the sites in the region, and the high market value of these archaeological finds encouraged the looting of numerous sites in this region. Marjorie proposed to the SAR Board of Managers that the initial survey should be done by a trained anthropologist accompanied by a biologist, both of whom were "rugged enough to ride a horse for days at a time." Even though she claimed that "it is a man's job, and he would have in mind that in this survey, there are remains to be noted from the Ice Age to fairly recent Apache remains.... A good photographic record should be made. Sherd samples and lithic materials should be noted. The flora and fauna, and the ecological aspects of Luna County should be noted. I think that much should be done. We should stake our claim."[4] Even though she said that "it is a man's job," she also assured them that she was rugged enough to do the survey. She went on to suggest that they should go ahead and start the survey and then seek funding for at least a five-year project in Hidalgo County. "I have also indicated that I think that the School should insist on publications. These projects are not worth anything unless the findings are presented to the public."[5]

Despite the split between the two institutions, Marjorie continued to have a positive relationship with the SAR and was able to secure support for a project that she had long dreamed of being carried out in southwest New Mexico. Marjorie did in fact convince the SAR Board to sponsor research in Hidalgo County, and in 1960 she was given a $10,000 grant-in-aid to support the implementation of the "Hidalgo Project for archaeological investigations in the southwestern corner of the state."[6] As the project's supervisor, Marjorie led a team that included two graduate students and six laborers into the barren landscape of the boot heel of southwestern New Mexico. From July to September 1960, they surveyed more than one hundred rock shelters and caves that revealed twelve ancient sites. A brief archaeological survey of the Alamo Hueco Mountains was carried out from July 13 through July 20 to locate caves and rock shelters for possible excavation. It was decided that the team would excavate three cave sites and three small shelters. Marjorie noted:

*I had the help of the Baker boys [Bob and Russell Baker of Deming] as assis-
tants and that nice Dick Ambler. Dick was very helpful and in fact I couldn't
have gotten along without him. I wrote to [Emil] Haury and asked him for two
of his best graduate students [from the University of Arizona]. Ambler was
one of them. . . . The sad thing is, even in spite of what that preliminary study
did, we only had six weeks. I got a grant from the school. They were to give me
another grant but Fred Wendorf [director of the Laboratory of Anthropology]
told the director of the school, Ed Weyer, that he wanted me for another project. . . . There was no reason why I couldn't have gone on with it because it
was just getting good. But anyway, it was a productive season and I met some
pretty wonderful friends for the museum all through Deming and Silver City.[7]*

Recalling her experience on the survey, Marjorie was reminded of what
one of her colleagues had said to her.

*Jesse Jennings used to say, "The best way to survey is to pick up one foot and
put it down and lift up the other one and keep walking." We did an awful lot
of that. We did a lot of it beforehand because we knew that there were flint
knapping areas. We knew that ancient hunters had been all through that
area. We picked up a lot of lithic material all around the areas we concen-
trated on to study and then we walked all those overhangs where there were
remains of Apache occupation. We knew where the caves were. We picked
U-Bar Cave, which is where the human hair net came from and the artifacts
connected with it, and the Pinnacle Cave and Buffalo Cave. Buffalo Cave
had been tested earlier by the Cosgroves [Harriet S. "Hattie" and Cornelius B.
"Burt"]. They did a lot of cave work down in that general area.[8] I think the
significant thing about Buffalo Cave is the picture of that great big black
buffalo on the back side of that cave. Now the question is, Were there buffalo
there or was there a Buffalo Clan or did it signify something else? There were
lots of problems that might have been solved had we been allowed to go on
with the project.[9]*

In the introduction to their report on the Hidalgo County Project, Marjorie and Richard Ambler wrote that "three caves were excavated: U-Bar
Cave (LA 5689), Buffalo Cave (LA 5690), and Pinnacle Cave (LA 5691). . . .
In brief, excavations showed that Buffalo and Pinnacle Caves were occupied
as temporary habitations, whereas the larger U-Bar Cave was primarily a

ceremonial spot. As far as could be determined, all three were, at least in part, contemporaneous. They were utilized by inhabitants of nearby villages, most of whom can be assigned to the Animas Phase of the Casas Grandes Culture." They were not ready "to elaborate on the intercultural relationships of the area, on the development or sequence of the cultures through time, or on the exact cultural relationship of this area to the surrounding regions."[10] This was one of the reasons Marjorie wanted to continue her work in the area. She wanted more than anything to try to put the pieces of the ancient cultural puzzle together for this region.

While Marjorie and Richard Ambler were excavating U-Bar Cave in Hidalgo County, they found a hunting net made of human hair. Within the cave was a hunting shrine that had been destroyed by pot hunters prior to the survey. Buried deep in bat guano was a cache. The assemblage in this cache consisted of a rolled and tied hunting net made of human hair, four hanks of human hair carefully wrapped in thirty unused hunting snares, and a coiled basket containing two ringtail cat skins.[11] This exceptional human hair net spans an area of approximately 777 square feet and is 151 feet long and 5.15 feet wide. It is composed of 8,140 feet of hair cordage, measuring 1.5 miles. It is estimated that approximately sixty-nine full heads of hair would have been required to make the net. There are 25 knots per square foot, with an estimate of 19,425 square knots in this net. Weighing 7.25 pounds, they suggested that it could be slung over a shoulder and easily carried, but it was unused. The four hanks of hair were more than likely for repairing the net should it tear.[12]

U-Bar Cave's "Wooden Katchina" or Tlaloc?

Another unique find in U-Bar Cave was the "wooden katchina" that they referred to as "the remarkable little figure, found in U-Bar Cave in the ceremonial area." Marjorie showed this to her Pueblo friends and colleagues, either in person or in a photograph, and they all told her:

Although they all recognized it as a sacred being, none so far have been able to identify it. They say it is unlike any in their pantheon. It is interesting to note, however, that two Rio Grande Pueblo Indians, without knowing where the katchina came from, said, "It is not from here." They explained that it belonged to the south. The red paint was the most significant color, they said, and it signified "south." The black mask was synonymous with omnipotent power. Both red and black paint (on this Katchina) were for the "hunt" and the black splashes on the back were for "rain." This katchina is powerful for all Indians, they asserted, and is for the animals that were hunted, and for all the crops.... [B]oth Rio Grande and Western Pueblo Indians recognized the figure as being predominantly male; and whatever its meaning, they agreed that it was taken to the cave for ceremonial purposes—to play its part in hunting and increase rituals.[13]

More recent research suggests a strong linkage between the Southwest and Mesoamerica through the comparison of the Mesoamerican Tlaloc complex with that of the Southwest kachinas.[14] The conceptual systems and shared metaphors described by Polly Schaafsma "indicate that the kachina complex of the protohistoric farmers in the Pueblo Southwest is a northern manifestation of a Mesoamerican constellation of ideas in the realm of Tlaloc."[15] One of the examples that Schaafsma uses to demonstrate this premise is the "Wooden Katchina" Marjorie and her team recovered from U-Bar Cave.

Schaafsma describes the images of Tlaloc as represented throughout Mesoamerica:

> Tlaloc is represented in the codices, murals and architectural sculpture as an anthropomorphic deity. Carved wooden and turquoise inlay masks were worn by religious impersonators of Tlaloc in festivals dedicated to rain and fertility. . . . [R]epresentations of Tlaloc are characterized by goggle eyes, sometimes shown with brows formed by serpents that intertwine over the nose to create a "cruller" effect. He may also be portrayed with an upturned mouth or with a mustache-like upper lip above a cavernous maw and in either case is equipped with long fangs. . . . Changes in Tlaloc iconography through time are inevitable, but the goggle eyes, the volute over the mouth, and the fangs are relatively constant.[16]

Another important feature related to Tlaloc are the caves throughout the Mesoamerican landscape, regarded as points of access to the underworld and places of origin. Schaafsma found that "caves are often viewed as entrances and thus as providing access to the watery Underworld as such. The realm of Tlalocan was accessed via caves, especially caves in mountains . . .

mountain caves, often housing springs and shrines, were regarded as especially sacred."[17]

In making a comparison between Mesoamerican and southwestern iconography, Schaafsma argues that

> Juxtaposed to this intricate web of landscape and other symbolism surrounding Tlaloc is the Southwest kachina complex, with a parallel set of concepts and metaphors. . . . It is the general belief that the anonymous ancestors come in the form of clouds to bring rains to the fields of the living, and when they are impersonated on the Pueblo plazas as kachinas, they wear masks. . . . Kachina masks appear around A.D. 1300 in Pueblo rock art and on ceramics. Along with masks, goggle-eyed figures resembling Tlaloc, often with their torsos covered with cloud symbolism, are prominent in Jornada Mogollon-style rock art in the Chihuahuan desert of southern New Mexico between ca. A.D. 1000 and 1400. The presence of a Tlaloc image on a Mimbres Black-on-white bowl confirms the presence of this figure in southern New Mexico between A.D. 1000 and 1150.[18]

Further evidence of ceremonial or prestige goods characteristic of Casas Grandes, in particular, was the large number of scarlet macaw feathers found at U-Bar and Pinnacle caves dating to the Animas Phase.[19] Marjorie and Ambler concluded that "this area should be a good location for the study of the early development of the Mogollon, as well as early contacts between the Southwest and Mesoamerica."[20]

Changes at the SAR and Hidalgo County Project

The first director of the SAR after the split from the MNM, Dr. Edward Weyer Jr., reported on the status of the Hidalgo Project to the Board of Managers in November 1960:

> The investigations were carried out under the supervision of Mrs. Marjorie Lambert of the Laboratory of Anthropology, who led the field party with two graduate students as field assistants and six laborers. No fewer than 200 caves giving promise of containing archeological remains were sighted. It is a virtually unexplored section from an archaeological point of view. One cave,

the largest excavated, was 280 feet long by about 70 feet wide. It had been used as a ceremonial center, and a most spectacular thing was discovered—a net made entirely of human hair, used for capturing animals. . . . No other net of this type, composed of human hair, has previously been found.

Another interesting item is a wooden katchina, painted red, turquoise, yellow and black; it is likewise a rarity and may shed light on the early religious beliefs in this region.

These and a quantity of other specimens show that the season's work was a signal success. Other excavations and samplings in the Hidalgo region showed that Pleistocene animals, and perhaps Ice Age man, were in the area at some period before the time of Christ. The people who used the caves were expert textile and basket makers. The excavations of the so-called Pinnacle Cave showed to some extent how people slept, what they ate, and what they wore. I refer you to the Preliminary Report for many other details connected with this Hidalgo Project.[21]

Weyer went on to say that "one of the important results of this expedition has been the effect of retarding or eliminating the 'pot-hunting' in the area by amateurs, which was very serious. The support of local ranchers and personnel of the local BLM was secured toward this end. Thus an area rich in archeological materials representing a great time span but subject in recent years to some of the worst pot-hunting in the Southwest has been made secure for scientific investigation." He added that "a prospectus has been prepared for the continuation of work in Hidalgo County, and we are eagerly awaiting the answer to a request for financial support to sustain this work from a company that has strong financial interest in that region."[22]

In response to Weyer's report on the Hidalgo Project, Miss Amelia Elizabeth White commented that she wanted to make sure that Marjorie received credit "as author of the [Hidalgo Project] idea."[23] Miss White wanted it to be on the record that Marjorie was the one who had conceived of the project, supervised the fieldwork, and was analyzing the materials brought back to the Laboratory of Anthropology, and that she should receive credit for the project. She had a good ally in Miss White, who was a powerful woman in Santa Fe and was a highly respected member of the SAR's board.

Unfortunately, Miss White was not able to help Marjorie continue with the Hidalgo Project. Marjorie's male colleagues at the Laboratory of Anthropology saw to it that she would not continue on the project. Marjorie contended that *[Fred] Wendorf was head of the LAB at that time and not on the side of the school. He came right out and said so. He laughed about it. I heard him talking about it. He had told Ed Weyer, "I guess it's going to make her pretty mad when she finds out about it." He told him that I couldn't go because I was working for him on the Navajo Reservoir Project. Trouble is, I never worked on that project! . . . Blame it on the museum. Blame it on the one person [Fred Wendorf].*[24] This was only the beginning of bad blood between Marjorie and Wendorf that lasted for the rest of her career, even after he went to Southern Methodist University in Texas.

In the 1961 annual report of the SAR, Ed Weyer reported that "a second season of field work in Hidalgo County is being organized. Because the Laboratory of Anthropology found it impossible to release Mrs. Marjorie Lambert under Museum salary to serve as Principal Investigator as she did on the first Hidalgo Project, the School of American Research has decided to conduct the coming season's work independently."[25] Sharing Marjorie's sentiments, Weyer expressed a sense of urgency in continuing with this project due to the high level of pot hunting that was occurring in the area. To keep the project moving forward, "Weyer hired archeologist Eugene B. McCluney, a Ph.D. candidate at the University of Colorado, to direct the second Hidalgo project, which began in June 1962."[26]

Marjorie was upset that she was not able to continue with the research she had started in Hidalgo County even though Miss White came to her defense. The SAR was interested in Marjorie's original proposal to carry out fieldwork in Hidalgo County over a period of years; however, she unfortunately was not involved in future projects. As Lewis and Hagan report,

the Hidalgo project continued for several more seasons. Excavations revealed a link between Hidalgo County sites and the imposing ruins of Casas Grandes one hundred miles south. McCluney excavated the Joyce Well Site the following year [1963], and in 1964 he examined outlying Mimbres sites and surveyed the Animas-Hachita and Playas Lake areas to determine the presence of early humans in the area.[27] . . . McCluney's excavations at the Clanton Draw, Box Canyon, and Joyce Well sites revealed T-shaped doorways, pottery styles, adobe structures, and other traits similar to those at Casas Grandes, a massive fourteenth century ruin with ball courts and platform mounds to the south in Mexico.[28]

With the resignation of Edward Weyer in November 1964, Eugene Mc-Cluney was made acting director of the school. Along with several other programs, the Hidalgo Project was put on hold as the school prepared to go through another transition. Financially recovering somewhat, the school initiated its fifth archaeological season in southwestern New Mexico in June 1966 with the excavation of Bobcat Cave south of Lordsburg.[29]

In her original proposal for the Hidalgo County survey, Marjorie stressed the need to get the reports out as soon as possible. Even though Marjorie and J. Richard Ambler completed their extensive and detailed report *A Survey and Excavation of Caves in Hidalgo County, New Mexico* in 1961, one year after their fieldwork, it was not published by the SAR until 1965.[30] McCluney took much longer getting the results of his fieldwork published. As Lewis and Hagan note, "the results of McLuney's 1962 excavations were published three years later, but nearly forty years would pass before he finished his final report. It was included in *The Joyce Well Site: On the Frontier of the Casas Grandes World*, published in 2002 by James Skibo and William Walker, who carried out further excavations at the site. They concluded that Joyce Well was not politically dominated by Casas Grandes but shared with it common religious beliefs and practices."[31]

The Hidalgo County monograph was the last project Marjorie would work on for the School of American Research, and the site report was the last major publication that she worked on. Most of her published works in the 1960s and 1970s consisted of book reviews and articles for *El Palacio*, *American Antiquity*, *Archaeology*, *Ethnohistory Magazine*, and *Plains Anthropologist*, as well as pamphlets, leaflets, and gallery guides. From the mid-1970s to 1990 Marjorie was a regular contributor of articles to the *Collected Papers* series published by the Archaeological Society of New Mexico.

Jemez Site of Giusewa in 1965

It had been thirty-five years since Marjorie had worked in the Jemez Mountains as a budding archaeologist in UNM's Battleship Rock Field School. In 1965 Marjorie was part of an archaeological crew from the Museum of New Mexico sent to excavate part of Giusewa (LA 679) in what is known today as Jemez Springs.

When Spanish explorers first arrived in the southern Jemez Mountain region of north-central New Mexico in 1541, they counted seven Hemish

(Jemez) Pueblo villages in the vicinity of Jemez Springs, which they called *Aguas Calientes*. Over the next sixty years, foreign visits to the area were sporadic. A Franciscan priest named Fray Alonso de Lugo, who came with don Juan de Oñate in 1598, was the first European to live among the Hemish. Fray Alonso established a small, two-room mission at Giusewa. He left after three years. The Hemish people managed to keep the Spanish at bay until the 1620s, when Fray Gerónimo Zárate Salmerón arrived in the Jemez Province and built the massive fortress-like mission church at Giusewa called San José de los Jemez Church. He also founded a new settlement at the southern end of the valley called Wâala Tûuwa (Walatowa), today's Jemez Pueblo,[32] where he established a second mission church.

As the Franciscans established missions in Pueblo villages, the Spanish consolidated the scattered Hemish communities into villages called Astialakwa, Giusewa, and Patoqua. Navajo raids resulted in the abandonment of Giusewa and Patoqua by 1622, and the new church at Giusewa was destroyed. Under the leadership of Fray Martín de Arvide, the Hemish people were reassembled and the San José de los Jemez Church was rebuilt.[33] After Fray Martín was transferred to Zuni in early 1632, the church in Giusewa was abandoned. The second church that had been built at the same time in the principal Hemish village of Walatowa, the Church of San Diego, became the principal mission.[34]

The SAR and MNM excavated a section of Giusewa in 1921 and 1922 and found that the Pueblo predated the church by at least three hundred years. Even though twenty rooms and two kivas were excavated during these initial excavations, little scientific information was recorded.[35] Additional fieldwork by these two institutions was done in 1936–37. When the Museum of New Mexico returned in 1965, they did some stabilization work on the San José de los Jemez church and excavated four pueblo rooms and several other features. Marjorie noted that "since excavations have been limited, the exact size of Giusewa is undetermined. One house block rose to a height of three stories, touching the church on the west side. Giusewa is known to have extended westward across the present highway under parts of the modern Via Coeli Monastery and beyond."[36]

During the excavations in the early 1920s, a series of frescoes on the walls of the church nave was discovered. They included fleur-de-lis and other floral patterns, as well as Indian motifs. Also found were remnants of windows made of selenite, a translucent form of gypsum.[37] Marjorie discusses these frescoes in great detail in her article "Mural Decorations in San José De Los Jemez Mission Church, Jemez State Monuments, New Mexico," along with additional details about the church ruins.[38] She noted that the San José church was constructed entirely of sandstone, with the exception of a few adobe bricks in the walls and beneath the edifice. She goes on to suggest that the church and monastery were built on top of an earlier pueblo. The remains of the San José de los Jemez Church and Monastery can be seen today at the Jemez Historic Site.

Marjorie also did an analysis of the available sherds and ceramics from the three excavations.[39] She was surprised that there was an almost total lack of European artifacts and/or pottery. She was certain that there should have been European, especially Spanish, artifacts from the church excavations since they had been found at other Spanish mission sites throughout the Southwest. A single San Luis Blue-on-cream sherd, a little gypsum serpent head, and a fired adobe brick are the only evidence, other than the architecture, that would suggest that the Spanish had ever been at Giusewa.[40]

Despite the lack of field notes and artifacts from the excavations of the 1920s and 1930s, Marjorie was able to make a couple of observations based on the 52,192 sherds that she examined. She reported:

> Seventeenth century Giusewa people were using and/or making vast quantities of Jemez Black-on-white and Jemez culinary ware. The Jemez Black-on-white pottery of this pueblo, as well as Jemez Black-on-white throughout the region, show little change from that which was being manufactured three centuries earlier. This can only mean that Jemez potters were strongly provincial and that they chose to keep old traditional colors, forms, and designs. The only exceptions, though very rare, were the borrowing of a few cup, plate and perhaps pitcher forms. Potters also made an attempt to copy rims of imported Glaze F bowls. Infrequently the rim designs of (Kotyiti) Glaze F bowls were also poorly produced.

She concludes that the "abundance of local wares, and the paucity of imported Indian pottery and Iberian ceramics is further proof that the resident Giusewatowans, and neighboring Jemez Indians who were rounded up and brought here for missionary purposes, combined forces to resist any and all changes, be they of a material or religious nature."[41]

Twin Hills Site: A Final Excavation

The Twin Hills site (LA 8866), located to the west of Santa Fe, consists of an open volcanic pipe, one of several throughout the state of New Mexico.[42] A Santa Fe High School student, Kenneth Hansen, discovered archaeological materials in a volcanic pipe in the Twin Hills formation in March 1967. Marjorie was not that thrilled about working on this site, but as usual she followed the orders of her male superiors. As she recalled,

the last excavation, if you want to call it that, that I was involved with for the Museum of New Mexico were those blow holes west of Santa Fe. I guess it was Joe Allen on our staff out at the LAB who knew of a young boy who had gone down one of those blow holes and had come out with a broken arrow, and some faunal and human skeletal remains. A. E. Dittert, the director of the LAB, thought it would be important if we could do a little bit of work there. Sallie Wagner and I with some others [Jack Lambert and Joe Allen] went over in that area and we walked around. There were a lot of pinon trees and a few scrubby pine trees. It was obvious that Indians had been hunting all through there because you could pick up broken projectile points. Nothing very early, but it was interesting.

There was this one blow hole, and I let Joe handle that. I wasn't really keen on it. I thought it was a waste of time because we didn't have the money. But we built a platform with a contraption that would let people down and back up. We didn't find very much, but we did take a lot of soil samples and I guess that they're still out at the LAB. I guess the unstudied faunal remains would be too. There were lots of examples of snakes that had fallen down there. There was a turkey that had an arrow shot through it. The carcass of it was found there. The radiocarbon dates that came back did not conform to the age of a tree stump from there. It was so much earlier. . . . I think some of those blow holes would be interesting to study. There are a lot of them throughout New Mexico out in the lava bed near Laguna and the Badlands and out west of Santa Fe too. It was a very active volcano. The Indian boy we had on that project was terrified of it because of its relation to a Sipapu. I think it was after that he began to have psychological problems. . . . I didn't like that dig. I didn't want to have anything to do with it, but I had to.[43]

It was during her work at the Laboratory of Anthropology that her eye problems began.

Some of the stuff would come in at the LAB and there was a screen out in the back, and Sue Wells was supposed to be taking most of the dirt off the stuff and then sacking it. I went out to help her one day just for a break from what I was doing in the office, and a little piece of metal flew into my eye and the secretary, Terry Resnick, sent me down to see an eye specialist. That was the beginning of the story of my eye problem. It was just superficial. I was told that he was the bright boy of Santa Fe, that he was the bright boy of Johns Hopkins, the top ten in his class, and now he has lost his license and blinded me.[44]

Afterward, Marjorie started having problems with her eyesight. As she started to slowly lose her eyesight, she made the difficult decision to retire earlier than she wanted from the Museum of New Mexico.

PART III

In Recognition of
a Legacy

CHAPTER 10

Postretirement Activities

1970s–1990s

> When I retired from the museum, I thought it was about time to
> get out and let some of the younger people carry on.
>
> —MARJORIE LAMBERT[1]

Marjorie retired in 1969 after thirty-two years with the Museum of New
Mexico. Even though she was having increased problems with her eyesight,
Marjorie was not one to spend her retirement in a rocking chair on the
front porch. She continued to be active professionally, serving on boards and
mentoring young archaeologists and museum professionals. She served as
a research associate professor at Eastern New Mexico University from 1969
to 1972. She also became a research associate at the SAR again in 1969 and
held that position until 1978. She was invited to join the SAR's board in 1970.

Ongoing Involvement with the School of American Research

Marjorie found her participation on the board of the SAR to be rewarding.
In 1985 she acknowledged that

> *I have been on the board since 1970, and I have found it a most delightful and*
> *rewarding experience. I feel that I contribute to that board. Doug [Schwartz]*
> *and I are the only anthropologists on the board. There are not any others.*
> *They are mostly bankers and lawyers, businessmen. . . . I am on the Execu-*
> *tive Committee and I am on the Indian Arts Collections Committee too. Of*
> *course, I love Indian art; it's one of my sidelines. So, it has been a very happy*
> *experience. I love the school. Both Jack and I were so devoted to that whole*
> *complex down there. . . . We have very close ties to the school. . . . I think that*
> *it's good for me to be on that board. Then, too, I know so much of the ancient*
> *history of the school.*[2]

Marjorie shared her thoughts about her lifelong association with the SAR.

One of the things I am most proud of is to see the School of American Research come back into its own. That has been a really rewarding experience for me. I feel particularly strongly about the school because when I first came to New Mexico I lived on $58.80 a month on a graduate fellowship. At that time Hewett, who certainly didn't have much money and the school didn't either, would give us these little scholarships and these little fellowships to help us with our research and our work. I had one for $150, which saw me through a very tight period. I also got one for $300. You can see how I am grateful for what was done for me early in my career. And then to see this great campus develop and all the wonderful things they are doing.[3]

After her retirement, Marjorie continued to stay active in the many organizations she was involved in throughout her career. When interviewed at the age of eighty-nine, Marjorie recalled:

Up until not too long ago, I was still an active participant in the Spanish Colonial Arts Society of New Mexico. I'm still on their board. I'm in an emeritus status though. I have not done too much participating in the Museum of New Mexico, although I'm always willing to give them suggestions if they call on me. Up until not too long ago I was still active in the Southwestern Association for Indian Arts and certainly the Indian Market, which was the love of my life, particularly pottery, up until I began to have really bad problems with my eyes. I had to resign from that. The Old Santa Fe Association. I was very active in that up until just a short time ago. And certainly the School of American Research year after year has been the love of my life. Probably it's at the top of my list and the one that I'm most interested in. I think that's partly because of the history of where they're situated and hearing Jack talk about the development of the property when he first became the estate manager. I've been very active in the Archaeological Society of New Mexico up until recently. It's changed quite a bit and it isn't quite my cup of tea anymore. There aren't any archaeologists, to begin with. They have a lot of active members who are learning something about archaeology and prehistory. They have a good lecture program, which was one of my chief responsibilities for many years.[4]

During Marjorie's tenure on the SAR board, the ownership of the Indian Arts Fund (IAF) collection came up. At the request of the members of
the IAF, the SAR took ownership of the group's collection in 1965 and an
agreement was drawn up between the SAR and the MNM stating that the
collection would continue to be stored at the Laboratory of Anthropology.
Marjorie was still an active board member in 1972 when the Indian Arts
Fund disbanded as a legal entity and the collection of 4,280 textiles, baskets,
pottery, paintings, jewelry, and clothing was moved to the basement of the
Museum of Fine Arts. This was the same year that the SAR staff and board
were starting to plan their move from their offices in the old Hewett House
on Lincoln Avenue to their new home in the White estate on Garcia Street.

In 1972 Amelia Elizabeth White passed away at ninety-four and left her
estate on Garcia Street, *El Delirio*, to the SAR. The SAR president, Douglas
Schwartz, started making plans to convert the estate into an anthropological
research center. As part of his vision for expanding the school's programs,
Schwartz also saw the need to get the Indian Arts Fund collections out of the
basement of the Museum of Fine Arts and into a building that would house
both the IAF and SAR collections. In 1978 the new Indian Arts Research
Center was added to the SAR campus specifically to house the IAF and growing SAR collections.[5] During his tenure, Doug Schwartz also introduced the
renowned scholar program that brings together anthropologists on the SAR
campus to discuss important topics as part of the seminar series resulting
in SAR publications. He also secured funding to develop a resident scholars
program, where individuals come to the SAR campus for a nine-month period or during the summer to research and write. Another program provides
fellowships for Native American artists and scholars to conduct research in
the Indian Arts Research Center's collections or to create works of art while
living on the SAR campus. The Katrin H. Lamon bequest supported a Native
American resident scholar each year and provided short-term fellowships for
Native American artists from 1984 to 1994.

Marjorie and Jack sold their home to the SAR in 1977. The main house
and box stalls were renovated into a house and an apartment for resident
scholars and fellows. As a resident scholar at the SAR during the summer
of 1997, I had hoped to stay in the Marjorie F. Lambert resident scholar
apartment, but it was already occupied by Hopi/Tewa basket weaver Kevin
Navasie, who had a Dubin fellowship that summer. Having a Native Ameri-

FIGURE 28 Greg Cajete (Santa Clara Pueblo) was the first Katrin H. Lamon Native American resident scholar and Ramona Sakiestewa (Hopi) was the Lamon artist fellow at the SAR's Indian Arts Research Center in 1984. Photo by Deborah Flynn. Courtesy of the School for Advanced Research. Resident Scholars Photos, SAR Records, 1984–85 Lamon Fellows.

can artist staying at the converted scholar's apartment in her name pleased Marjorie very much.

Reflecting on her relationship with Douglas Schwartz, president and CEO of the SAR until his retirement in 2001, Marjorie said:

> *I think that Doug Schwartz is in a class by himself. I don't know how anyone could really describe anyone with Doug's qualities. There's no doubt about it. He's a genius. He's the only anthropologist that I have known throughout my long life that is also a good businessman. And that's just unheard of. You're in your little adobe tower, your ivory tower, and you may be the best professor in the world, you may be the best researcher or field man, but you aren't any good at keeping things together. Doug had the ability to administer and organize, too. And on top of that, I think he's absolutely charming and a lovable person. . . . As far as developing the school, which was really about to go out of*

existence when Dr. Schwartz came here, look at it today. It's one of the leading organizations that's internationally known, and people from everywhere that have ever been here want to come back again and be part of it. I always sort of look on Doug as being part of my family, or that I'm part of his. Certainly, with the whole family. I admire him. He has such extraordinary qualities. How many anthropologists do you know—and I've known some brilliant ones— when they get up to give a lecture, they're the deadliest speakers? Doug can charm any audience and what he says sticks because it's factual as well as beautifully presented. . . . He has always been that way. Then too, he has a lot of fun about him. Let's put it this way: I think Doug has a wonderful sense of humor. I think he's a great person.[6]

It was during this time that Marjorie was asked to join the Collections Committee of the SAR Board. She recalled that during the Collections Committee meetings, *we would take up matters of business. . . . They had already read the minutes of the previous meeting and what was going to be talked about, the agenda, and so on, to each one of us beforehand so that we would know pretty much what was going to be involved. . . . And then we would discuss the collections that had come in and we'd vote on whether to accept them or not. Sometimes we would reject some. We also had to address the matter of de-accessioning things that didn't particularly fit the collection.*[7]

Since the SAR received federal funding through grants, it was required to comply with the Native American Graves Protection and Repatriation Act (NAGPRA), passed into law in 1990.[8] In reply to repatriation requests from Native American groups culturally affiliated with the items in the SAR collections, Marjorie said, *It comes along all the time. There are things that we are quite willing to see repatriated. The Indians are not hard to deal with. We've [SAR] had no problem at all. We negotiate with tribes right along. We negotiate with the Cheyenne. We negotiate with the Hopi. We negotiate with Cochiti and so on. So far it's been very amicable.*[9]

When NAGPRA was passed in 1990, the SAR and the museum were both aware of the concerns that Native Americans had about their ancestors and sacred items being stored in museum collections. While working as the assistant collections manager at the SAR's Indian Arts Research Center, I researched and wrote a master's thesis on the repatriation of sacred materials and developed a set of guidelines for the SAR in 1985.[10] Much has been written since the passage of NAGPRA, but some museums have been slow to come into compliance with the law. Over the past thirty years, the SAR and the museum have been at the forefront by hiring Native American staff and actively consulting with descendant Native American communities regarding their collections.[11]

During the time when Marjorie was on the SAR Collections Committee, these NAGPRA related negotiations and repatriation requests also involved discussions with the Laboratory of Anthropology. This is no surprise because as late as 1997 there was still confusion over ownership and stewardship responsibilities. As Marjorie noted at the time, *Quite a lot of the school property is still within the confines of the Museum of New Mexico. We like to know how it is being cared for. We ask for a report now and then. It's an ongoing thing contracted between the two organizations.*[12] Finally, in 1999 the previous agreements and loans were resolved and the SAR collections were moved to the Indian Arts Research Center, and the museum's anthropological, archaeological, and ethnographic collections were either housed in the Laboratory of Anthropology and the Museum of Indian Arts and Culture, or in off-site storage facilities. Today the archaeology collections are stored and cared for at the Center for New Mexico Archaeology, an off-site, state-of-the-art repository and research facility located south of Santa Fe.

In addition to her ongoing active role at the SAR, Marjorie continued her memberships and participation in professional organizations such as the American Anthropological Association and Society for American Archaeology. She also attended conferences when she could. Marjorie and I attended the annual Pecos Conference held at Pecos National Historical Park in 1987. As Nancy Fox points out, Marjorie "always found time for groups serving causes close to her heart. Concern for the preservation of Santa Fe's unique historical and architectural character is expressed through her membership in the Old Santa Fe Association."[13]

Old Santa Fe Association

Marjorie was involved in historic preservation in Santa Fe long before the National Historic Preservation Act was passed in 1966. She recalled: *Early on I met Margretta Dietrich, Mrs. Charles Dietrich, who was the powerhouse behind the New Mexico Association on Indian Affairs at the time, and of course Miss White. Miss White and her small group before my time had founded this organization called the Old Santa Fe Association with the hope of preserving the best in what was called Santa Fe architecture. That included the interiors as well as exteriors of historic buildings.*[14]

The Old Santa Fe Association was founded in 1926 by a group of like-minded residents, artists, writers, and architects, in an attempt to protect the unique flavor, built environment, and cultures in Santa Fe. This new group was led by Mary Austin, John Gaw Meem, Carlos Vierra, Gustave Baumann, Alice Corbin, and William Penhallow Henderson, among others. They formed to fight the City Council to save a parcel of land around St. John's College from being developed into a proposed cultural colony, or Chautauqua. They organized themselves "into a permanent body to be known as the Old Santa Fe Association, for the purpose of working for the preservation of Old Santa Fe, and of guiding new growth and development and advancement in material welfare, in such a way to sacrifice as little as possible of the unique charm and distinction of this city, born of age, tradition and environment, of which are Santa Fe's priceless assets."[15]

By the time Marjorie joined the Old Santa Fe Association, they were involved in other projects. She notes:

One of our purposes was to try and preserve buildings like the Borrego House, which is a restaurant now. . . . And the old Morley house. Most people don't know that there are two Morley houses. There is one on Arroyo Tenorio and there is an older one way up on the hill above Fort Marcy. Anyway, we did the best we could in preserving them, but it's not very active now because of the Santa Fe Historic Foundation. That has taken over and I think that's an awfully good idea because it's a bigger organization. It has more money. I think the Old Santa Fe Association is probably just more or less a name in the history of Santa Fe these days. There are some little books that they put out. . . . I helped them all I could. I would write publicity for them and I would send out notices for some of their meetings and I would go to the meetings. Kenneth Chapman and Dr. Frank Mera were both prominent in that organization, and I guess Morley in his day too.[16]

Spanish Colonial Arts Society

In 1926 a small group in Santa Fe held a small Spanish Market to support and promote the local New Mexico art forms, and the women and men who created them. To continue these markets the Spanish Colonial Arts Society was founded on October 29, 1929, by authors Mary Austin and Frank G. Applegate and a group of friends and collectors in Santa Fe who incorporated it as a nonprofit. Two weeks prior to the official signing of the society's incorporation paperwork, it purchased a privately owned chapel in the village of Chimayo. The chapel was given to the Archdiocese of Santa Fe. The society provided basic maintenance for almost twenty years and later refurbished the chapel. This chapel, known as El Santuario de Chimayo, has become known throughout the world and is visited by hundreds of thousands of tourists each year. It is best known for the pilgrimages people make there during Holy Week, especially on Holy Thursday and Good Friday, some seeking blessings and some in fulfillment of a vow. Some pilgrims walk from as far away as Albuquerque, about ninety miles away. Many visitors to the church take a small amount of "holy dirt" found in a *pocito* in the floor of a side room, often in hopes of a miraculous cure for themselves or a loved one. Originally built in 1816, it was declared a National Historic Landmark in 1970.

A second major purchase by the Spanish Colonial Arts Society was an altar screen by nineteenth-century master *santero* José Rafael Aragón, originally from the Nuestra Señora del Carmen church at Llano Quemado, New Mexico. The altar screen was sold to the society by a church committee after it had replaced it with a millwork altar screen. This altar screen has been on long-term loan to the Palace of the Governors since 1929 and continues to be exhibited in the Spanish Colonial chapel room.

During the Great Depression of the 1930s, several people in New Mexico received skills and training by participating in the Works Progress Administration's (WPA) projects. Marjorie recalled:

We had some Spanish American men who made some of the furniture for the museum. Some of these were copies of Spanish colonial chairs and things that were used in offices. Many were made by people who came from a santero family or from a Spanish artistic family. In the beginning, most of them had Anglo supervisors. There was what was called the State Vocational Guide Office, I think, that got them started. Carmen Espinosa was responsible for getting some of the tin work and so on redone. Some of the best tin work is in public buildings here in Santa Fe. The Spanish Colonial Arts Society is very much a part of Santa Fe and New Mexico history.[17]

In the 1930s the society operated the Spanish Shop, where they sold works made by the Spanish American artists.

Marjorie was delighted to be asked to join the Spanish Colonial Arts Society shortly after she arrived at the museum:

> *I certainly had a different kind of education from what I'd had up to that point. Of course, I'd had southwestern and Mesoamerican history and I had known Spanish American students on the campus of the University of New Mexico, which I thought was so neat because for the first time in my life I was associated with not only Indians but with Spanish American people—a trilingual sort of atmosphere. I knew that they had what were called* santeros *from reading and so on, but I didn't know very much about them. There was a very strong lady that was in this part of the country known as Mary Cabot Wheelwright, who had a big place at Los Luceros in Alcalde, New Mexico, and she was a powerhouse in the Spanish Colonial Arts Society. She said, "I have a young friend we should have. She works in the museum, and we ought to have her in our organization. She's certainly a good worker." So, Mary brought me to my first meeting.*[18]

Many of Marjorie's contacts with Spanish Americans were outside the museum, especially through the Spanish Colonial Arts Society.

> *I have been a member and a board member for many years. I collected Spanish colonial art for them and then too I got things for the museum and the Historical Society. They would bring in things now and then. I think the Spanish American people for a long time felt that they were the poor relations and second-class citizens. They didn't seem to have any interest in the International Folk Art Museum when it first opened. They didn't seem to have much interest in Spanish Colonial ecclesiastical art. . . . It has just been in the last few years [ca. 1990] with the Spanish Market growing as part of their economy that they are beginning to take great pride in their cultural background.*[19]

Spanish American Friends

Given Marjorie's position in the museum and the range of collections she worked with, she was in a unique position to meet and work with the diverse peoples and cultures of northern New Mexico. Marjorie's relationships were not just with Native Americans but extended to Spanish Americans as well. Some were dear friends while others worked for her in the field as part of Marjorie's archaeological excavation crews and in the museum. She respected her Spanish American crew members and museum employees and said:

> I've had and still have great friends among the Spanish Americans. Some of my most loyal colleagues in the museum have been people that were on the maintenance staff. I don't think I could have done the exhibits that I did. I don't think that I could have had the success that I had because they were always so loyal to me, and they were always good to me. They worked hard and used to get so mad at the Anglo male staff that I worked with because they would be upstairs someplace drinking coffee and talking theory all the time. One of them told the museum director; I heard him say, "She does twice the work that they do! They don't do nothing! She does all the work!" . . . They were that loyal to me.[20]

Marjorie depended on her Spanish American staff to help her with exhibit installations. She had fond recollections of working with them.

> They were helpful in scrounging things up for the exhibits. . . . We would go around to the different stores that were changing window displays to see if we could have the old props. It was nothing to see a whole group of us walking across the plaza with all these dress forms. Mr. Dendall gave us some old female forms and we had different heads put on them for costumes and so on. . . . We didn't have any budget for exhibits so we found you could save grapefruit cans and paint them adobe color or whatever and then you could set a pot on it and so on. They were responsible for helping with the Huichol exhibit of mine. . . . one of my very best exhibits.[21]

As her relationships with the museum staff grew, Marjorie was invited to christenings and other family celebrations, and helped her Spanish American friends in any way that she could.

> I'm not sure that I wouldn't have been fired for this, but they would come to me of all people in the museum to help them with their income taxes. And if there

*is anyone who is stupid about figures it's me. The only reason I think I didn't
go to Leavenworth [Prison] is because most of them had so many children, it
turned out that they didn't have to pay any taxes. Then too, the forms were
simpler then. I know that Jack would be a little disturbed after I married him
to have me down there at night making out their income taxes. . . . I'm glad I
did. I was glad that I could reciprocate.*[22]

Marjorie loved everything the Spanish Colonial Arts Society was doing,
especially in how it was helping to promote the preservation of the culture,
arts, and crafts of the Spanish Americans in Santa Fe.

*The thing that I thought was so interesting were these first little markets. The
markets were very small. Once a year we had what was called the Spanish
Market. These came about through the talks we had at our monthly board
meetings. The first one—I hadn't been in the museum very long—was upstairs
in the Art Museum, very small. The board room upstairs was where it was
held. And then someone said, "Well why don't we try to have the [Spanish]
markets before the Indian Market and have one on the Plaza?" So we talked
and we talked about that and then along came people like Eleanor Biddell,
who was a trader here in town, Jim McMillan of the Spanish Indian Trading
Post, Dorothy McKibben, who was working with him then, and the Meems, and
Alan Veder, was one of them, and Al Packard's father, Frank Packard. And so
we started our markets, which were small to begin with. We would raise the
money for the prizes among ourselves. . . . It has grown to be a market that is
comparable to any in the country, and it has done a great deal toward revital-
izing Spanish local, New Mexico santero art. It's an outlet for their creativity.*[23]

Marjorie was not only buying and collecting pieces for herself and the society, but she supported many of the youth who were starting out. *One thing
I always like to do, and I offered to do nearly every year, was to give the prize
money for the little ones. I think the little Spanish or Indian children, or any
children, should be encouraged to do their artwork. So I would give the little
prize money for these little ones that had their little table full of their stuff to
sell. And they did some pretty good stuff.*[24] In 1965 the Spanish Market was
resurrected as an annual event, and over several years it expanded and grew
from the portal of the First National Bank of Santa Fe to the whole plaza and
side streets of Santa Fe today.

In the early 1950s the Spanish colonial art scholar Elizabeth Boyd White, known as E. Boyd, was appointed as the first curator of the newly established Spanish colonial arts department at the New Mexico Museum of International Folk Art. E. Boyd, along with a small group of the original founders, was involved in the reinvigoration of the Spanish Colonial Arts Society and she served as the curator of the society's collections for many years.

As the society's collections had grown to several hundred pieces, the board expressed a desire to find a permanent home to house the collection and exhibit it. At the time the collections were being stored in the homes of society members and there were concerns about their storage and security. Finally, in 1998 the society received an anonymous gift of 2.6 acres of land and a historic residence to be used as a core gallery space of a proposed museum. After a successful building campaign, the Museum of Spanish Colonial Art opened to the public in July 2002, becoming the only museum in the world dedicated to Spanish colonial art, with a special emphasis on the unique art styles of New Mexico.[25]

Marjorie took great pride in what was accomplished by the Spanish Colonial Arts Society over the years.

> Today we have the finest collection of Spanish Colonial material I think anywhere. I don't know of any other place that could rival our collection. Nice, old Spanish southwestern—either southern Arizona or northern Mexico, but mostly New Mexico. My connection with that gave me a chance to get out into the Spanish American villages, which I hadn't really paid too much attention to until then. We'd go out and talk to people like George Lopez and his family at Cordova and of course George Lopez was the senior santero then. I think most people are still working very hard in that organization.[26]

Given her love of history and her close relationships with so many Spanish Americans, it is no surprise that Marjorie would become so involved with the Spanish Colonial Arts Society. She was involved in the society from her early years at the museum but it wasn't until she retired that she became a trustee in 1970 and continued to serve on the board until 1998. She has fond memories of her work with the Spanish Colonial Arts Society. *I think the society has done a wonderful job. One thing we did do, mostly just people like ourselves who were pushing it, and it suddenly dawned on us, Why don't we get Spanish American people involved in this? At first they didn't seem interested at all. . . . Now they are all interested. They are proud of what their ancestors have given to the state.* [27]

The Spanish Colonial Arts Society continues to sponsor the Traditional Spanish Market in late July on the Historic Santa Fe Plaza. Featuring hand-made traditional arts from hundreds of local Spanish American *santeros*, weavers, potters, and carvers, it is a popular event for residents as well as tourists.

CHAPTER 11

Friends Among the Pueblos and Northern New Mexico Villages

> My archaeology would be nothing without the present-day
> Indians. The whole thing makes a complete picture in my mind.
>
> —MARJORIE LAMBERT[1]

In addition to enjoying her career working in a museum and as a southwestern archaeologist, Marjorie has valued the friends she made over the years. As her coworker for many years Nancy Fox wrote, "Aside from ties with an international circle of anthropologists, residence in Santa Fe brought wide acquaintances among celebrated personalities of the local art colony, as well as enduring friendships among the nearby Indian Pueblos."[2] Marjorie was often heard saying, *I've enjoyed very much my contact with the Indians particularly and the Spanish American people. I wouldn't exchange those contacts for anything, and I think I'm a better person for having had those contacts. I think it's been wonderful, and I think there would be more understanding in this country if we all had the opportunity to work closely with people of different ethnic backgrounds.* She met many of her Native American and Spanish American friends through her work as well as through her husband Jack. They were all friends and *the pueblos and reservations have always been so much a part of Jack's and my life.*[3]

Learning from Native Americans

Marjorie's early experience was much like most American children with the stereotypic notion that the Nation's Indigenous inhabitants were "noble savages." She described one of her earlier childhood experiences when she saw Native Americans in a parade in Colorado Springs.

I thought all Indians had to be like them. I thought that they had to be big. They had to have a feathered headdress. They had to be on beautiful horses. There was a Cheyenne Indian dressed in full regalia, and I had never seen anything more beautiful in my life. You can say it's corny and so on if you want to, but he was a storybook picture of an Indian. Proud. It was a rodeo parade and they had an Indian procession. That was my experience with Indians until I came to New Mexico, so you can see how thrilled I was to become friends with them.[4]

Many of the Native Americans that Marjorie worked with as a student in Hewett's summer field schools in the Jemez Mountains became lifelong friends. One of those early contacts was with Jose Rey Toledo from Jemez Pueblo. Marjorie recalled that

Hewett would take us to ceremonies at either Jemez or Zia, and I became very friendly with many of the Zia people. Trinidad Medina and her family at Zia and Florence Shije's family. While at the University of New Mexico I also got to know some of the Indian students who were attending the university. There were quite a few Indians that were at the University of New Mexico and that to me is what made that campus so exciting. . . . I had never been where I would get to know a lot of Indians as friends. The Marmon girls from Laguna and Indians coming from Isleta and Sandia—those associations just as students. Then we would be invited to their homes, and I thought it was absolutely fascinating the way they lived. The simplicity of it and the generosity and the warmth. Of course, to me every time I went it was a feast day. . . . I'd never had posole and frijoles and tamales that would be made just for lunch. Then I'd go to Cochiti and see Trinidad Herrera and Carolyn Pecos, all those nice people. And Lorencita Herrera's family.[5]

Marjorie got to know many of her lifelong Pueblo friends when she became a field supervisor and hired them as crew members to work on excavations in the northern Rio Grande Valley.

I think of some of the first people I hired to help me on small excavations. They were Indians that I had known through Hewett who were from San Ildefonso Pueblo. I knew the Gonzalez family. Joe Aguilar was one of my very best friends. I knew the Aguilars until the end of their lives, really. I don't know whether their daughter Florence is still alive or not, but one of the sons became a very fine painter. Florence became a potter. Her mother Rose was a good potter, but Joe was my real friend. He was the one I always looked to as someone who would protect me in the field if I made a mistake or something. He would quietly give me a sign to go that way or this way. There were others that I knew from San Ildefonso, Tesuque, and San Juan [Ohkay Owingeh Pueblo]. It's just been an ongoing thing throughout the years. I think that I am a better person from having these wonderful associations with the Indians of the Southwest.[6]

It was her work as an anthropologist and archaeologist that brought her into contact with so many Native Americans throughout her career. Over the years she has seen a major shift in the number of Native Americans entering the museum profession.

I think it's great to have a such a wonderful profession where I've spent most of my life, really, among Indians. I don't think anyone could be any luckier than I am. One way museums have progressed, I think, is that you see a lot more Indians on the staff than you would see in my day. We had the janitorial group and we had the guards that were Spanish American, but we didn't have any Indians. They would come in to see Dr. Hewett, old friends from Santa Clara and San Ildefonso, but they didn't have the freedom in the museum complex that they have today. I am very happy about that.[7]

In 1985 Marjorie was invited by the contract archaeologists from the Museum of New Mexico who were working on a project near Jemez Pueblo to join them at a meeting with some of the members of the Pueblo. She recalled that *the first thing I did was reestablish an old relationship with Jose Rey Toledo. He was the second Indian I ever met when I came to New Mexico as a girl. It was a very emotional reunion. We hadn't seen each other in years. He's just like a brother to me. These Indian friends I have are probably my best friends. Jack and I had a good social life here in Santa Fe and in New Mexico, but that's superficial compared to the relationships we had with our Indian friends.*[8]

After decades of knowing so many Native Americans and making so many lifelong friendships, Marjorie made this observation: *I've never felt that I was superior to them or that I was the scholar and they were my subjects. I always immediately tried to be friends with them. I wanted them for friends, and I think they then decided to accept me as a friend too.*[9] Here she shares some stories of her dear friends.

Helen and Kenneth Shupla

Recalling some of her dearest friends from the Pueblos, Marjorie often said how much she deeply appreciated their friendships and how much she learned from them. Well-known Santa Clara potter Helen Baca Shupla (1928–85) and her Hopi katsina carver husband Kenneth (1918–88) were two people Marjorie considered special friends to both her and Jack.

> *The Shuplas, of course, were lifelong friends. Helen and Kenneth Shupla. . . . I knew them as early as 1936 when they were out there at the [Santa Fe] Indian School. They were married at the time, and he was the farmer in charge of the gardens out there and she was the mama of their four children. She was firing these funny little pieces of pottery in the kitchen oven. To have relationships develop and to see her go on to be one of the masters of ceramic art among the Pueblos was special.[10]*
>
> *Helen and Kenneth Shupla were two of our very dearest friends. Helen just adored Jack. Well, I couldn't blame her, I adored him too. I know one of the things that touched me the most. . . . Helen and Kenneth went to the nursing home where I had taken Jack first and she went to the head of the nursing home and said, "We don't want Jack to stay here anymore. We have not spoken to Marjorie about this yet, but we want to have him come out to Santa Clara where we can take care of them." This was at a time when they were living in a two-room adobe house with their grandchildren and some of their own children, and it just touched me so much.[11]*

Throughout the years Marjorie confided:

> *We'd go out there just for fun, just to visit, and watch them work in the studio. Kenneth would sit there and talk and tell you Indian stories while he was carving one of her [Helen's] big jars and never make a mistake. . . . One of the things that touched me was when Jack brought out some of his polishing stones that an old Indian from Santa Clara had given to him when he was a young man and gave them to Helen for her to use in her polishing.[12]*
>
> *[Helen] makes the best melon bowls of any of the Indian potters. Not that she doesn't do other kinds of pottery. I did do one little paper on Helen Shupla for the Southwestern Association on Indian Affairs, but then I got the idea to amplify the paper when I found so many examples [of melon bowls] when I was in Peru. I have been sort of tracing the melon bowl as a type of pottery all up*

*through South America . . . into Mexico. There are examples at Casas Grandes,
although [Charles] DiPeso didn't recognize them as melon bowls. They occur in
the Mississippi Valley, and I have found that the people who have written on
the archaeology of the eastern United States called them fluted bowls. Actually,
they are not bowls. They are a type of agricultural thing really.*[13]

 *I was particularly fond of little Helen Shupla. I know that she had a very
difficult and very sad childhood and I planned to really do a biography of
Helen. . . . Her mother was Papago [Tohono O'odham] and her father was from
Santa Clara. Her mother died when she was born, or just a baby, and then her
father had to bring her up here to the Pueblo and she was raised by Santiago
Naranjo's family. Santiago was her grandfather. I think of her always as being
sort of a neglected little child. Kenneth said she really was neglected. She was
dressed in rags. And here out of this came this student from the [Santa Fe] Indian
School out here in the studio painters and artists group. I was always impressed
by some of her pots. She had the tiniest hands, but she was the strength of that
family. Kenneth you thought of as being the father of that family, and you got the
idea he was very strong until you knew Helen personally. She's the one that held
that family together. When Helen died he [Kenneth] didn't last any time at all.*[14]

 *I've heard Helen argue with people like Dick Spivey over the price of her
pottery. You would be surprised how tough those little women can be sometimes. I don't have half the courage they have. One thing she did that I will
never forget. She came to me after I had to put Jack in that first nursing home.
She said, "Kenneth and I know that you are having eye trouble and if you ever
need a home or if Jack needs a home too we will take care of you." I can hardly
talk about it now, it makes me cry. That's why Helen is special to me. But she
had great wit too. You could say most anything to her. She would laugh. She
had a good, earthy sense of humor.*[15]

Santiago Naranjo (Oyegepi)

Santiago Naranjo (1856–1945), of Santa Clara Pueblo, was an old friend of
Hewett's, and very much a father figure to Marjorie. *He was Hewett's foreman
at the Puye excavations and also in the Rito de los Frijoles. That goes back,
believe it or not, before my birth. . . . He was a wonderful old man. He was a
handsome old fellow.*[16]

When Hewett was in his eighties and his health was failing, Santiago, who
was quite a few years older, would walk to Santa Fe from Santa Clara Pueblo

to visit with him. It often fell to Marjorie to take Santiago back home after each visit. Marjorie recalls that during this time

it was my job as curator of archaeology . . . to get Santiago back to the Pueblo. It was during World War II and Hewett would send over enough ration tickets so I could buy some gasoline. Then [one day] came the news of the Trinity experiment and that the first atomic bomb had been successfully detonated. It was that morning that Hewett had said that he wanted me to get the old man back to the Pueblo. Santiago had been in town all night. He was staying at Sam Hudleston's workshop. Of course, Santiago was one of my dearest friends and one of the Indian father figures. He blessed me when we found out that first morning what Los Alamos had been doing, making a bomb![17]

Marjorie described the trip back to Santa Clara Pueblo with Santiago Naranjo on August 7, 1945, the day after the first atomic bomb had been dropped on Hiroshima.

Santiago and I started out to the Pueblo. It had been raining during the night and there were these great big clouds in the sky and everything was kind of scary. Santiago looked up and he said, "You know, Marjorie, it's started. One of these days all the white people are going to be gone from here and the Indians will come back into their own." When we got back to the Pueblo he did not want to go to Helen's and Kenneth's or his daughter's place. He wanted to go to the old home where he had been when his wife was alive. I remember this dresser with the abalone shell with carnelian and fetishes in it. He said something and was talking to them in Tewa and put his hands over them. Then he walked toward me, and he put his hands on my head and said a prayer for me. Of course, I am not a linguist, so I don't know what he said, but I was incredibly touched by the whole thing.[18]

Geronima Cruz Montoya (P'otsúnú)

A lifelong friend of Marjorie's was painter Geronima Cruz Montoya (1915–2015) of Ohkay Owingeh Pueblo.[19] *She [was] married to Juan Montoya, who's dead now, who was from Sandia Pueblo. She [was] Tewa. Relationships like that just can't be duplicated.*[20]

One lovely northern New Mexico day in July 1997, Marianne Kocks and I took Marjorie to see two of her dear friends at Ohkay Owingeh, Geronima Montoya and her sister Romancita Sandoval. We met them at the Ohkay Owingeh Cultural Arts Center, where they were both working that day. After a while, we went to the senior citizens' center for lunch. Geronima said that she remembered walking across the plaza in Santa Fe and seeing a pretty young woman around the museum. That pretty young woman was Marjorie, and after they met they became close friends—a friendship that continued throughout their long lives. Marjorie recalled seeing Geronima during Indian Market when she was judging. *She was one of the Indians from way back when that I always stopped to see.*[21]

Both Jack and Marjorie valued their friendships with the Native Americans in New Mexico. Many of them were artists, others worked for them in one capacity or another. Marjorie met some as students while working on various excavations, and others worked with her in the museum or at various times for Jack. During a 1990 interview Marjorie pointed out, *Now most of them are dead. But I still love and have affection for the ones that are left. People have asked, "Well, how do you talk to the Indians? We're so different, don't you find we're different?" You know they aren't any different from us. Two women, you and an Indian woman, can talk on just about the same things that you and I talk about. Things that go on in their lives, the Pueblo, what they're doing in the way of their arts or their painting and so on.*[22] These close relationships informed much of Marjorie's work in archaeology, at the museum, and in her activism on behalf of the Pueblos in New Mexico.

Indian Visitors at the Museum

Often people from the Pueblos came to the museum to ask Marjorie and others for their assistance in protecting their sacred areas as well as to see what information and objects might be in the collections that could assist them in renewing or reviving ceremonies. One incident that Marjorie recalled was in the 1940s when Hewett's health was failing.

> *I remember that some from Santa Clara and San Ildefonso came into the museum about that time—the Palace of the Governors. Hewett kept two offices . . . one in the Palace and one in the Art Museum. When he was feeling*

*up to it, he'd be working in one or the other. The San Ildefonso, particularly
Robert Gonzales, who was the spokesman . . . [they] wanted something done
about their sacred springs, which are up in the Los Alamos area. It was off
limits to them, and they had been cemented over. That's where they used to
have their ceremonies. One of their springs is an emergence place. Hewett,
if he had been a younger man [might have helped them], but there weren't
any men [staff members] in the museum that were willing to fight for them. I
think they should have. Of course, we couldn't go to the government because
we didn't really know what was going on there [Los Alamos] most of the time
due to the Manhattan Project.*[23]

Several Indian artists sold their jewelry and pottery under the portal of
the Palace of the Governors while Marjorie had her office there. Oftentimes
she had friendly visits from the vendors while others would come to her with
their complaints. Monica Silva would visit her now and then. *Monica Silva of
Santa Domingo, one of the famous masa bowl makers and one of the famous
Indian potters . . . I think she was from Santa Clara, but she married as a
very young girl into Santo Domingo and she learned to make Santo Domingo
[style] pottery and became famous. . . . She was one of my friends from under
the portal at the Palace. . . . Monica was really a character. She used to come
to my office quite a bit and we would chat. Once in a while there would be a
squabble out there for space, but it wasn't as crowded as it is now.*[24]

Another woman from Santo Domingo that Marjorie got to know was
Linda Calabasas. Marjorie recalled that *she sold jewelry and she sold little,
not very good, pieces of Santo Domingo pottery. She was a real character. . . .
She came into my office one day and she was popping her chewing gum . . . and
she said, "Marjorie, I don't like tourists." And I said, "Well, they're part of every
museum. You can't do anything about it. Why don't you like them?" She said,
"They called me a bad name." I said, "I can't believe that. What did they call
you?" She swished her arms around and she said, "What does 'typical' mean?
They said, 'There sits a typical Indian.'"*[25] Marjorie was always disturbed by
the attitudes of the non-Native residents in Santa Fe and the tourists, especially when they made derogatory comments about the local Puebloans and
members of other Native communities.

Marjorie described the time when a young Jicarilla Apache man, who
had been appointed by the tribal council to start a museum in Dulce, New
Mexico, came to ask for her assistance.

He didn't have the faintest idea of how to get the money from the govern-
ment, except that the government said they ought to have one [a museum].
He thought that the Museum of New Mexico and probably the Laboratory of
Anthropology would furnish all the Apache material. I suggested that "know-
ing your people, and I don't know them too well, I think you ought to get to-
gether with different people on the reservation and talk to them and get them
interested in a museum, get them to donate things from their homes and their
collections." You could see his face light up and he began to get the idea. He
took notes. He came in several times, and he was going to come again and he
never did. I couldn't find out anything about him at the headquarters there, so
I guess they never did really get a museum. . . . All the Indians of that period
seemed to want to start museums. Geronima, who is so much more capable
in that respect than so many others, wanted to have [a museum] at San Juan.
I don't think they know how to get the grants. They don't know how to prepare
them. I think they need help in that direction.[26]

There have been starts and stops in the planning of a museum at Ohkay
Owingeh Pueblo since the early 2000s.

In her position as curator she would receive some interesting requests.

I was in the museum, and this was during WWII, and it was a very, very
snowy Saturday morning. We worked Saturdays then. The librarian, I think
her name was Leslie Murphy, called me and said, "There is a group of old
Indians in here and they say they are from Zuni and they want to know where
to look in Matilda Cox Stevenson's studies of the Zuni for certain ceremonies
that have to do with war." I was a little bit uneasy. I went up there and the
thing that was so sad was that there had not been any communication from
places that were closer to Zuni, like Gallup. They could have gotten the same
annual report of the Bureau of American Ethnology there but they didn't
know it. . . . I helped them. Of course, we didn't have any fancy machines to
do the Xeroxing or word processing, but Leslie stayed overtime, and I did too.
I did some reading and this young interpreter with them copied it down. They
were going to reenact one of the ceremonies that was no longer given. I told
them where they could get the BAE report on interlibrary loan if they would
get the nearest librarian in the Indian School at Zuni or somewhere to get it
for them, so they would know just how to set up the altars and so on. . . . This
was medicine to take care of their young people who were serving in the war.[27]

Marjorie also depended on the advice of her Native American friends in planning exhibits.

I never put anything of a prehistoric nature, nothing which might now be called sensitive material, on exhibit without going out to Joe Aguilar or to speak to Ambrosio Calabasas, an old Santo Domingo man. I went to them quietly and I would have the things there and say, "What would you call this?" And they would tell me and I would say, "Well, that's what I thought it was. Is it all right to show it?" And they would say, "Yes." I don't think they would now. The whole picture has changed. Of course, we don't show inhumations or cremations or anything like that now. The Indians wouldn't permit it. But for one of the exhibits, I did ask them if it would be all right and they said it would be okay. I showed a Hohokam cremation and I showed little Oscar of Jemez Cave and a mummified burial that Jess Jennings had sent me from Utah. I like the Indians and I didn't want them to get into trouble and I didn't want to get in trouble either. I don't know how they would feel now about putting that hunting net that we found at U-Bar Cave on exhibit. I think the museum has had it in an exhibit but I don't know that I would show it without asking the Indians. I certainly wouldn't show the stuff that was with it.[28]

Picuris Pueblo Museum

Marjorie had a special interest in Picuris Pueblo and the development of a museum there. Located on the western slopes of the Sangre de Cristo Mountains in northern New Mexico, the people of Picuris Pueblo speak a northern Tiwa language that is closely related to the language spoken at Taos Pueblo and the southern Tiwa spoken at Sandia and Isleta. Its remote location limited interactions with other Indigenous groups historically. Since the eighteenth century, Picuris Pueblo has been surrounded by Spanish American neighbors who were generally friendly.[29]

Marjorie got to know several people at Picuris Pueblo through her work as a member of the planning committee for the Picuris Pueblo Museum in the 1960s. Marjorie and Al Schroeder both served on the committee along with others such as Geronima Montoya and staff from the Bureau of Indian Affairs. *I often think of the Indians that we associated with when we were trying to get the Picuris Pueblo Indian Museum started. All the Picuris people . . . I was so impressed by the way they expressed them-*

selves.[30] Marjorie was especially taken with the mannerisms of the Picuris people. *They were so moving in the way they talked. None of us, I don't care whether we had stage experience or had been trained actors and actresses, we couldn't have had movement like they had in their talks which just occurred naturally.*[31]

When Marjorie started working on the planning committee, she and others were concerned about the welfare of Picuris Pueblo. According to Donald N. Brown, "Picuris Pueblo in the 1960s was only a reflection of the traditional community. Paved roads, electricity, television sets, and telephones linked the Pueblo to the outside world on which the residents had become dependent. Most of the ceremonial association has disappeared."[32] Marjorie justified the museum committee's work because

> *Picuris was off the beaten track and the BIA and the Eight Northern Pueblos Indian Agency wanted to do something that would improve their economy. One of the things was to put in that big fish pond [Pu-La Lake], and they would sell tickets to people who wanted to come out there [to fish for trout]. They also got the use of a museum. Herb Dick had been doing all that wonderful archaeological work in the old pueblo there. He had the old part exposed and the idea was that it would be partly an outdoor museum and then exhibits in this building. The building I never really cared for because it was BIA architecture. It didn't look Puebloan at all. Anyway, the archaeological part of it was fine because there would be good material for exhibits.*[33]

Finally, the new Picuris Pueblo Museum was completed in 1968. Marjorie recalled:

> *The museum was built and Al Schroeder and I were two of the advisors. Along with Geronima Montoya and a woman who had a trading post up along the river there, I don't remember her name. Anyway, we'd go every three weeks up to a meeting with the old people, the heads of the Pueblo, for discussions and so on. And finally, it was opened. . . . The museum was lovely, the part that had the exhibit cases. Herb Dick and his students at Adams State University did all the work for the Indians. Then our idea was that they would sell their pottery and their aprons and things that they make, the women there, and some of their arts and crafts and jewelry. But the sad thing was that the old*

women were not willing to teach the younger ones how to do micaceous culinary pottery anymore. It was just a sad situation. Now there's a grocery store there and there's a nice little restaurant, but as far as there being a museum it's nothing. . . . But, that's how I became involved with Picuris. That, of course, was mostly after I had retired from the museum.[34]

According to various websites, the Picuris Pueblo Museum sells beadwork, pottery, and weavings by local artisans, and they give tours of the archaeological site.

Santa Fe Indian Market

Marjorie recalled that in the past there used to be more Indians involved in the meetings and serving on committees of the New Mexico Association on Indian Affairs, now the Southwestern Association for Indian Arts (SWAIA), when she was working with Margretta Dietrich. It was their goal to have the Indians be full participants in the decision-making process. Marjorie commented on the non-Indians in attendance at these meetings: *There would be lots of Indians at those meetings. I remember when some anthropologists from Harvard came to one of our meetings where there were lots of Indians— blanket Indians, the kind who wore Pendleton blankets. This one anthropologist was walking back and forth and he said, "Now when the Indian child begins to verbalize and ambulate. . . ." And this old fellow turned to another Indian and said, "Why doesn't he say 'walk and talk'?"*[35]

In the early days of her association with Margretta Dietrich and the NMAIA, Marjorie was approached about the conditions that the Indian artists had to endure when they came to Santa Fe for Indian Market. One major concern was finding a place for them to camp for a couple of days during the market. *They used to camp on Marcy Street. There was a parking lot. At the time this started, this seems incredible now, but during my association anyway in the late 1930s and early 1940s, there was not a place in town for the Indians to go to the bathroom either. They sat out under that portal or they slept on the ground over in that parking lot. So we worked very hard on that. We worked with the market.*[36]

The NMAIA sponsored Indian dances in the courtyard of the Palace of the Governors. Marjorie recalled that back then,

Margretta Dietrich had a stack of the most beautiful Indian blankets you ever saw and she would have her handyman, Moises, bring them down from her property . . . and they would line the patio of the Palace of the Governors, excepting for the center, and the Indians were allowed to dress in my little office which was there. This was before we had the Hall of the Modern Indian. Then spectators would come in to see the Indian dances, that's where we made most of the money every year, carrying on with this little fee we charged. They'd come in through those big double blue gates. That went on until it became what you see today, a great big market.

As with most organizations that have a long history, change is inevitable and not everyone agrees. As Marjorie argues,

the big disagreement at the time was this. We wanted the New Mexico Association on Indian Affairs to stay New Mexico only. Charlie Minton came in as director that year and he said that he thought it would be nice if we allowed Arizona Indians to be part of it. That was all right. That was the Southwest. We thought that would be just perfect and we would also spread out a little bit and we thought, well, Southern Utes in Colorado and the Navajo in Utah too. Then, the next thing we knew, the Institute of American Indian Arts came to Santa Fe [in 1962] and they started fussing because they said the Indians who supported their organization wanted to be included too. We had some awful fights about that. Most of us, the old-timers, did not want it to change to a national market. It shouldn't be called the Southwestern Association for Indian Arts anymore. It is not. It's an American Indian extravaganza![37]

This change in the Southwestern Association for Indian Arts and the Santa Fe Indian Market caused much heartache for Marjorie.

I always got along so well with Indians and I feel that they have had such a raw deal ever since they made contact with the first white person. . . . My Indian friends like the Shuplas and people like that . . . wouldn't always get their application for their booth in on time so the Plains Indians would have it, or the Oklahoma Indians, they always got theirs in right after the first of the year. They were organized. New Mexico's Indians are different. It's always been a casual thing here in the Southwest. I don't know how many times I'd go to the office and beg them to give people like the Shuplas a chance, but they wouldn't. So, they'd have to be on the outskirts of town somewhere, maybe way up there on Marcy Street or somewhere. You go to that Market today and as spectacular as it is, and as hard as it is to get near the booths . . . I think it's probably good, but I think it has outgrown the Plaza.[38]

Marjorie started judging at Indian Market around 1938–39 and only judged pottery. She was involved in judging for over thirty years, and she encouraged the museum staff to get involved as well.

My association was mostly with people like Margretta Dietrich, [the] Pack-ards and Kenneth Chapman. I was so honored and I just thought I had really arrived. I thought maybe I really knew something about Indian art the first time when Dr. Mera and Kenneth Chapman asked me to be a judge of pottery with them. . . . I remained a part of that organization and worked very hard for them up to the early 1970s. My eyesight wasn't good enough and I just didn't think I was capable of judging anymore. . . . We gave prizes and different people like Henry Dendall and the Packards and the curio dealers would give money for prizes. That was our fun thing. . . . I used to love to go around and see my old Indian friends in the market. That was the highlight of the whole thing. Shaking hands with them. Giving them their prizes.[39]

At the time the museum did not have an acquisition fund to purchase Indian art for the collection. So, Marjorie often *bought some pieces and gave them to the collection. I think there are quite a few things in that collection that I started getting early on. Of course, the prize piece is that great big, decorated black-on-black San Ildefonso jar . . . one of the last big ones that Maria Martinez made and is on [the cover of] Dick Spivey's book. I wasn't responsible for that personally, though it is one of the most beautiful she ever made.*[40] This spectacular jar signed "Marie & Julian" won first place at the 1942 Santa Fe Indian Market and is in the collection of the Museum of Indian Arts and Culture in Santa Fe.

Marjorie was at the forefront of seeking advice from her Native American friends and set the stage for those who have followed in her footsteps. She considered these friends as advisors and collaborators during archaeological excavations, while documenting and cataloging the collections, and when planning and installing her exhibits. Since the 1980s some museums in the Southwest have formed Indian Advisory Boards or Councils who work with museum staff as advisors and collaborators on exhibits and programming. In particular, the Museum of Indian Arts and Culture in Santa Fe, New Mexico (MIAC), convened a group of tribal representatives to assist with the planning and installation of the "Here, Now, and Always" exhibit. This Indian Advisory Board continues to meet with the MIAC staff quarterly and advises on exhibits, collection acquisitions, and questions regarding NAGPRA compliance. The Arizona State Museum at the University of Arizona in Tucson worked with a similar group of Native American advisors and collaborators on its exhibit "Paths of Life." Other museums such as the Museum of Northern Arizona in Flagstaff, Arizona, and the Center of Southwest Studies at Fort Lewis College in Durango, Colorado, co-curate exhibitions with Native artists and scholars. These collaborations offer opportunities for museum staff to learn more about their collections and for Native artists and scholars to gain a better understanding of museum operations and best practices, while building lifelong friendships.

When Marjorie talked about her Native American friends, in particular, she has often said, *They were part of my life. . . . I think I am a better person because of my association with American Indians.*[41]

CHAPTER 12

A Trail Blazed for Others to Follow

We loved our work and were in it for the love of the work.

—MARJORIE LAMBERT[1]

In the past museums offered viable career opportunities for anthropologists and archaeologists, especially women, much as they continue to do today. As Nancy Parezo and Margaret Hardin point out, "Women curators were dedicated and provided a great service to anthropology. . . . Claiming that anthropology was the basis for a way of life and museums were institutions from which to apply anthropology to life was a common sentiment."[2] Reflecting on the time when she entered the museum field, Marjorie made this observation:

> When I left the university and the teaching jobs—I'd had approximately three years of it—there were two aspects of anthropology that a woman might look forward to. It could be involved with, for me, the University of New Mexico, or it could be the Museum of New Mexico. In other words, you could be with academe the rest of your life as a teacher in the department of anthropology, and perhaps be lent now and then to the psychology department, and maybe a little extension work. And in a museum, you took care of what I've already described—exhibits and some fieldwork, writing, and so on—which is all right, but those were the only two fields. Perhaps you could have a job in a high school teaching. But nowadays . . . there are many aspects of anthropology open for women as well as men for that matter. You have to consider the fact that you can work now in hospitals as an anthropologist. You can work in police departments as an anthropologist. You can set up your own company and not only do archaeological work, but you can do anthropology, generally

speaking, from the standpoint of it as a general science. There are all kinds of
futures now for women in anthropology.[3]

At the time that Marjorie was beginning her career as a museum curator,
some young women were finding employment with federal agencies, but
they primarily held positions as secretaries. She noted that *the girls in the*
Park Service at that time when I was young had desk jobs. Now [1997] they can
go out as guides. They can go out and be one of the rangers. The Park Service
is one of the examples that's changed very much for women.[4] Recently women
have been assigned to high-level positions in the National Park Service in the
Southwest. For example, in 2021 Kayci Cook Collins was selected to be the
new superintendent of Mesa Verde National Park and Yucca House National
Monument in Colorado. She also supervises Denise Robertson, the superintendent of Chaco Culture National Historic Park and Aztec Ruins National
Monument in New Mexico.

Over her career, Marjorie observed an increase in the number of women
entering the field of anthropology and staying; she also witnessed a change
in the attitude towards women, in particular women of color.

> *I was very loyal to both the American Anthropological Association and the*
> *Society for American Archaeology. But there weren't too many women when*
> *I first started going to meetings. But as the years went on and as they began*
> *to get more participants from different universities, I noticed more and more*
> *women coming. Another thing, I noticed that men who hadn't been hiring*
> *women before were beginning to hire them. Paul Martin and Emil Haury,*
> *they began to hire more and more women. And I noticed too, something that*
> *pleased me very much, for years and years I had never seen any African*
> *Americans at our national meetings. I noticed more and more, particularly*
> *in the field of anthropology, not archaeology, there were noticeable numbers*
> *of African American women. I felt pretty good about that.*[5]

In thinking about the future, Marjorie felt positive about the different
opportunities available to women anthropologists. *I don't know what the*
best fields are for women today. There's medical anthropology. There are some
aiming toward the directorship of museums. And they are very good at what
they do. I think that men are recognizing that too. I think that some of them
are recognizing them [women] as true partners. I don't think anthropology is

just a man's field anymore. They say that anthropology is the Science of Man. It's the Science of People. It will be interesting to see where we go in the next century.[6]

Marjorie also commented on how anthropological and archaeological practices have changed over time.

I think of the concepts of archaeological and ethnological work, how it is changing. It used to be that you would study archaeology and that was it. You wrote your report and you turned it in. If you studied a group of people, you wrote a monograph or you wrote a book about them. Now, when anthropologists go in to work with a people, they try to do something for the people. You might say that the Peace Corps in a way is anthropology. These people go all over the world and they're working with cultures and they're trying to help the people and perhaps the animals and the environment they live in. It's a big thing now and it's a matter of our survival if we don't work on it.[7]

This type of applied anthropology that Marjorie is referring to is a growing field in academia and outside the realm of universities. It also has its own professional membership organization, the Society for Applied Anthropology, and is taught as a separate subfield in some major colleges and universities.

Reflecting on Her Life's Work

Based on her own experiences, Marjorie made this observation as to how women were treated in the profession:

I think we were treated well enough in graduate school as well as in my early professional years, with the exception of the salary discrimination. I think that women in those jobs were made to do things that the men in the Department or in the museum didn't want to do. They worked in a roundabout way so the women would have to do that. For example, if there wasn't enough money in the budget to hire somebody to keep the museum open during the noon hour [they would ask Marjorie to stay and guard the museum]. Why should the women curators be made to stand at the desk while the men went out to lunch, and late lunches at that! That sort of discrimination has gone on all through my career. The women knew it. But I think women are much better at standing up for their rights now than in the years when I first started. We wouldn't have dared because jobs were scarce.[8]

Marjorie often mentioned the fact that she was making less than her male colleagues throughout her career. This pay inequity also affected her relationship with Hewett. When describing her feelings about this issue, she said, *I was hurt because Dr. Hewett was so good to me and he thought the world and all of me. He was sort of a father figure to all of us. It was like your own father doing a dirty trick on you.* She felt that it would have helped if Hewett had explained to her why her salary was lower than her male colleagues and why she was having to use her own money to keep the archaeological equipment in proper working condition and to cover exhibit installation expenses. *That's the only thing I hold against that man. . . . He was a wonderful teacher and a good friend. I think men were like that then. They thought they were giving us a break by having us in the profession.*[9] Unfortunately, subsequent MNM directors did not provide her with an equitable salary either.

Marjorie also recognized the fact that there were times when she may have been passed up for a promotion or a pay raise. She observed that

anthropology as a whole, and museum work especially, has had the reputation of being very poorly paid professions [something she always referred to as "genteel poverty"]. We knew that when we went into it. We loved our work and we were there for the love of the work. Florence [Hawley Ellis] and I have always said this when talking about the really terrible salaries that we all made. But we knew it. We thought we were there for the work and I still think that the work was more important. But gosh, you've got to live. It's harder to live now. There are many things now that take your money than when we were all poor and starting out.[10]

Unfortunately, the disparities in salaries for women in both academe and museums continue to this day, not just in anthropology, but also in the sciences and in Ivy League law schools.

Noting how much the gender dynamics had changed over time, Marjorie said, *I know of two or three museums that have almost totally, if not all, female staff. You wouldn't have found that when I first went into anthropology. They wouldn't have allowed it.* There were women who worked in the Southwest who did gain top positions in colleges, such as Dorothy Keur at Hunter Col-

lege. Marjorie points to another successful archaeologist who started out in
the Southwest but ended up moving in a different direction.

> *I think of some of the pioneers in my generation. I think of what one of my col-
> leagues did in the way of breaking the ice—and I'm not making a pun, because
> she did most of her work in Greenland—that was Frederica de Laguna. I had
> a tremendous respect for that little lady. She was with Bryn Mawr [a women's
> liberal arts college in Bryn Mawr, Pennsylvania]. She was head of the depart-
> ment there. The only person that would hire her—she tried everywhere to get
> an academic job—was this elderly Norwegian anthropologist who was really
> gung ho about the Eskimo and their culture. He hired her and one Eskimo
> to go with him. . . . There's a wonderful book written by her called* Voyage to
> Greenland[11] *about the trials and tribulations of a woman in the field at that
> time. She made it and she became one of the world's leading authorities on
> Eskimo prehistory. That was her main field of teaching at Bryn Mawr. Not
> knowing her at all, I have the feeling that I would have admired her tremen-
> dously if I could have worked with her. . . . She was an excellent teacher and
> she was head of her department of anthropology.*[12]

New Era of Women in Leadership Roles

In the past four decades, women have finally come out of the shadows to
become leaders in the field as museum directors, heads of anthropology departments, the primary investigators of archaeological research projects, and
owners of cultural resource management companies. Nevertheless, there is
still a long way to go in the areas of diversity, equity, and inclusion.

Often overlooked are the women who made their contribution to southwestern archaeology by working alongside their husbands. Two women of
note are Harriett Cosgrove with husband Burton, known for their Mimbres research, and Ann Axtell Morris, wife of Earl Morris, who successfully
popularized anthropology with her publication *Digging in the Southwest*.[13]
Another is Florence Lister, who worked along with her husband Robert and
wrote about their lives and work together in *Pot Luck: Adventures in Archaeology*. This autobiographical form of writing provides a glimpse into
the important roles that women played as wives to what is assumed to be
the larger-than-life "Indiana Jones" ideal of the male archaeologist. In many
cases, it was the "wife" who was a partner in the field as a camp cook and

crew member, and then back home she served as the able assistant, writing and typing up field notes and reports and helping with publications—all of which was overlooked for many years. Today, there are numerous couples working alongside each other in the field or on different projects altogether, where the women receive the same accolades as their husbands.

Much has changed for women in anthropology and archaeology since I interviewed Marjorie in the 1990s. Since the 1970s and 1980s women have taken advantage of the new opportunities that have opened up in academia. More women have achieved full tenured professorships in major universities across the nation. Some have been appointed as heads or chairs of their departments, as well as elected to presidencies in professional organizations such as the American Anthropological Association, Society for American Archaeology, and Society for Applied Anthropology. Others have become college presidents.

Even though women have been directors of museums since the 1960s, these have been primarily children's museums or small art museums. Eventually, women were hired to direct museums in the Southwest, such as the Wheelwright Museum of the American Indian and the Laboratory of Anthropology in Santa Fe. For the first time, in 2006 all four museums in the Museum of New Mexico system were under women directors. Shelby Tisdale was the director of the Museum of Indian Arts and Culture / Laboratory of Anthropology, Joyce Ice was the director of the Museum of International Folk Art, Frances Levine was the director of the New Mexico History Museum and the Palace of the Governors, and Marsha Bol was the director of the New Mexico Museum of Art. This trend has continued in other museums, including university museums.

As both universities and museums are working toward being more diverse, equitable, and inclusive of women, especially women of color, there have been some advances in this area as well. American anthropologist Johnnetta Betch Cole is an educator, museum director, and college president. Cole was the first female African American president of Spelman College, a historically Black college, from 1987 to 1997. She was president of Benne College from 2002 to 2007. From 2009 to 2017 Cole was the director of the Smithsonian Institution's National Museum of African Art. She continues to serve as a positive role model for young women of color pursuing careers in anthropology and museums. The January 2022 appointment of Cynthia Chavez Lamar, a member of San Felipe Pueblo, to the directorship of the National Museum of the American Indian is yet another example where a woman of color is leading a major museum on the National Mall in Washington, D.C. She is the first Native American woman to be named as a Smithsonian museum director.

Incorporating Indigenous Knowledge into Her Work

Marjorie was an ethnoarchaeologist long before the term became popular, and she incorporated the wisdom she received from her Native American friends and colleagues in all that she did in archaeology and in the museum. She often said:

> I don't see what good archaeology is alone. I don't see what good ethnography is alone. They go together. They're [Native Americans] part of the history of the Southwest. It's about all of what's been going on here in the Southwest and in Mexico and in the Americas generally from the Ice Age right down to the present. It's an ongoing evolutionary thing. It's all the same. It's the art of human history. It's the art of the history of a very great people. I'm speaking of the American Indian. . . . I feel very deeply about them and I have a feeling of such shame when I think of what we have done to them in the past. There's no point in dwelling on it. It happened and I hope it doesn't continue to happen.[14]

Marjorie didn't live long enough to be part of, or aware of, the exciting work being done by Indigenous archaeologists and scholars today. The recent publication *The Continuous Path: Pueblo Movement and the Archaeology of Becoming*, edited by Samuel Duwe and Robert W. Preucel in 2019,[15] provides a new lens into how we approach southwestern archaeology and addresses some of the questions Marjorie had about people moving across the southwestern landscape through time. Indigenous and non-Indigenous archaeologists and scholars collaborated throughout this volume in support of the editors' premise that "this book is the result of [their] desire to rethink aspects of a southwestern archaeology by taking Pueblo conceptions of history and philosophy seriously. . . . [Their] aim was to present a series of collaborative papers of wide geographical breadth (from Hopi to Taos) that explored Pueblo movement and history and that emphasized continuities from ancient times to the present day."[16]

Another groundbreaking publication that is inclusive of the Indigenous perspectives is *Footprints of Hopi History: Hopihinintiput Kukveni'at*, edited by Leigh J. Kuwanwisiwma, T. J. Ferguson, and Chip Colwell in 2018. In the preface to this publication, the editors note that the "footprints" are considered to be "archaeological remains of former settlements, pottery sherds, stone tools, petroglyphs, and other physical evidence of past use and occupation of the land."[17] These "footprints" were left by the Hopi ancestors as they migrated across the landscape from their place of origin to their present-day homes on the Hopi Mesas in Arizona. Part of their heritage today is as stewards of these ancestral lands. This is the type of inclusive archaeological practice that Marjorie advocated for and would be fully engaged in if she were alive today.

A Lifetime of Recognition

When Marjorie retired in 1969 she received the "Certificate of Appreciation" from New Mexico's Department of Education. In her brief biography on Marjorie, Nancy Fox wrote, "Her many past contributions to her profession have elicited the respect of colleagues throughout the nation. A member of Phi Gamma Nu, honorary scholastic and social science fraternity, she is listed in *American Men of Science, Who's Who in the West, American Women's Who's Who*, and the *International Directory of Anthropologists*."[18] Nancy Fox went on to note that Marjorie's "Membership in the Archaeological Society of New Mexico reflects her continuing support for an organization to which she devoted many years as a Trustee and Secretary."[19] Volume 3 of the *Papers of the Archaeological Society of New Mexico*, edited by Albert H. Schroeder, was dedicated to Marjorie in 1976.

In 1984 she received local and regional recognition when she was made an Honorary Life Member of the Archaeological Society of New Mexico and the School of American Research. She was also made Curator Emeritus of the Laboratory of Anthropology by the Museum of New Mexico's Board of Regents in 1984. At the national level, Marjorie was the recipient of the Fiftieth Award for Outstanding Contributions to American Archaeology by the Society for American Archaeology that same year.

In 1988 Marjorie was both humbled and honored to receive the Louis T. Benezet Award from her alma mater, Colorado College, in Colorado Springs. She was also given the New Mexico Heritage Preservation Award. That same year both Marjorie and Jack Lambert were recognized as Living Treasures of Santa Fe for the contributions they both had made throughout the years as valued Santa Fe community members.

Marjorie continued to be recognized both locally and regionally for her philanthropic work as well as her professional contributions. In 1990 she was given the Spanish Colonial Arts Society Award for her years as a trustee but also for her ongoing care and preservation of the collections when they were housed at the Museum of New Mexico. In 1995 Marjorie was inducted into the Palmer High School Alumni Hall of Fame in Colorado Springs.

In writing about Marjorie, Linda Cordell best summarizes Marjorie's archaeological legacy.

> In her long and productive career, Marjorie Lambert has made contributions to the fields of history, pre-Columbian art, and museum work, in addition to archaeology. Yet, as she herself has said, "If I had my choice of taking just one of the things I did, it would probably be the fieldwork." . . . Indeed, I think she is best known among southwestern archaeologists for being a meticulous and successful fieldworker. She excavated at Chaco Canyon in 1932 with the University of New Mexico field program. She also worked at Battleship Rock field camp in the Jemez Mountains, at Tecolote Ruin near Las Vegas, New Mexico, at San Gabriel del Yunque near San Juan Pueblo, and at a series of important Archaic cave sites in Hidalgo County, New Mexico. Although each of these projects contributed importantly to New Mexico prehistory, I think Lambert is best known for her work at Paa-ko, which exemplifies the particular kind of research for which she is known.[20]

The Byron S. Cummings Award was presented to Marjorie by the Arizona Archaeological and Historical Society in 1996 in recognition of her contributions to southwestern archaeology. She especially treasured this award, a trowel mounted on a plaque that she showcased on her wall for many years.

A Life Fulfilled

A large inventory of experiences has provided Marjorie with a full and satisfying life, in spite of the numerous obstacles that she had to overcome. As she concluded, *I think it has been a great life*. When asked "What if you had it to do it all over again?," she replied, *I'd probably end up doing the same thing. Never as a museum administrator, though. I have been offered them, you know. I have been told by colleagues, people like Paul Martin and J. O. Brew, that when Hewett died, I should have gone on to Chicago or Harvard and really become a big wheel in the museum field. I never wanted to live anyplace but Santa Fe. . . . I don't have any regrets about being the small wheel in the Santa Fe picture. I loved it. It's my life here.*[21]

Marjorie, like many scholars in museums and academia, planned to catch up with her writing when she retired. Unfortunately, the loss of her eyesight prohibited her from doing the kind of writing she had hoped. Regardless, throughout her career she was quite prolific, with 137 articles for *El Palacio*, which included brief site reports, information about the collections and exhibits, and book reviews. She also wrote articles for professional journals such as *American Antiquity, Archaeology, New Mexico Anthropologist, Plains Anthropologist, New Mexico Historical Review, Ethnohistory Magazine*, and many more. She additionally wrote articles for local magazines and newspapers. She completed two monographs for the SAR—one on Paa-ko and the other on the work she and Richard Ambler did in Hidalgo County. She also contributed the chapter on Pojoaque Pueblo for the *Handbook of North American Indians* published by the Smithsonian Institution.[22]

Parezo and Hardin concluded that "in spite of the odds against them and the marginalization, women realized that they had played an important role by working in museums. In many ways, Marjorie Lambert summed up the feelings of all the women who worked in museums: 'I don't see how you could regret a career in anthropology, no matter where it leads.'"[23] Nancy Fox asserted that "by example, as well as through publication and her activities as teacher, lecturer, and exhibit curator, Marjorie has lent inspiration to a generation of young archaeologists."[24]

When asked what her mother would say to her now, Marjorie replied, *She would probably say that I am a schoolteacher or a librarian gone bad. She said once, "I might have known that you were going to do something like that. You were always making mud pies." Maybe that's true. Maybe I just like to play in the dirt!*[25] And as she reflected on her life, her work, and her legacy, Marjorie thought about it for some time before saying,

> *I don't know if it was the right decision or not, but I have certainly had a productive and interesting life. I don't think any of us regret it. I don't see how you*

could regret a career in anthropology. I encouraged so many young people that I have taught or who have come to me for advice throughout the years that even if you don't go on into anthropology as your major field of endeavor, the background in anthropology is perfect for so many other professions. I know of two fairly young women, one who is practicing law now, I think with the Navajos, and the other with a law firm in Albuquerque. Both of them had a degree in anthropology first. I think that makes a wonderful background, no matter what you go into.[26]

Throughout her career and especially after retiring, Marjorie encouraged many young women and men to pursue higher goals in their anthropological and museum careers. She was always supportive of women in archaeology despite the pitfalls and some of the hardships she endured. Marjorie, like many of the other invisible women in the development of anthropology, deserves her place in the written history of southwestern anthropology, archaeology, and museology for her contributions to archaeological inquiry into the ancient past of the Southwest; for her ability to bring about a public appreciation for anthropology and southwestern archaeology through public lectures, museum exhibits, and *El Palacio* articles over the years; and for her unfailing support of the arts of Native Americans in the Southwest and the Spanish Americans in northern New Mexico. It is hoped that Marjorie Ferguson Lambert's experiences as a young woman in a male-dominated field will provide insight for those young women entering the field today and tomorrow. By tracing Marjorie's footprints as one of the "Daughters of the Desert," we may be able to relate her experiences to our own as we follow our own paths through history as the "Granddaughters of the Desert."

Through her field excavations and historic research, she has added to our knowledge of the history of human occupation in the Southwest. To Marjorie, the "study of man" was always fascinating, and if she had to choose a lifetime career all over again it would be anthropology. *I think that anthropology is important. That's my final statement. It's super important. I don't think we're going to survive as a culture unless we understand anthropology and what anthropology is about. Human history.*[27] Marjorie passed away on December 16, 2006, at the age of ninety-eight in Santa Fe. She will be remembered as a true role model and beloved mentor. There is much to be learned from those who have gone before.

FIGURE 29 Marjorie Ferguson Lambert in 1986. Photo by David Grant Noble. Courtesy of the Photographer.

APPENDIX A

Awards and Fellowships

1930	Alice Van Diest Award for Excellence in Social Studies, Colorado College
	Pi Gamma Mu, honorary social science fraternity
1930–34	Graduate Fellowship, University of New Mexico
1934–37	Research Grant, School of American Research
1960	Grant-in-Aid, School of American Research
1969	Certificate of Appreciation, State of New Mexico, Department of Education
1984	Honorary Life Member, Archaeological Society of New Mexico
1984	Honorary Life Member, School of American Research
1984	Curator Emeritus of the Laboratory of Anthropology by the Board of Regents of the Museum of New Mexico
1984	Fiftieth Award for Outstanding Contributions to American Archaeology, Society for American Archaeology.
1988	Louis T. Benezet Award, Colorado College, Colorado Springs
1988	Marjorie and Jack Lambert—Living Treasures of Santa Fe Award
1988	New Mexico Heritage Preservation Award
1990	Spanish Colonial Arts Society Award
1995	Alumni Hall of Fame, Palmer High School, Colorado Springs
1996	Byron S. Cummings Award, Arizona Archaeological and Historical Society

APPENDIX B

Archaeological Field Schools and Site Excavations

1930	Unshagi and Nanishagi in the Jemez Mountains (UNM field camp at Battleship Rock)
1931–35	Chetro Ketl at Chaco Canyon (UNM Field School in Anthropology)
1932	Tecolote (New Mexico Normal School, now Highlands University in Las Vegas)
1934–35	Puaray
1935–39	Kuaua
1935	Giusewa
1936	Paa-ko
1944	Yuque Yunque
1956	Well I, Palace of the Governors
1960	Hidalgo County
1965	Giusewa
1967	Twin Hills Site

Publications

Ferguson, Marjorie E.

1931 "The Acculturation of Sandia Pueblo." A thesis submitted for the master of arts degree in archaeology and anthropology. Illust. 100 pages. Albuquerque: University of New Mexico.

1933 "Preliminary Report on Tecolote Ruin." *El Palacio* 34 (25–26): 196–98.

Tichy, Marjorie F.

1935 "The Material from Kuaua." *El Palacio* 38 (22, 23): 119–22.

"Puaray and Kuaua Cultural Material." *Annual Report of the School of American Research.* pp. 15–17.

1936 "Observations on the Mission Uncovered at Puaray." *El Palacio* 41 (11–13): 63–66.

1937 "The Excavation of Paa-ko Ruin, a Preliminary Report." *El Palacio* 42 (19–21): 109–16.

"A Preliminary Account of the Excavation of Paa-ko, San Antonio, New Mexico." *New Mexican Anthropologist* 1 (5): 73–77.

1938 "The Kivas at Paako and Kuaua." *New Mexico Anthropologist* 2 (4–5): 71–80.

"In the Footsteps of Coronado." *New Mexico Magazine* 16 (3): 16–17, 35–37.

1939 "The Archaeology of Puaray." *El Palacio* 46 (7): 145–63.

"Yesterday's People." *New Mexico Magazine* 17 (1): 12–13, 40, 46–47.

"Report of the Curator of Southwestern Archaeology." *Annual Report of the School of American Research*. pp. 10–14.

1940 "New Pots for Old." *New Mexico Magazine* 18 (3): 16–17, 39–40.

Articles in *Landmarks of New Mexico* by Edgar L. Hewett and Wayne L. Mauzy. Albuquerque: University of New Mexico Press.

"Coronado Monument—Kuaua Ruins" (p. 88)

"The Kuaua Frescoes" (pp. 90–91)

"Puaray (Bandelier) Ruins" (p. 92)

"Ruins of Paa-ko" (p. 100)

1941 "Six Game Pieces from Otowi." *El Palacio* 48 (1): 1–6.

"An Unusual Specimen from Paa-ko." *El Palacio* 48 (7): 155–57.

Review of "Anasazi Painted Pottery" by Paul S. Martin and Elizabeth Willis. Field Museum of Natural History Anthropology Memoirs, vol. 5 (1940). *El Palacio* 48 (2): 32–33.

"Cummings Book on Kinishba." Review of *Kinishba, A Prehistoric Pueblo of the Great Pueblo Period* by Byron Cummings. Tucson: The Hohokam Museums Association and the University of Arizona (1940). *El Palacio* 48 (3): 59–60.

Review of "The Cochise Culture" by E. B. Sayles and Ernst Antevs. Medallion Papers, No. 29. *El Palacio* 48 (8): 175–77.

"Navajo Archaeological Study." Review of *Big Bead Mesa: An Archaeological Study of Navaho Acculturation, 1745–1812* by Dorothy Louise Keur. Memoirs of the Society for American Archaeology, no. 1, Supplement to American Antiquity, vol. 7, no. 2, pt. 2 (1941). *El Palacio* 48 (11): 250–53.

"Notes on the Southwestern Science Meeting" (with Hulda R. Hobbs). *El Palacio* 48 (5): 110–16.

"New Archaeological Loans." *El Palacio* 48 (10): 236–37.

"Eisele Collection Catalogued." *El Palacio* 48 (11): 258.

1942 "Report of the Curator of Archaeology." *Annual Report of the School of American Research*. pp. 10–12.

"An Arizona Ceremonial Cave." Review of *A Ceremonial Cave in the Winchester Mountains, Arizona* by William Shirley Fulton. No. 2. Dragoon, Ariz.: Amerind Foundation (1941). *El Palacio* 49 (2): 42–44.

"Robert's Hunt for Early Man." Review of *Archaeological and Geological Investigations in the San Jon District, Eastern New Mexico* by Frank M. Roberts. Smithsonian Miscellaneous Collection, vol. 103, no. 4 (1942). *El Palacio* 49 (11): 253–55.

"Changes in Historical Exhibits." *El Palacio* 49 (8): 170–72.

"Further Museum Reinstallations in Governor's Palace." *El Palacio* 49 (11): 247–48.

1942 "Man's Poor Relations." Review of *Man's Poor Relations* by Earnest Hooten. Garden City, N.Y.: Doubleday, Doren & Co. (1942). *El Palacio* 50 (4): 89–91.

"Archaeology." *Annual Report of the School of American Research.* pp. 12–14.

"Recent Fieldwork in Peru." Review of *Archaeological Studies in Peru* by W. Duncan Strong, Gordon R. Willey, and John M. Corbett. New York: Columbia University Press (1943). *El Palacio* 50 (7): 164–66.

1944 "Archaeology." *Annual Report of the School of American Research.* pp. 8–10.

"Taakaa, Pueblo Indian Dwarf." *El Palacio* 51 (2): 21–25.

"San Felipe Saint's Day Fiesta." *El Palacio* 51 (5): 100.

"Exploratory Work at Yuque-Yunque." *El Palacio* 51 (11): 222–224.

"Additional Gifts from the San Juan Region." *El Palacio* 51 (11): 207.

"A Penetrating Study of Old Oraibi." Review of *Old Oraibi: A Study of the Hopi Indians of Third Mesa* by Mischa Titiev. Papers of the Peabody Museum of Archaeology and Ethnology, vol. 22, no. 1. Cambridge, Mass.: Harvard University (1944). *El Palacio* 51 (6): 114–17.

"Autobiography of a Hopi Indian." Review of *Sun Chief*, ed. Leo Simmons. New Haven: Yale University Press (1942). *El Palacio* 51 (1): 15–17.

"Outworn Nomenclature of Archaeology." Review of article by T. A. Richards in *American Journal of Archaeology* (Spring 1944). *El Palacio* 51 (8): 146–47.

1945 "Annual Feast Day at Tsia Pueblo." *El Palacio* 52 (1): 11–13.

"The Cahita Indians of Mexico." Review of *The Aboriginal Culture of the Cahita Indians* by Ralph Beals. Berkeley and Los Angeles: University of California. *El Palacio* 52 (3): 55–57.

"The Distribution of Early Elbow Pipes." *El Palacio* 52 (4): 70–73.

"Haury Report on Hemmingway Expedition." Review of *The Exca-vations of Los Muertos and Neighboring Ruins of the Salt River Valley, Southern Arizona* by Emil Haury. Papers of the Peabody Museum of American Archaeology and Ethnology, vol. 14, no. 1 (1945). *El Palacio* 52 (8): 160–63.

"The Archaeology of Sinaloa and Jalisco." Review of *Excavations at Cuilcan, Sinaloa, Ibero-Americana: 25 and The Archaeology of the Autlam-Tuxcacuesco Area of Jalisco Ibero-Americana: 26* by Isabel Kelly (1945). *El Palacio* 52 (12): 258–64.

"Luhrs' Study of Pueblo Adolescents." Review of "An Anthropo-logical Study of the Sources of Maladjustment Among Eastern Pueblo Adolescents" by Dorothy L. Luhrs. PhD dissertation, University of Southern California. *El Palacio* 52 (12): 262–64.

1946 "Indians Used Cigar-Like Pipes." *Science Service.* Janu-ary 27–February 2, cols. 1–2. (Reprint of "The Distribution of Early Elbow Pipes" article in *El Palacio* 52 (4): 70–73.)

"State Flag from Bomber Santa Fe Donated." *El Palacio* 53 (1): 15.

"Pun-Ku, Kiva Ringing Stones." *El Palacio* 53 (2): 42–43.

"New Exhibit on Ecuador." *El Palacio* 53 (2): 56–57.

"Lectures on New Mexico Indians." *El Palacio* 53 (3): 68.

"Indian Affairs Lecture Series." *El Palacio* 53 (5): 121.

"First National Bank Exhibit." *El Palacio* 53 (6): 166–67.

"Turquoise Gift of Mrs. Schmidt." *El Palacio* 53 (7): 186.

"Wisconsin Archaeology." Review of *Preliminary Report on the Upper Mississippi Phase in Wisconsin* by W. C. McKern. *Bulletin of the Public Museum of Milwaukee*, vol. 16, no. 3, pp. 109–285 (1945). *El Palacio* 53 (7): 196–97.

"First Capital Suffers Further Damage." *El Palacio* 53 (11): 324.

"New Mexico's First Capital." *New Mexico Historical Review* 21 (2): 140–44.

"Archaeology." *Annual Report of the School of American Research.* pp.7–13.

1947 Review of *Frijoles: A Hidden Valley in the New World* by J. W. Hendron, ed. Dorothy Thomas. Santa Fe: Rydal Press (1946). *El Palacio* 54 (1): 19–21.

"A Painted Ceremonial Room at Otowi." *El Palacio* 54 (3): 59–69.

Review of *The Sinagua, A Summary of the Archaeology of the Region of Flagstaff, Arizona* by Harold S. Colton. Museum of Northern Arizona, Bulletin 22 (1946). *El Palacio* 54 (3): 77.

Review of *Indians Before Columbus* by Paul S. Martin, George I. Quimby, and Don Collier. Chicago: University of Chicago Press (1947). *El Palacio* 54 (7): 172.

Review of *Frances Drake and the California Indians, 1579* by Robert Heizer. University of California Publications in American Archaeology and Ethnology, vol. 42, no. 3 (1947). *El Palacio* 54 (8): 198–99.

Review of *The SU Site: Excavation of a Mogollon Village, Western New Mexico, Third Season, 1946* by Paul Martin and John Rinaldo. Anthropological Series, Field Museum of Natural History, vol. 32, no. 3 (1947). *El Palacio* 54 (9): 220–22.

"Death of Rosalee Aguilar" (obituary). *El Palacio* 54 (9): 208.

"A Ceremonial Deposit from the Pajarito Plateau." *El Palacio* 54 (10): 227–37.

"Tin-Work Collection Acquired." *El Palacio* 54 (10): 246–47.

Review of *Prehistoric Indians of the Southwest* by H. M. Wormington. The Colorado Museum of Natural History, Popular Series, no. 7 (1947). *El Palacio* 54 (11): 268–69.

"Archaeology." *Annual Report of the School of American Research.* pp. 36–39.

1948 "Kelly Moves to McGill University." *El Palacio* 55 (1): 29.

"Famous Mexican Visitors." *El Palacio* 55 (2): 42.

"A Recent Tour of Central America." *El Palacio* 55 (2): 43–51.

"Lehmers Visit Museum." *El Palacio* 55 (2): 51.

"Sun Chief Visits Museum." El Palacio 55 (2): 61.

"Navajo Miracle Presented in St. Francis." *El Palacio* 55 (4): 122.

"Bonampak Mural Exhibition Launched with Special Program." *El Palacio* 55 (9): 295.

"Recent Gift to Archaeology Department." *El Palacio* 55 (10): 301.

"Word for Seal (Pinnipedia) Traced." Review of *Linguistics—The Word for Seal (Pinnipedia) in Various Languages* by J. P. Harrington. Journal of the Washington Academy of Sciences, vol. 37, no. 4 (1947). *El Palacio* 55 (5): 140.

Review of *The Tres Alamos Site on the San Pedro River, Southeastern Arizona* by Carr Tuthill. Amerind Foundation, no. 4. Dragoon, Ariz. (1947). *El Palacio* 55 (5): 153–54.

Review of *An Ancient Site at Borax Lake, California* by Mark R. Harrington. Southwest Museum Papers, no. 16. Los Angeles (1948). *El Palacio* 55 (5): 154–55.

"Dr. Mera Speaks Before Art Fund Group." *El Palacio* 55 (5): 155.

"Florence Dibell Bartlett Collection Exhibition Opens in Old Palace." *El Palacio* 55 (6): 182–83.

"The Florence Dibell Collection of New Mexico Colonial Art." *El Palacio* 55 (7): 195–200.

Review of *Temples of Yucatan—a Camera Chronicle of Chichen Itza* by Laura Gilpin. New York: Hastings House (1948). *El Palacio* 55 (7): 209–11.

"Notes on the Possible Occurrence of Graving Tools in a New Mexico Pueblo Site." *El Palacio* 55 (8): 257–61.

"Valuable Northern Rio Grande Valley Spanish Colonial Colchas Received." *El Palacio* 55 (11): 331–33.

"Historic Pistol Given Museum." *El Palacio* 55 (11): 359.

Review of *Prehistoric Men* by Robert J. Braidwood. Chicago Natural History Museum, Popular Series, Anthropology, no. 37 (1948). *El Palacio* 55 (12): 381.

"Archaeology." *Annual Report of the School of American Research.* pp. 31–34.

1949 "Historical Society Receives Interesting Old Trunk." *El Palacio* 56 (2): 51.

"Prehistoric 'Compact' Shown in Old Palace." *El Palacio* 56 (2): 59.

"Hawley Writes on Rio Grande Pueblo Acculturation." Review of *An Examination of Pueblo Problems Basic to Acculturation in the Rio Grande* by Florence Hawley. *American Anthropologist* 50 (4): 612–24 (1948). *El Palacio* 56 (2): 61.

"Ancient Burial Near Santa Fe's Public Welfare Building." *El Palacio* 56 (3): 80–81.

"McCormick Spanish Colonial Pieces on Display." *El Palacio* 56 (3): 95–96.

"Archaeological Society of New Mexico Holds Biennial Meeting." *El Palacio* 56 (4): 105.

Review of *Tepexpan Man* by Helmut de Terra, Javier Romero, and
T. D. Stewart. Viking Fund Publications in Anthropology, no. 11
(1949). *El Palacio* 56 (5): 150–53.

"A Comparison of Paa-ko Clay Artifacts Other than Pottery with
Similar Material from Pecos." *El Palacio* 56 (7): 202–7.

"John Gaw Meem's Present Ecclesiastical Pieces to Museum." *El
Palacio* 56 (10): 300.

"Museum and Historical Society Receive Historic Santa Fe Memorabilia." *El Palacio* 56 (10): 315–16.

"Maya Specimens Given School." *El Palacio* 56 (10): 319.

"Report of the Curator of Archaeology and Associate in Charge."
Annual Report of the School of American Research. pp. 34–37.

1950 "The Florence McCormick Collection of Spanish Colonial Art." *El
Palacio* 57 (12): 35–40.

"Society Purchases Retablo." *El Palacio* 57 (2): 52.

"Spanish Colonial Jewelry Exhibit in Museum." *El Palacio* 57 (3): 87.

"Museum Purchases Rare Old Samplers." *El Palacio* 57 (6): 172.

"Marcy's Military Regalia Comes to Museum of New Mexico as
Gift." *El Palacio* 57 (6): 186.

"Twenty-Sixth Annual AAA Meeting." *El Palacio* 57 (7): 212–14.

Review of *Proceedings of the Fifth Plains Conference for Archaeology.* Assembled by John L. Champe. Notebook no. 1, Laboratory
of Anthropology. Lincoln: University of Nebraska (1949). *El
Palacio* 57 (7): 219–20.

Review of *Franciscan Awatovi: The Excavation and Conjectural
Reconstruction of a Seventeenth-Century Spanish Mission Es-
tablishment at a Hopi Indian Town in Northwestern Arizona* by
Ross Gordon Montgomery, Watson Smith, and John Otis Brew.
Papers of the Peabody Museum of American Archaeology and
Ethnology, vol. 36, no. 3 of the Awatovi Expedition. Cambridge,
Mass.: Harvard University. *El Palacio* 57 (9): 286–91.

"Archaeology." *Annual Report of the School of American Research.*
pp. 40–42.

Lambert, Marjorie F.

1951 "Acquisitions and Present and Future Needs." *Biennial Report of the
Historical Society of New Mexico.* 1949–50. p. 7.

Reviews of "Turkey Foot Ridge Site" and "Sites of the Reserve
Phase" by Paul S. Martin and John B. Renaldo. *Fieldiana: Anthropology* 38: 2–3 (1950). *El Palacio* 58 (1): 27–30.

"New Quarters for Historical Collections." *El Palacio* 58 (6): 190.

"Meetings of the American Anthropological Association, Central
States Branch and the Society for American Archaeology." *El
Palacio* 58 (7): 222–23.

Review of *Archaeology of the Bynum Mounds* by John L. Cotter and
John M. Corbett et al. Archaeological Research Series, no. 1,
Natchez Trace Parkway, National Park Service, U.S. Department
of the Interior. Washington, D.C.: U.S. Government Printing
Office (1951). *El Palacio* 58 (9): 292–95.

"Archaeology." *Annual Report of the School of American Research.*
pp. 45–47.

1952 "Oldest Armor in United States Discovered at San Gabriel del
Yunque." *El Palacio* 59 (3): 83–87.

"Bank Exhibit of Maxwell and Carson Mementos." *El Palacio* 59 (9):
295.

"Installations and Acquisitions, Department of Archaeology." *Biennial Report of the Historical Society of New Mexico*, 1951–52. pp.
8–10.

"Archaeology." *Annual Report of the School of American Research.*
pp. 50–53.

1953 "Historic Portrait Comes to Society." *El Palacio* 60 (2): 70.

"Paul David Reiter, 1909–1953" (obituary). *El Palacio* 60 (2): 71–72.

"Archaeology." *Annual Report of the School of American Research.*
pp. 61–64.

"Prehistoric Maya Civilization Is Termed Greatest in Americas," a
review of the Giles G. Healey lecture. *Santa Fe New Mexican*,
March 17, 1953, p. 5, cols. 4–5.

"End Beams Given to Historical Society." *El Palacio* 60 (2): 74.

"Former School of American Research Fellow Tours Europe." *El
Palacio* 60 (3): 111.

"Luhrs Heads Los Angeles State College Anthropology Department." *El Palacio* 60 (4): 153.

"Historical Society Receives Nineteenth-Century Doll." *El Palacio*
60 (4): 174–75.

Review of "Excavations in Big Hawk Valley, Wupatki National Monument, Arizona," by Watson Smith. Museum of Arizona, Bulletin 24. Flagstaff: Northern American Society of Science and Art (1952). *El Palacio* 60 (6): 243–44.

"Marjorie Lambert Attends Annual Meetings at Urbana." *El Palacio* 60 (6): 244.

"The Oldest Armor Found in the United States—The San Gabriel del Yunque Helmet." *Archaeology* 6 (2): 108–10.

"Cities Before Columbus: Prehistoric Town Planning in the Puebloan Southwest." *Landscape* 3 (2): 12–15. (Winter 1953–54).

"Necrology. Jerome William Hendron" (obituary). *El Palacio* 60 (10): 360–62.

"Museum Receives Two Gifts of Interest." *El Palacio* 60 (12): 420.

1954   Review of *Kiva Mural Paintings at Awatovi and Kawai-ka-a, with a Summary of Other Wall Paintings in the Pueblo Southwest* by Watson Smith. Reports of the Awatovi Expedition, no. 5. Peabody Museum of American Archaeology and Ethnology (1952). *El Palacio* 61 (2): 52–57.

"Camman Lecture on Cambodian Jungle City of Angkor." *El Palacio* 61 (3): 89.

"Old Spanish Sword Discovered." *El Palacio* 61 (3): 94.

"Nineteenth Annual Meeting, Society for American Archaeology, Albany, New York, May 7–8, 1954." *El Palacio* 61 (6): 192–94.

"A Recently Discovered Sword of the Late Seventeenth or Early Eighteenth Century." *El Palacio* 61 (9): 300–305.

"Archaeology." *Annual Report of the School of American Research.* pp. 48–50.

"Athens to Rome Covered in Talk by Noted Student." *Santa Fe New Mexican*, November 5, 1954, p. 5, col. 1.

"Paa-ko, Archaeological Chronicle of an Indian Village in North Central New Mexico (Parts I-V)"; "The Physical Type of the Paa-ko Population (Part VI)" by Spencer Rogers. *School of American Research Monograph*, no. 19.

"Installations and Acquisitions, Department of Archaeology." *Biennial Report of the Historical Society of New Mexico*, 1953–54. pp. 8–11.

1955   "Early Man in the Southwest Exhibit Installed in the Palace of the Governors." *El Palacio* 62 (10): 290–93.

"William Wallace Postlethwaite, 1870–1955" (obituary). *El Palacio*
62 (10): 293–95.

Review of *Clay Figurines of the American Southwest, with a Description of the New Pillings Find in Northeastern Utah and
a Comparison with Certain Other North American Figurines*
by Noel Morse. Papers of the Peabody Museum of American
Archaeology and Ethnology, no. 49 (1). *El Palacio* 62 (10):
298–305.

"Archaeology." *Annual Report of the School of American Research.*
pp. 49–53.

1956 "Rare Glaze I-Yellow Potsherd from San Cristobal." *El Palacio* 63
(2): 35.

"A Prehistoric Stone Elbow Pipe from the Taos Area." *El Palacio* 63
(2): 67–68.

"Prehistoric Pueblo Indian Cache Exhibited." *El Palacio* 63 (5–8):
145.

"Old Palace Well Restored." *El Palacio* 63 (5–8): 249–50.

"William Wallace Postlethwaite Memorial Dedication, Colorado
College Museum." *El Palacio* 63 (5–8): 250.

"Some Clay and Stone Figurines from the Mogollon-Mimbres Area,
Luna County, New Mexico." *El Palacio* 63 (9–10): 259–83.

"Biennial Meeting of the Archaeological Society of New Mexico to
be Held in January." *El Palacio* 63 (11–12): 332.

"Archaeology." *Annual Report of the School of American Research.*
pp. 45–47.

1957 "Mogollon-Mimbres Exhibition Opened in Palace of the Governors." *El Palacio* 64 (1–2): 29–40.

"Biennial Meeting of the Archaeological Society of New Mexico." *El
Palacio* 64 (1–2): 40–42.

"A Rare Stone Humpbacked Figure from Pecos Pueblo, New Mexico." *El Palacio* 64 (3–4): 93–108.

"Sherman S. Howe" (obituary). *El Palacio* 64 (11–12): 366.

"Palace of the Governors." *Annual Report of the School of American
Research.* pp. 29–30.

1958 "Erwin and Kelly Collections Come to Museum." *El Palacio* 65 (4):
156.

"The Curators Say." *El Palacio* 65 (4): 157–58.

"Harroun Family Memorabilia Received as a Gift." *El Palacio* 65 (6): 239–40.

"Museum Exhibits Tell Story of Man in the Southwest." *Santa Fe Scene*, September 20, 1958. p. 19.

"A Pottery Bell from Northwestern New Mexico." *American Antiquity* 24 (2): 184–85.

"Palace of the Governors: Archaeology." *Annual Report of the School of American Research.* pp. 29–30.

1959 "Education Through Exhibition, Part I." *Santa Fe Scene*, April 4, p. 12.

"Education Through Exhibition, Part II." *Santa Fe Scene*, April 11, p. 14.

1961 (with Richard Ambler) "A Survey and Excavation of Caves in Hidalgo County, New Mexico." *School of American Research Monograph*, no. 25. Santa Fe.

"John Champe, A Founder of the Plains Conference." *Plains Anthropologist* 6–12, pt. 1, pp. 73–75.

"Karl Ruppert." *American Antiquity* 27 (1): 101–3.

Man the Hunter. Catalog and text for MOIFA-MNM Traveling Exhibit.

1963 "Alfred Vincent Kidder, Sr., 1885–1963" (obituary). *El Palacio* 70 (3): 36–39.

Review of *The Sculpture of Ancient Mexico. La Ecultura del Mexico Antigua* by Paul Westheim. Garden City, N.Y.: Anchor Books, Doubleday & Company (1963). *American Antiquity* 29 (2): 252.

Review of *Papago Indian Pottery* by Bernard Fontana et al. *Ethnohistory Magazine* pp. 301–3.

1965 *Southwestern Indians Today: A Gallery Guide.* Santa Fe: Museum of New Mexico Press.

"San Jose de los Jemes Mission Church and Monastery." Leaflet for distribution at Jemez State Monument.

1966 "Pueblo Indian Pottery: Materials, Tools, and Techniques." *Popular Series Pamphlet*, no. 5. Santa Fe: Museum of New Mexico Press.

The Rain Cloud Callers. Catalog for a special exhibition at the Fine Arts Museum, June 5–July 24, 1966. Santa Fe: Museum of New Mexico Press.

"A Unique Kokopelli Jar." *El Palacio* 73 (2): 21–25.

"Lucy M. Lewis—Pottery of Acoma." *The Quarterly of the Southwestern Association for Indian Arts, Inc.* Summer 3 (3).

Thirty-Ninth Pecos Conference of Southwestern Anthropologists.
El Palacio 73 (3): 47.

1967 "Excavations at Twin Hills Site, Santa Fe County, New Mexico: A
Preliminary Report of Research Conducted on LA 8866." *Laboratory of Anthropology Notes*, 45. Santa Fe.

Review of *This Land Was Theirs: A Study of North American Indians* by Wendell H. Oswalt. New York: John Wiley & Sons (1966).
El Palacio 74 (1): 44–45.

"A Kokopelli Effigy Pitcher from Northwestern New Mexico." *American Antiquity* 32 (3): 398–401.

"A Unique Prehistoric Anasazi Pipe." *El Palacio* 74 (4): 41–42.

Review of *Ancient Hunters of the Far West* by Malcolm J. Rogers,
ed. Richard F. Pourade. San Diego: Union Tribune Publishing Co.
(1966). *El Palacio* 74 (4): 39–40.

Winter Scenes from Pueblo and Navajo Land in *Winter Solstice*.
Albuquerque: Museum of Albuquerque. pp. 5–8.

1968 Review of *The Excavation of Hawikuh* by Frederick Webb Hodge—
Report of the Hendricks-Hodge Expedition, 1917–23. Contributions from the Museum of the American Indian, Heye Foundation. Vol. 20, by Watson Smith, Nathalie and Richard Woodbury.
Contribution by Ross Montgomery. New York (1966). *El Palacio*
75 (1): 46–48.

1969 "Casas Grandes: Bygone Metropolis of the Gran Chichimecas."
In *Twentieth Field Conference of the Geological Society of New Mexico*, eds. Diego A. Córdoba, Sherman A. Wengerd and John
Shoemaker. Albuquerque: University of New Mexico Press. pp.
56–60.

"Foreword" to *Tonque Pueblo: A Report of Partial Excavation of
an Ancient Pueblo IV Indian Ruin in New Mexico* by Franklin
Barnett. Albuquerque: Albuquerque Archaeological Society.

1972 "The Wonderful Wit of Harry Mera." *El Palacio* 76 (4): 20–30.

1973 "Christmas Day in Jemez." *El Palacio* 79 (3): 6–7.

1974 (with Martha Bogert) Review of *The Four Churches of Pecos* by
Alden Hayes. Albuquerque: University of New Mexico Press
(1974). *El Palacio* 80 (4): 46–47.

1975 Review of "Collected Papers in Honor of F. H. Ellis." *Archaeological
Society of New Mexico, Paper no. 2*. Albuquerque.

1976 "Recollections of Jesse L. Nusbaum." *Exploration Magazine*. Santa
Fe: School of American Research.

1979 "Some Thoughts on the Origin of Basketry and the Textile Arts."
Chimp Chatter 4 (3) January–February.

"Mural Decorations in the San Jose de los Jemez Mission Church."
In Collected Papers in Honor of Bertha P. Dutton. *Archaeological Society of New Mexico*, no. 4. Albuquerque.

"Pojoaque Pueblo." In *Handbook of North American Indians, Southwest*, vol. 9. Alfonso Ortiz, vol. ed. Washington, D.C.: Smithsonian Institution.

1981 "Spanish Influences on Pottery of San Jose de los Jemez and Giusewa, Jemez State Monument (LA 679), Jemez Springs, New Mexico." In Collected Papers in Honor of Erik K. Reed. pp. 215–236. *Archaeological Society of New Mexico*, no. 6. Albuquerque.

1983 "Charlie R. Steen: A Biography." In Collected Papers in Honor of Charlie R. Steen. pp. 1–11. *Archaeological Society of New Mexico*, no. 8. Albuquerque.

1985 "The Wells in the Palace of the Governors Patio and the Excavation of Well I." In Collected Papers in Honor of Albert H. Schroeder. pp. 207–22. *Archaeological Society of New Mexico*, no. 10. Albuquerque.

1986 "Alden C. Hayes: A Biography." In Collected Papers in Honor of Alden C. Hayes. pp. 1–5. *Archaeological Society of New Mexico*, no. 11. Albuquerque.

1989 "Foreword" to *I Am Here: Two Thousand Years of Southwest Indian Arts and Culture*, by Andrew Hunter Whiteford, Stewart Peckham, Rick Dillingham, Nancy Fox, and Kate Peck Kent. pp. ix. Santa Fe: Museum of New Mexico Press. p. ix.

1990 "Bits and Pieces from the Past." In *Clues to the Past: Papers in Honor of William M. Sundt. Archaeological Society of New Mexico*, no. 16. pp. 155–71. Albuquerque.

Notes

Introduction

1. Cynthia Irwin-Williams, "Women in the Field: The Role of Women in Archaeology before 1960," in *Women of Science: Righting the Record*, ed. G. Kass-Simon and Patricia Farnes (Bloomington: Indiana University Press, 1990), 1–41.

2. In their "Series Editors' Introduction" to David Browman's *Cultural Negotiations: The Role of Women in the Founding of Americanist Archaeology* (Lincoln and London: University of Nebraska, 2113), vii, Regna Darnell and Stephen O. Murray observe that "by identifying otherwise unrecognized women, this work sets a new standard for feminist archaeological historiography."

3. Nancy J. Parezo, ed., *Hidden Scholars: Women Anthropologists and the Native American Southwest* (Albuquerque: University of New Mexico Press, 1993).

4. Barbara A. Babcock and Nancy J. Parezo, *Daughters of the Desert: Women Anthropologists and the Native American Southwest 1880–1980* (Albuquerque: University of New Mexico Press, 1988).

5. See the "Introduction" to *Women in Archaeology*, ed. Cheryl Claassen (Philadelphia: University of Pennsylvania Press, 1994), 1–8.

6. From the introduction to *Women Anthropologists: A Biographical Dictionary*, eds. Ute Gacs, Aisha Khan, Jerri McIntyre, and Ruth Weinberg (New York: Greenwood Press, 1988), xvi.

7. The approach used here focuses on the incorporation of the voices of Marjorie Ferguson Lambert and other women in the development of Southwest archaeology. Marjorie's voice, noted in italics throughout the book, is based on approximately eighteen hours of tape-recorded interviews from 1990 to 1997. Direct quotes from these interviews inform most of what is written here. Overall, Marjorie's "voice" is complemented with information gleaned from literary and archival sources and taped interviews by scholars, colleagues, and friends.

8. In her two volumes on *Women Scientists in America* (Baltimore and London: Johns Hopkins University Press, 1982, 1995), Margaret Rossiter claims that the acceptance of women into the field of science "was the result of the partial convergence of two major, though essentially independent, trends in American history between 1820 and 1920. On the one hand there was the rise of higher education and expanded employment for middle-class women; on the other

there was the growth, bureaucratization, and 'professionalization' of science and technology in America."

9. Alice B. Kehoe and Mary Beth Emmerichs, eds., *Assembling the Past: Studies in the Professionalization of Archaeology* (Albuquerque: University of New Mexico Press, 1999).

10. James Snead's *Ruins and Rivals: The Making of Southwest Archaeology* (Tucson: University of Arizona Press, 2001) provides an overview of the environment in which southwestern archaeology developed and the rivalries that resulted in differing philosophies between the early relic hunters and eastern "museum men" who were collecting to fill the halls of their museums and those who were promoting their scholarly endeavors.

11. Nancy J. Parezo, "Conclusion: The Beginning of the Quest," in *Hidden Scholars*, 359–60.

12. Marjorie Lambert to Jennifer Fox, September 2, 1985.

13. This is well documented in Barbara Babcock and Nancy Parezo, *Daughters of the Desert*, and Parezo's edited volume *Hidden Scholars.*

14. Darnell and Murray, *Cultural Negotiations*, ix. This issue, along with other obstacles, is discussed by Alice B. Kehoe and other contributors to *Assembling the Past.*

15. Darnell and Murray, *Cultural Negotiations*, ix.

16. Alfred V. Kidder's "Introduction" in *Prehistoric Southwesterners from Basketmaker to Pueblo*, by Charles Avery Amsden (Los Angeles: Southwest Museum, 1949), xi–xvi.

17. J. Ned Woodall and Philip J. Perricone, "The Archaeologist as Cowboy: The Consequences of Professional Stereotypes," *Journal of Field Archaeology* 8 (1981), 506–7.

18. Linda S. Cordell, "Women Archaeologists in the Southwest," in *Hidden Scholars*, 204.

19. Joan Gero, "Socio-Politics and the Woman-at-Home Ideology," *American Antiquity* 50 (1985), 344.

20. Irwin-Williams, "Women in the Field," 25.

21. Florence Hawley Ellis to Jennifer Fox, August 4, 1985. Cited in Babcock and Parezo, *Daughters of the Desert*, 124.

22. Dorothy Keur to Jennifer Fox, August 6, 1985. Cited in Babcock and Parezo, *Daughters of the Desert*, 143.

23. Nancy Parezo and Margaret Hardin, "In the Realm of the Muses," in *Hidden Scholars*, 281–82.

24. Irwin-Williams, "Women in the Field," 25.

25. See Babcock and Parezo, *Daughters of the Desert*, 171.

26. Katherine Bartlett to Jennifer Fox, August 24, 1985. Cited in Babcock and Parezo, *Daughters of the Desert*, 172.

27. H. Marie Wormington to Jennifer Fox, August 10, 1985. Cited in Babcock and Parezo, *Daughters of the Desert*, 150.

28. Jennifer Fox, "Women Who Opened Doors," in *Hidden Scholars*, 294–310
29. Lambert to Fox, September 2, 1985.
30. See Babcock and Parezo, *Daughters of the Desert*, and Parezo, *Hidden Scholars*.
31. Hawley Ellis to Fox, August 4, 1985.
32. Babcock and Parezo, *Daughters of the Desert*, 131.
33. Shelby J. Tisdale discusses how women anthropologists who attempted to educate the public about anthropology and the Southwest through popular writings were stigmatized and peripheralized by the discipline in "Women on the Periphery of the Ivory Tower," in *Hidden Scholars*, 311–33.
34. Hawley Ellis to Fox, August 8, 1985.
35. Nancy J. Parezo and Margaret Hardin, "In the Realm of the Muses," in *Hidden Scholars*, 271.
36. Lambert to Fox, September 2, 1985.

Chapter 1

1. Marjorie Lambert was interviewed by Jennifer Fox on September 2, 1985, as part of the "Daughters of the Desert Project," directed by Barbara A. Babcock and Nancy J. Parezo. The project was sponsored by the Wenner-Gren Foundation for Anthropological Research and resulted in a conference at the University of Arizona, a traveling exhibition, and a publication, *Daughters of the Desert: Women Anthropologists and the Native American Southwest, 1880–1980*, edited by Barbara A. Babcock and Nancy J. Parezo (Albuquerque: University of New Mexico Press, 1988).
2. Margaret W. Rossiter provides an extensive history of the struggle that women had in gaining recognition in the sciences, including anthropology, in *Women Scientists in America: Struggles and Strategies to 1940*, vol. 1 (Baltimore and London: Johns Hopkins University Press, 1982). Rossiter (p. xvi) saw this change in the role of women in science as the convergence of two trends: "the emergence of women and of science," which fall "into three main periods in the United States: before 1880, 1880 to 1910, and after 1910. Of these the second period is both the most interesting and the most important, for it was then that acceptable conditions for women's presence in science were worked out. . . . By 1910, however, this period of great fluidity and innovation had ended, and new rigidity set in. Despite much protest by feminists of both sexes, women's subsequent experience in science was more one of containment within previously demarcated limits than expansion into newer and greater opportunity beyond them."
3. Lambert to Fox, September 2, 1985, with edits. Throughout this book I have incorporated Marjorie Lambert's voice based on interviews collected by various scholars and myself over the years. Direct quotes from these interviews are noted in italics. Some of the quotes are edited to convey the original intent more clearly and to make it easier for the reader. The content and structure are Marjorie Lambert's own words and true voice.
4. *Colorado Springs Gazette Telegraph*, January 25, 1965.

5.   Interview with Louise Stiver, former curator of the Museum of Indian Arts and Culture / Laboratory of Anthropology, Santa Fe, New Mexico, in 1989. James Henry Breasted was an American Egyptologist, archaeologist, and historian who promoted research on ancient Egypt and the ancient civilizations of western Asia. He was a professor at the University of Chicago, and with financial aid from John D. Rockefeller, he organized the Oriental Institute there in 1919. "James Henry Breasted, American Archaeologist," Encyclopedia Britannica, accessed January 20, 2013, http://www.britannica.com/EBchecked/topic/78551/James-Henry-Breasted.

6.   Alfred V. Kidder would have a great influence on Marjorie's archaeological career, beginning with his publication *An Introduction to the Study of Southwestern Archaeology* (New Haven, Conn.: Yale University Press, 1924).

7.   James E. Snead, *Ruins and Rivals: The Making of Southwest Archaeology* (Tucson: University of Arizona Press, 2001), xxiii.

8.   Sylvanus Griswold Morley became both mentor and friend to Marjorie, and after reading Morley's *The Inscriptions at Copan* (Washington, D.C.: Carnegie Institution of Washington, 1920), she dreamed of one day going to Mesoamerica to see the Mayan sites.

9.   The School of American Research was changed to the School for Advanced Research in the Human Condition in 2006, the second name change in its hundred-year history. For the purposes of this publication, I have chosen to use School of American Research where appropriate, which was the name of this institution throughout Marjorie's association with it.

10. Alice B. Kehoe, "Introduction," in *Assembling the Past: Studies in the Professionalization of Archaeology*, eds. Alice B. Kehoe and Mary Beth Emmerichs (Albuquerque: University of New Mexico Press, 1999), 6.

11. Lambert to Fox, September 2, 1985, with edits.

12. Two years before Colorado became a state, Colorado College was established as a coeducational institution in 1874. The driving force behind the founding of the college was the combination of Christian outreach and the development of the railroad. General William Jackson Palmer, founder of the Denver and Rio Grande Railroad, reserved land and contributed funds for a college in the new city of Colorado Springs located along its north-south line.

13. For an overview of Hewett and his relationship with the "Eastern Establishment" and Harvard University, see Don D. Fowler's contribution "Harvard vs. Hewett: The Contest for Control of Southwestern Archaeology, 1904–1930," in Kehoe and Emmerich, *Assembling the Past*, 161–211.

14. Don D. Fowler, *A Laboratory for Anthropology: Science and Romanticism in the American Southwest, 1846–1930* (Albuquerque: University of New Mexico Press, 2000), 265–68. For more on Hewett's 1907 summer field schools in southwest Colorado, see Snead, *Ruins and Rivals*, 85.

15. Lambert to Fox, September 2, 1985.

16. Lambert to Fox, September 2, 1985.

17. Lambert to Stiver, November 11, 1989.
18. Lambert to Fox, September 2, 1985.
19. Lambert to Fox, September 2, 1985.
20. Lambert to Tisdale, July 10, 1997.
21. Malinda Elliott, *The School of American Research: A History, The First Eighty Years* (Santa Fe: School of American Research, 1987), 30–31.

Chapter 2

1. Lambert to Fox, September 2, 1985.
2. Don D. Fowler, *A Laboratory for Anthropology: Science and Romanticism in the American Southwest, 1846–1930* (Albuquerque: University of New Mexico Press, 2000), 261.
3. Malinda Elliott, *The School of American Research: A History, The First Eighty Years* (Santa Fe, N.M.: School of American Research, 1987), 20.
4. Elliott, *The School of American Research*, 21.
5. Fowler, *A Laboratory for Anthropology*, 268.
6. Elliott, *The School of American Research*, 21.
7. Lambert to Stiver, November 1, 1989.
8. Lambert to Tisdale during an interview with Katherine Halpern, Courtney Reeder Jones, and Marjorie Lambert in Santa Fe, New Mexico, on July 3, 1997.
9. Lambert to Tisdale, July 3, 1997.
10. Michael L. Elliott reports that the "greatest period of archaeological and ethnological activity and investigation in the Jemez area was from the 1910s through the 1930s. Representatives of the School of American Archaeology (School of American Research), the Museum of New Mexico, the Bureau of American Ethnology, The Royal Ontario Museum of Archaeology, and the Museum of New Mexico all performed fieldwork, including both surveys and excavations." Michael L. Elliott, "Large Pueblo Sites Near Jemez Springs, New Mexico," *Cultural Resources Report 3* (Santa Fe National Forest, November 1982), 6.
11. "Summer Field School," *El Palacio* 24, no. 2. (August 25, 1930), 80.
12. Edwin Ferdon, cited in Carol A. Gifford and Elizabeth A. Morris, "Digging for Credit: Early Archaeological Field Schools in the American Southwest," *American Antiquity* 50, no. 2. (April 1985), 406.
13. Lambert to Tisdale, August 6, 1997.
14. "Summer Field School," 81.
15. Jane Howard, *Margaret Mead: A Life* (New York: Simon and Schuster, 1984).
16. Lambert to Tisdale, August 6, 1997.
17. "Summer Field School," 79–80.
18. "Digs," *El Palacio* 35, no. 5–6 (1933), 40–41.
19. Paul Reiter, "The Jemez Pueblo of Unshagi, New Mexico: With Notes of the Earlier Excavations at Amoxiumqua and Giusewa." Part I and II, Monograph Series, vol. 1, no. 5, University of New Mexico and the School of American Research (Albuquerque: University of New Mexico Press, 1938), 42.

20. Michael L. Elliott, "Overview and Synthesis of the Archaeology of the Jemez Province, New Mexico," *Archaeology Notes* 51 (Santa Fe: Museum of New Mexico Office of Archeological Studies, 1986), 17.

21. Lambert to Tisdale, August 6, 1997.

22. Michael L. Elliot noted that Reiter reported, "One hundred and ninety-one burials were recovered from Unshagi. . . . Seventy-eight (41 percent) of the skeletons were infants and children." Reiter, "The Jemez Pueblo of Unshagi, New Mexico," 20.

23. Lambert to Fox, September 2, 1985, with edits.

24. Lambert to Tisdale, August 6, 1997.

25. Hartley Burr Alexander was a well-known philosophy professor from Scripps College in Claremont, California. He published two volumes in the *Mythology of All Races* series, a thirteen-volume book series edited by Louis Herbert Gray from 1916 to 1932 and published by Marshall Jones Company in Boston. Volume 10 on North America, published in 1916, focused on Native American mythology and volume 11, published in 1920, focused on Latin America.

26. Lambert to Tisdale, August 6, 1997.

27. Jeanne O. Snodgrass, *American Indian Painters: A Biographical Directory* (New York: Museum of the American Indian, Heye Foundation, 1968), 192–93; Clara Lee Tanner, *Southwest Indian Painting: A Changing Art*, 2nd ed. (Tucson: University of Arizona Press, 1973), 164–67.

28. Lambert to Fox, September 2, 1985.

29. Lambert to Tisdale, August 6, 1997.

30. Reiter, "The Jemez Pueblo of Unshagi, New Mexico," 81.

31. Elliott, "Overview and Synthesis of the Archaeology of the Jemez Province, New Mexico," 21.

32. Lambert to Tisdale, August 6, 1997.

33. Lambert to Tisdale, August 6, 1997.

34. Lambert to Tisdale, August 6, 1997.

35. Lambert to Tisdale, August 6, 1997.

36. Marjorie F. Lambert, "A Pottery Bell from Northwestern New Mexico," *American Antiquity* 24, no. 2 (1958), 184–85.

Chapter 3

1. Douglas W. Schwartz, "Foreword," in "New Light on Chaco Canyon," ed. David Grant Noble, *Exploration* (SAR Annual Bulletin, 1984), ix.

2. David Grant Noble, "New Light on Chaco Canyon," ed. David Grant Noble, *Exploration* (SAR Annual Bulletin, 1984).

3. Out of respect for living Native peoples in the Southwest, I use their preferred term *Ancestral Puebloan* to refer to the cultural group that has been referred to in earlier archaeological literature as the *Anasazi*. The only time *Anasazi* may appear is in a direct quote from earlier publications.

4. See Snead, *Ruins and Rivals*.

5. Don D. Fowler, "Harvard vs. Hewett: The Contest for Control of Southwestern Archaeology, 1904–1930," in *Assembling the Past: Studies in the Professionalization of Archaeology*, ed. Alice B. Kehoe and Mary Beth Emmerichs (Albuquerque: University of New Mexico Press, 1999), 165–66.

6. Fowler. "Harvard vs. Hewett," 185. Also see Peter Hare, *A Woman's Quest for Science: A Portrait of Anthropologist Elsie Clews Parsons* (Buffalo, N.Y.: Prometheus Books, 1985); Delsey Deacon, *Elsie Clews Parsons: Inventing Modern Life* (Chicago and London: University of Chicago Press, 1997); Babcock and Parezo, *Daughters of the Desert*; Nancy J. Parezo, ed., *Hidden Scholars*; and Margaret M. Caffrey, *Ruth M. Benedict: Stranger in a Strange Land* (Austin: University of Texas Press, 1989).

7. Fowler, "Harvard vs. Hewett," 185.

8. Fowler, "Harvard vs. Hewett," 189–90.

9. *Field School Announcements* (1929), 7, 8, 11, cited in Carol Joiner, "The Boys and Girls of Summer: The University of New Mexico Archaeological Field School in Chaco Canyon," *Journal of Anthropological Research* 48 (1992), 51.

10. See Barbara J. Mills, "Cultural Matters: The Impact of Field Schools on Southwest Archaeology," in *Southwest Archaeology in the Twentieth Century*, eds. Linda S. Cordell and Don D. Fowler (Salt Lake City: The University of Utah Press, 2005), 60–80; Carol Joiner, "The Boys and Girls of Summer: The University of New Mexico Archaeological Field Schools in Chaco Canyon," *Journal of Anthropological Research* 48 (1992), 49–66; and Frances Joan Mathien, "Women of Chaco: Then and Now," in *Rediscovering Our Past: Essays on the History of American Archaeology*, ed. Jonathan E. Reyman (Aldershot, U.K.: Avebury Press, 1992), 103–30.

11. Barbara A. Babcock and Nancy J. Parezo, *Daughters of the Desert: Women Anthropologists and the Native American Southwest* (Albuquerque: University of New Mexico, 1988), 128.

12. Babcock and Parezo, *Daughters of the Desert* (1988), 57.

13. Katherine Spencer Halpern participated in a taped interview with Shelby Tisdale, along with Courtney Reeder Jones and Marjorie Lambert, in Santa Fe on July 3, 1997.

14. Babcock and Parezo, *Daughters of the Desert* (1988), 63.

15. Halpern to Tisdale, July 3, 1997.

16. Malcolm Carr, Katherine Spencer, and Dorianne Wooley, "Navaho Clans and Marriage at Pueblo Alto," *American Anthropologist* 41, no. 2 (1939), 245–57.

17. Halpern to Tisdale, July 3, 1997.

18. Jones to Tisdale, July 3, 1997.

19. Jones to Tisdale, July 3, 1997.

20. Jones to Tisdale, July 3, 1997.

21. Jones to Tisdale, July 3, 1997. The letters that Courtney Reeder Jones wrote during this time are published in *Letters from Wupatki*, ed. Lisa Rappaport (Tucson: University of Arizona Press, 1995).

22. Lambert to Tisdale, August 6, 1997.
23. Lambert to Tisdale, August 6, 1997.
24. Lambert to Tisdale, August 6, 1997.
25. Lambert to Tisdale, August 6, 1997.
26. Lambert to Tisdale, August 6, 1997.
27. Lambert to Tisdale, August 6, 1997.
28. Lambert to Tisdale, August 6, 1997.
29. Lambert to Tisdale, August 6, 1997.
30. Annual Report of the School of American Research (1931), 21. Marjorie was also mentioned as having taken her master's exam at Chaco Canyon that year in "Summer Field School at Chaco Canyon," *El Palacio* 31, no. 3 (July 22, 1931), 31.
31. "Summer Field School at Chaco Canyon." (1931), 31.
32. Lambert to Tisdale, July 25, 1990.
33. Marjorie Ferguson, "The Acculturation of Sandia Pueblo," unpublished master's thesis, University of New Mexico (1931).
34. Ferguson, "The Acculturation of Sandia Pueblo," 56.
35. Lambert to Fox, September 2, 1985.
36. Marjorie E. Ferguson, "A Study of the Architecture of the Chaco Canyon Indians, the Province of Tusayan, and the Indians of the Seven Cities of Cibola," Chaco Canyon Archives, University of New Mexico.

Chapter 4

1. Linda Cordell, "Women Archaeologists in the Southwest," in *Hidden Scholars: Women Anthropologists and the Native American Southwest*, ed. Nancy Parezo (Albuquerque: University of New Mexico Press, 1993), 214.
2. The Laboratory of Anthropology was incorporated in 1927 with a pledge of funds from John D. Rockefeller to construct a building designed by architect John Gaw Meem and to support five years of operation. Hewett, who had been primarily focused on institution building in the Southwest, could not take credit for this project. Instead, it was Jesse L. Nusbaum and Kenneth Chapman who were instrumental in getting the Laboratory underway. For an overview of the history of the Laboratory of Anthropology's first fifty years, see the special issue of *El Palacio*, vol. 87, no. 3 (Fall 1981). Of course no one could have predicted the impact the Great Depression would have on the future of the LAB, but after fifteen years of management by scientists and scholars and barely making ends meet, it became a unit of the Museum of New Mexico in 1947. It has been supported by the state of New Mexico since and is now part of the Museum of Indian Arts and Culture.
3. Don D. Fowler, *A Laboratory for Anthropology: Science and Romanticism in the American Southwest, 1846–1930* (Albuquerque: University of New Mexico Press, 2000), 262.
4. Lansing B. Bloom, "Edgar Lee Hewett: His Biography and Writings to Date," in *So Love the Works of Men, Seventieth Volume Honoring Edgar Lee Hewett*, eds.

Donald D. Brand and Fred E Harvey (Albuquerque: University of New Mexico, 1939), 13–34. Also see Beatrice Chauvenet, *Hewett and Friends: A Biography of Santa Fe's Vibrant Era* (Santa Fe: Museum of New Mexico Press, 1983); Fowler, "Harvard vs. Hewett"; Fowler, *A Laboratory of Anthropology*; Snead, *Ruins and Rivals*; James E. Snead, "Paradigms, Professionals, and the Making of Southwest Archaeology, 1910–1920," in *Southwest Archaeology in the Twentieth Century*, eds. Linda S. Cordell and Don D. Fowler (Salt Lake City: University of Utah Press, 2005), 27–46; Jeffrey Allen Thomas, "Promoting the Southwest: Edgar Lee Hewett, Anthropology, Archaeology and the Santa Fe Style," unpublished PhD dissertation, Department of History, Texas Tech University, Lubbock, 1999; and Raymond H. Thompson, "Edgar Lee Hewett and the Political Process," *Journal of the Southwest* 42, no. 2 (2000), 271–318.

5. Fowler, *A Laboratory for Anthropology*, 262–63. In her biography on Edgar L. Hewett, Beatrice Chauvenet describes Hewett's relationship with Frank Springer and his disappointment when he was dismissed by the Board of Regents in 1903. Beatrice Chauvenet, *Hewett and Friends: A Biography of Santa Fe's Vibrant Era* (Santa Fe: Museum of New Mexico Press, 1983), 47.

6. New Mexico Normal School was changed to New Mexico Normal University in 1902, and then to New Mexico Highlands University in 1941.

7. Marjorie Ferguson, "Preliminary Report on the Tecolote Ruin," *El Palacio* 34, no. 25–26 (1933), 196–98.

8. Lambert to Tisdale, August 6, 1997.

9. Marjorie Ferguson, Unpublished "Report of Marjorie Ferguson, Research Fellow," report in the files of the Laboratory of Anthropology Archives, Santa Fe, N.M., n.d.

10. Ferguson, "Preliminary Report."

11. Severin Fowles and B. Sunday Eiselt, "Apache, Tiwa and Back Again: Ethnic Shifting in the American Southwest," in *The Continuous Path: Pueblo Movement and the Archaeology of Becoming*, eds. Samuel Duwe and Robert W. Preucel (Tucson: University of Arizona Press, 2019), 166–94.

12. Lambert to Tisdale, July 20, 1990.

13. These monuments were part of a system established in 1931 with the passage of the Preservation of the Scientific Resources of New Mexico. See Nancy Owen Lewis and Kay Leigh Hagan, *A Peculiar Alchemy: A Centennial History of the School of American Research, 1907–2007* (Santa Fe: School for Advanced Research, 2007), 46. New Mexico's State Monuments were renamed New Mexico Historic Sites when the State Legislature passed SB70 in 2013.

14. Lewis and Owen, *A Peculiar Alchemy*, 47.

15. Edgar L. Hewett, Annual Report of the School of American Research (1934).

16. Marc Simmons, "History of Pueblo-Spanish Relations to 1821," in *Handbook of North American Indians, Southwest*, vol. 9, ed. Alfonso Ortiz (Washington, D.C.: Smithsonian Institution, 1979), 179, notes that Tiguex was a cluster of twelve southern Tiwa Pueblos along the Rio Grande River north of Bernalillo,

New Mexico. It was here that Coronado camped during the winter of 1540–41. The depredations against the Tiwas were so severe that many abandoned their homes in the middle of the winter, resulting in the virtual depopulation of Tiguex Province.

17. Albert H. Schroeder, "Pueblos Abandoned in Historic Times," in *Handbook of North American Indians, Southwest*, vol. 9, ed. Alfonso Ortiz (Washington, D.C.: Smithsonian Institution, 1979), 242. For more recent information on the location of this pueblo, see Bradley J. Vierra and Stanley M. Hordes, "Let the Dust Settle: A Review of the Coronado Campsite in the Tiguex Province," in *The Coronado Expedition to Tierra Nueva: The 1540–1542 Route Across the Southwest*, eds. Richard Flint and Shirley Cushing Flint (Boulder: University Press of Colorado, 1997), 249–61.

18. Marjorie Tichy, "Observations on a Mission Uncovered at Puaray," *El Palacio* 41 (1936), 65.

19. Marjorie Tichy, "The Archaeology of Puaray," *El Palacio* 46, no. 7 (1939), 147.

20. Tichy, "Observations on a Mission," 66.

21. Tichy, "The Archaeology of Puaray," 154.

22. David Grant Noble, *Ancient Ruins of the Southwest: An Archaeological Guide* (Flagstaff, Ariz.: Northland Press, 1981), 133.

23. Annual Report of the School of American Research (1934).

24. Lambert to Tisdale, August 6, 1997.

25. Lambert to Tisdale, August 6, 1997.

26. Annual Report of the School of American Research (1935).

27. Marjorie Tichy, Annual Report of the School of American Research (1935).

28. Lambert to Tisdale, August 6, 1997.

29. Michael Elliott, "Large Pueblo Sites Near Jemez Springs, New Mexico," *Cultural Resources Report 3* (Santa Fe: Santa Fe National Forest, Southwest Region, November 1982), 4. George P. Hammond and Agapito Rey, *Narratives of the Coronado Expedition 1540–1542* (Albuquerque: University of New Mexico Press, 1940). For a description of the area and a history of excavations in the Jemez Province, see Michael L. Elliott's "Overview and Synthesis of the Archaeology of the Jémez Province, New Mexico," *Archaeology Notes 51* (Santa Fe: Museum of New Mexico Office of Archaeological Studies, 1986), and Paul Reiter's "The Jemez Pueblo of Unshagi, New Mexico: With Notes on the Earlier Excavations at 'Amoxiumqua' and Giusewa. Part 1," *The University of New Mexico Bulletin* 1, no. 4 (June 1, 1938).

30. Elliott, "Large Pueblo Sites of Jemez Springs," 4.

31. Lambert to Tisdale, August 6, 1997.

32. Marjorie F. Lambert, "Spanish Influence on the Pottery of San Jose de los Jemez and Giusewa, Jemez State Monument (LA 679), Jemez Springs, New Mexico," in "Collected Works in Honor of Erik Kellerman Reed," *Papers of the Archaeological Society of New Mexico* 6 (1981), 215–36.

33. Annual Report of the School of American Research (1936).

34. Marjorie Ferguson Tichy, "The Excavation of Paa-ko Ruin: A Preliminary Report," *El Palacio* 42 (January–June 1937), ff. 110.

35. Cordell, "Women Archaeologists," 214.

36. Information based on the Galisteo Basin Archaeological Sites Protection Act website, www.galisteo.nmarchaeology.org, accessed on February 24, 2022.

37. Lambert to Tisdale, August 6, 1997.

38. Lambert to Tisdale, August 6, 1997.

39. Lambert to Tisdale, August 6, 1997.

40. Nels C. Nelson, a University of California student hired by Clark Wissler of the American Museum of Natural History, excavated numerous sites in the northern Southwest over a six-year period in the 1910s. Paa-ko was one of the sites Nelson excavated. Nelson's use of stratigraphy to develop site chronologies no doubt had influenced Marjorie's use of this technique in her own field methodology. See Nels Nelson, "Chronology of the Tano Ruins," *American Anthropologist* 18 (1916), 159–80.

41. Marjorie F. Lambert, "Paa-ko, Archaeological Chronicle of an Indian Village in North Central New Mexico" (Parts I–V); "The Physical Type of the Paa-ko Population" (Part VI), by Spencer Rogers, *School of American Research Monograph, No. 19* (1954).

42. Lambert to Tisdale, August 6, 1997.

43. Lambert to Tisdale, July 20, 1990.

44. Lambert to Tisdale, August 6, 1997.

45. Tichy, "The Excavation of Paa-ko Ruin"; Marjorie Ferguson Tichy, "A Preliminary Account of the Excavation of Paa-ko, San Antonito, New Mexico," *New Mexico Anthropologist* 1, no. 5 (1937), 73–77; "The Kivas of Paako and Kuaua," *New Mexico Anthropologist* 11, no. 4–5 (1938), 71–80, and "Yesterday's People," *New Mexico Magazine* 17, no. 1 (1939), 12–13, 40.

46. Tichy, "The Kivas of Paako."

47. Lambert to Tisdale, August 6, 1997.

48. Cordell, "Women Archaeologists," 214.

49. Quoted in Lewis and Hagan, *A Peculiar Alchemy*, 47.

50. Malinda Elliott, *The School of American Research: A History, The First Fifty Years* (Santa Fe, N.M.: School of American Research, 1987), 28; also see Lewis and Hagan, *A Peculiar Alchemy*, 40.

51. Lambert to Tisdale, August 6, 1997

52. Lambert to Tisdale, August 6, 1997.

53. Lambert to Tisdale, July 31, 1997.

54. Lambert to Tisdale, July 20, 1990.

55. Tsankawi is an Ancestral Puebloan site located in a detached part of Bandelier National Monument near White Rock, New Mexico. A self-guided 1.5-mile loop trail provides access to numerous Ancestral Puebloan sites, caves carved into soft tuff, and rock art.

56. Lambert to Tisdale, July 31, 1991.

57. Lambert to Tisdale, July 20, 1990.
58. Cordell, "Women Archaeologists," 214.

Chapter 5

1. Lambert to Tisdale, July 25, 1990.
2. Lambert to Fox, September 2, 1985.
3. Lambert to Tisdale, August 6, 1997.
4. Lambert to Fox, September 2, 1985, cited in Nancy J. Parezo and Margaret A. Hardin, "In the Realm of the Muses," in *Hidden Scholars: Women Anthropologists and the Native American Southwest*, ed. Nancy Parezo (Albuquerque: University of New Mexico Press, 1993), 270–93.
5. Lambert to Tisdale, July 25, 1990.
6. Parezo and Hardin, "In the Realm of the Muses" (1993), 271. See Parezo and Hardin for an extensive discussion of the role that museums have played in providing employment to women anthropologists outside of the academy.
7. Lambert to Tisdale, July 25, 1990.
8. Lambert to Tisdale, July 25, 1990.
9. Parezo and Hardin, "In the Realm of the Muses," 281–82.
10. Lambert to Fox, September 2, 1985.
11. Lambert to Fox, September 2, 1985.
12. Marjorie's detailed report in the School of American Research (SAR) Annual Report (1939), 10–12, provides many details of her year's work in collections management and the nine special exhibitions that were installed that year.
13. Marjorie F. Tichy, SAR Annual Report (1943), 13.
14. Tichy, SAR Annual Report (1943), 13.
15. Tichy, SAR Annual Report (1943), 13.
16. *The Santa Fean* (1981), 39.
17. Lambert to Tisdale, July 25, 1990.
18. In 1937 the New Mexico State Legislature enacted a statute that provided for the distribution of the Museum of New Mexico collections to established branches in various towns throughout the state. Edgar L. Hewett, SAR Annual Report (1939), 13–14.
19. Hewett, SAR Annual Report (1939), 13–14.
20. Hewett, SAR Annual Report (1941), 21.
21. Tichy, SAR Annual Report (1942), 10–11.
22. Tichy, SAR Annual Report (1942), 10–11.
23. Tichy, "Changes in Historical Exhibits," *El Palacio* 49, no. 8 (1942), 170–72; "Further Museum Reinstallations in Governor's Palace," *El Palacio* 49, no. 11 (1942), 247–48.
24. Tichy, SAR Annual Report (1943), 12–13.
25. Marjorie Ferguson Tichy, "The Kivas of Paako and Kuaua," *New Mexico Anthropologist* 2, nos. 4 and 5 (1938), 71–80.
26. Lambert to Tisdale, July 10, 1997.

27. Lambert to Fox, September 2, 1985.
28. Marjorie F. Tichy, "The Archaeology of Puaray," *El Palacio* 46 (1939), 145–63.
29. Marjorie F. Tichy, "Yesterday's People," *New Mexico Magazine* 17, no. 1 (1939), 12–13, 40.
30. Marjorie F. Tichy, "New Pots for Old . . . ," *New Mexico Magazine* 18, no. 3 (1940), 16–17, 39–40.
31. Marjorie Ferguson (Tichy) Lambert, "Coronado Monument—Kuaua Ruins," "The Kuaua Frescoes," "Puaray (Bandelier) Ruins," and "Paako Ruins," in *Landmarks of New Mexico*, eds. Edgar L. Hewett and Wayne L. Mauzy (Albuquerque and Santa Fe: The University of New Mexico Press and the School of American Research, 1940), 78–83, 90–91. The book was reprinted in 1953, and Marjorie changed her initials at the end of each section to M.F.L. since she was by then married to Jack Lambert and she had taken his name.
32. Hewett, SAR Annual Report (1941), 21.
33. Marjorie F, Tichy, "Taakaa, Pueblo Indian Dwarf," *El Palacio* 51 (January–December 1944), 21–25.
34. Marjorie F. Tichy, "A Penetrating Study of Old Oraibi. Review of 'Old Oraibi: A Study of the Hopi Indians of Third Mesa,' by Mischa Titiev, *Papers of the Peabody Museum of Archaeology and Ethnology*, vol. 22, no. 1. Harvard University (1944)," *El Palacio* 51, no. 6 (1944), 114–17; "Autobiography of a Hopi Indian. Review of *Sun Chief*, ed. by Leo Simmons (New Haven, Conn.: Yale University Press, 1942)," *El Palacio* 51, no. 1 (1944), 15–17; and "Outworn Nomenclature of Archaeology. Review of article by T. A. Richards in American Journal of Archaeology (Spring 1944)," *El Palacio* 51, no. 8 (1944), 146–47.
35. Marjorie F. Tichy, "The Distribution of Early Elbow Pipes," *El Palacio* 52, no. 4 (1945), 70–73.
36. Tichy, SAR Annual Report (1939), 13.
37. David Grant Noble, *Ancient Ruins of the Southwest: An Archaeological Guide* (Flagstaff, Ariz.: Northland Press, 1981), 136–38.
38. Tichy, SAR Annual Report (1946), 9–10.
39. Lambert to Tisdale, August 6, 1997.
40. Lambert to Tisdale, August 6, 1997.
41. Stanley A. Stubbs, Bruce T. Ellis, and Alfred E. Dittert Jr., "Lost Pecos Church," *El Palacio* 64 (1957), 67–92.
42. Lambert to Tisdale, August 6, 1997.
43. Marjorie F. Lambert, "A Bare Stone Humpbacked Figurine from Pecos Pueblo, New Mexico," *El Palacio* 64, no. 3–4 (1957), 93–108.
44. Tichy, SAR Annual Report (1944), 9.
45. Marjorie F. Tichy, "Annual Feast Day at Tsia Pueblo," *El Palacio* 52 (1945), 11–13.
46. Hewett, SAR Annual Report (1944), 5.
47. Nancy Fox, "Marjorie Ferguson Lambert: A Brief Biography," in "Collected Papers in Honor of Marjorie Ferguson Lambert," ed. Albert Schroeder, *Papers of the Archaeological Society of New Mexico* 3 (1976), 3.

48. Lambert to Tisdale, July 24, 1997.
49. Lambert to Tisdale, August 6, 1997.
50. Lambert to Tisdale, July 24, 1997.
51. Lambert to Tisdale, August 6, 1997.
52. Lambert to Tisdale, August 6, 1997.
53. Don Juan de Oñate y Salazar (1550–1626) was a Spanish Conquistador, explorer, and colonial governor of the Santa Fe de Nuevo Mexico province in the Viceroyalty of New Spain.
54. Tichy, SAR Annual Report (1944), 9
55. Marjorie F. Tichy, "Exploratory Work at Yuque Yunque," *El Palacio* 51 (1944), 224.
56. Tichy, "Exploratory Work at Yuque Yunque," 223–24.
57. Florence Hawley Ellis, *San Gabriel Del Yunque: As Seen by an Archaeologist* (Santa Fe, N.M.: Sunstone Press, 1989), 19.
58. Marjorie F. Tichy, "First Capital Suffers Further Damage," *El Palacio* 53 (1946), 324.
59. Marjorie F. Tichy, "New Mexico's First Capital," *New Mexico Historical Review* 21, no. 2 (1946), 140.
60. Ellis, *San Gabriel del Yunque*, 19.
61. Ellis, *San Gabriel del Yunque*, 88–89.
62. Tichy, SAR Annual Report (1943), 13.
63. Lambert to Tisdale, July 10, 1997.
64. Lambert to Tisdale, July 10, 1997.
65. Lambert to Tisdale, July 24, 1997.
66. Lambert to Tisdale, July 25, 1990.
67. Lambert to Tisdale, July 10, 1997.
68. Tichy, SAR Annual Report (1943), 14.
69. Lambert to Tisdale, July 31, 1997.
70. Lambert to Tisdale, July 31, 1997.
71. Lambert to Tisdale, July 31, 1997.
72. Hewett, SAR Annual Report (1944), 5.
73. Lambert to Tisdale, July 31, 1997.
74. Lambert to Tisdale, July 31, 1997.
75. Tichy, SAR Annual Report (1944), 9.
76. Lambert to Tisdale, July 31, 1997.
77. Lambert to Tisdale, July 24, 1997.
78. Lambert to Tisdale, July 24, 1997.
79. Lambert to Tisdale, July 24, 1997.
80. Marjorie F. Tichy, "New Exhibit on Ecuador," *El Palacio* 53, no. 2 (1946), 56–57.
81. Marjorie F. Tichy, "First National Bank Exhibit," *El Palacio* 53, no. 6 (1946), 166–67.
82. Tichy, SAR Annual Report (1946), 11–12.

83. Beatrice Chauvenet, *Hewett and Friends: A Biography of Santa Fe's Vibrant Era* (Santa Fe: Museum of New Mexico Press, 1983), 219–20.
84. Malinda Elliott, *The School of American Research: A History, The First Eighty Years* (Santa Fe, N.M.: School of American Research, 1987), 27.

Chapter 6

1. Lambert to Tisdale, July 24, 1997.
2. Lambert to Fox, September 2, 1985.
3. Malinda Elliott, *The School of American Research: A History, the First Fifty Years* (Santa Fe, N.M.: School of American Research, 1987), 38
4. Elliott, *The School of American Research*, 37.
5. Elliott, *The School of American Research*, 37.
6. Elliott, *The School of American Research*, 37–38.
7. Lambert to Tisdale, August 14, 1997.
8. Lambert to Tisdale, August 14, 1997.
9. Lambert to Tisdale, August 14, 1997.
10. Lambert to Tisdale, July 25, 1990.
11. Lambert to Tisdale, August 14, 1997.
12. Lambert to Tisdale, August 14, 1997.
13. Lambert to Tisdale, August 14, 1997.
14. Lambert to Fox, September 2, 1985.
15. Lambert to Fox, September 2, 1985.
16. Lambert to Tisdale, August 7, 1997.
17. Lambert to Tisdale, August 6, 1997.
18. The collaborative work between archaeologists and descendant communities has provided opportunities to learn more about the implications of movement across the landscape as more than the result of economic exchange or a response to social conflict. The ongoing contact of different populations in the past to the present has also shaped the identities of contemporary Indigenous peoples as well. See *The Continuous Path: Pueblo Movement and the Archaeology of Becoming*, eds. Samuel Duwe and Robert W. Preucel (Tucson: University of Arizona Press, 2019).
19. Marjorie F. Tichy, SAR Annual Report (1948), 31–32.
20. Tichy, SAR Annual Report (1948), 31; Marjorie F. Tichy, "Florence Dibell Bartlett Collection Opens in Old Palace," *El Palacio* 55, no. 6 (1948), 182–83. "The Florence Dibell Bartlett Collection of New Mexico Colonial Art," *El Palacio* 55, no. 7 (1948), 195–200.
21. Tichy, SAR Annual Report (1948), 32–33.
22. Tichy, SAR Annual Report (1948), 32–33.
23. The annual fiesta in Santa Fe was revived in the fall of 1919, partly to celebrate the victorious end of the war. A strong proponent of the new fiesta Hewett felt it should reflect the history and culture of Santa Fe and the Southwest. The first

fiesta under the School of American Research's sponsorship included many Indian dances. Reflecting the growing commitment of the school and many Santa Feans to the Southwest's Indian artists and craftspeople, another major cultural event was inaugurated as part of the 1922 fiesta. Santa Fe's first Indian fair, the forerunner of today's summer Indian Market, was held at the east end of the Palace of the Governors. See Malinda Elliott, *The School of American Research: A History, The First Fifty Years* (Santa Fe, N.M.: School of American Research, 1987), 29.

24. Elliott, *The School of American Research*, 32.
25. Lambert to Andrew H. Whiteford, December 10, 1984. Transcript on file at the School for Advanced Research Library.
26. Elliott, *The School of American Research*, 62–63.
27. Lambert to Tisdale, July 10, 1997.
28. Lambert to Tisdale, July 10, 1997.
29. Lambert to Tisdale, July 10, 1997.
30. Lambert to Tisdale, July 10, 1997.
31. Lambert to Tisdale, July 10, 1997.
32. Lambert to Tisdale, July 14, 1997.
33. Elliott, *The School of American Research*, 62–63.
34. Lambert to Tisdale, July 10, 1997.
35. Tichy, SAR Annual Report (1949), 35–36.
36. Tichy, SAR Annual Report (1949), 35–36.
37. Tichy, SAR Annual Report (1949), 35–36.
38. SAR Annual Report (1949), 34.
39. Lambert to Tisdale, July 24, 1997.
40. The Mogollon controversy is discussed by J. Jefferson Reid and Stephanie M. Whittlesey, "Seven Years That Reshaped Southwest Prehistory," in *Southwest Archaeology in the Twentieth Century*, eds. Linda S. Cordell and Don D. Fowler (Salt Lake City: The University of Utah Press, 2005), 47–59.
41. Lambert to Tisdale, July 24, 1997.
42. Lambert to Tisdale, July 24, 1997.
43. Lambert to Tisdale, July 24, 1997.
44. Lambert to Tisdale, July 24, 1997.
45. Lambert to Tisdale, July 24, 1997.
46. Tichy, SAR Annual Report (1949), 36.

Chapter 7

1. Linda Cordell, "Women Archaeologists in the Southwest," in *Hidden Scholars: Women Anthropologists and the Native American Southwest*, ed. Nancy J. Parezo (Albuquerque, NM: University of New Mexico Press, 1993), 214.
2. Lambert to Tisdale, July 31, 1997.
3. Lambert to Tisdale, July 31, 1997.
4. Lambert to Tisdale, July 20, 1990.

5.   Lambert to Tisdale, July 31, 1997.

6.   Lambert to Tisdale, July 31, 1997

7.   Lambert to Tisdale, July 31, 1997

8.   For more on the relationship between Jack Lambert and the Pfäffles and their work at Bishop's Ranch, see Lesley Poling-Kempes, *Ladies of the Canyons: A League of Extraordinary Women and Their Adventures in the American Southwest* (Tucson: University of Arizona Press, 2015), 223–24.

9.   Lambert to Tisdale, July 31, 1997.

10. Poling-Kempes, *Ladies of the Canyons*, 232.

11. Poling-Kempes, *Ladies of the Canyons*, 226.

12. Poling-Kempes, *Ladies of the Canyons*, 233.

13. Lambert to Fox, September 2, 1985.

14. Lambert to Tisdale, July 31, 1997.

15. Poling-Kempes, *Ladies of the Canyons*, 286.

16. Gregory Stark and E. Catherine Rayne discuss this in their publication about the White sisters, *El Delirio: The Santa Fe World of Elizabeth White* (Santa Fe, N.M.: School of American Research Press, 1998), 103. The film footage discussed here is in the New Mexico State Archives.

17. Lambert to Tisdale, July 31, 1997.

18. Stark and Rayne, *El Delirio*, 103.

19. Lambert to Tisdale, July 31, 1997. Elizabeth White established a cemetery on the estate for her dogs in 1957. The cemetery is located across the arroyo from the old kennels, near Elizabeth's and Martha's final resting place. The dogs' graves are marked by individual wooden crosses.

20. Lambert to Tisdale, July 31, 1997.

21. Marian F. Love, "An Anthropologist Meets A Cowboy," *The Santa Fean Magazine* (1981), 39.

22. Lambert to Tisdale, July 31, 1997.

23. Lambert to Fox, September 2, 1985.

24. Nancy Fox, "Marjorie Ferguson Lambert: A Brief Biography," in Collected Papers in Honor of Marjorie Ferguson Lambert, ed. Albert H. Schroeder, *Papers of the Archaeological Society of New Mexico* 3 (1976), 3–4.

25. Lambert to Tisdale, July 20, 1990.

26. Lambert to Tisdale, July 31, 1997.

27. Lambert to Tisdale, July 31, 1997.

28. Lambert to Tisdale, July 31, 1997.

29. Lambert to Tisdale, July 31, 1997.

30. Lambert to Tisdale, August 14, 1997.

31. Lambert to Tisdale, August 14, 1997.

32. Lambert to Tisdale, July 31, 1997.

33. Lambert to Tisdale, July 31, 1997.

34. Lambert to Tisdale, July 31, 1997.

35. Lambert to Tisdale, July 31, 1997.

36. Lambert to Tisdale, July 31, 1997.
37. Lambert to Tisdale, July 20, 1990.
38. Lambert to Tisdale, July 31, 1997.
39. Lambert to Fox, September 2, 1985.
40. Lambert to Tisdale, July 31, 1997.
41. For more detailed information on Jack Lambert's first marriage to Lois Pfäffle, see Lesley Poling-Kempes's overview of the Pfäffle family and their relationship with Jack Lambert in *Ladies of the Canyons*.

Chapter 8

1. Lambert to Fox, September 2, 1985.
2. Marjorie Ferguson Lambert, SAR Annual Report (1950), 40–42.
3. Lambert, SAR Annual Report (1951), 45–46.
4. Lambert, SAR Annual Report (1951), 47.
5. Lambert, SAR Annual Report (1951), 47.
6. Lambert, SAR Annual Report (1952), 51.
7. Lambert, SAR Annual Report (1952), 52.
8. Lambert, SAR Annual Report (1952), 52.
9. Marjorie F. Lambert, "The Oldest Armor Found in the United States- San Gabriel del Yunque Helmet," *Archaeology* 6, no. 2 (1953), 108–110.
10. Nancy Fox, "Marjorie Ferguson Lambert: A Brief Biography," in "Collected Papers in Honor of Marjorie Ferguson Lambert," ed. Albert H. Schroeder, *Papers of the Archaeological Society of New Mexico*, vol. 3 (1976), 3.
11. Barbara A. Babcock and Nancy J. Parezo, *Daughters of the Desert: Women Anthropologists and the Native American Southwest, 1880–1980* (Albuquerque: University of New Mexico Press, 1988), 131. Linda Cordell, "Women Archaeologists in the Southwest," in *Hidden Scholars: Women Anthropologists and the Native American Southwest*, ed. Nancy J. Parezo (Albuquerque: University of New Mexico Press, 1993), 214.
12. Marjorie F. Lambert, "Early Man in the Southwest Exhibit Installed in the Palace of the Governors," *El Palacio* 62, no. 10 (1955), 290–93.
13. Lambert, SAR Annual Report (1955), 50. Stewart Peckham, Nancy Fox, and Marjorie Lambert, "The Laboratory's Modern Era: 1947–1981," *El Palacio* 87, no. 3 (1981), 32–42.
14. Marjorie F. Lambert, "William Wallace Postlethwaite," *El Palacio* 62, no. 10 (1955), 293–95.
15. Lambert, SAR Annual Report (1955), 51.
16. Lambert, SAR Annual Report (1955), 51.
17. Lambert, SAR Annual Report (1955), 51.
18. Lambert to Tisdale, July 10, 1997.
19. Lambert to Tisdale, July 10, 1997.
20. Lambert to Tisdale, July 10, 1997.

21. "Amendments to the By-Laws of the Archaeological Society of New Mexico," *El Palacio* 62, no. 11 (1955), 339–44.

22. Lambert, SAR Annual Report (1956), 45.

23. Marjorie F. Lambert, "Some Clay and Stone Figurines from the Mogollón Mimbres Area, Luna County, New Mexico," *El Palacio* 63 (January–December 1956), 259–83.

24. Marjorie F. Lambert, "Mogollón Mimbres Exhibition Opened in Palace of the Governors," *El Palacio* 64 (January–February, 1957), 29–40.

25. Lambert to Tisdale, August 6, 1997.

26. Marjorie is referring to the work of Historical Archaeologist John L. Cotter, who wrote of his work in the east in "Archaeological Excavation of Jamestown Colonial Historical Park and Jamestown National Historic Site, Virginia," *Archaeological Research Series 4* (Washington, D.C.: National Park Service, U.S. Department of the Interior, 1958).

27. Lambert to Tisdale, August 6, 1997.

28. Lambert to Tisdale, August 6, 1997.

29. Marjorie F. Lambert, "Old Palace Well Restored," *El Palacio* 63 (January–December 1956), 249–50. "The Wells in the Palace of the Governors Patio and the Excavation and Repair of Well I. LA 4451," in "Southwest Culture History: Collected Papers in Honor of Albert H. Schroeder," *The Archaeological Society of New Mexico 10*, ed. Charles H. Lange (Santa Fe: Ancient City Press, 1985), 207–22.

30. Lambert, SAR Annual Report (1956), 46.

31. Lambert to Tisdale, August 6, 1997.

32. Lambert to Tisdale, August 6, 1997.

33. Lambert, SAR Annual Report (1957), 30.

34. Lambert to Tisdale, August 6, 1997.

35. Lambert, SAR Annual Report (1958), 29–30.

36. Oliver Seth, Minutes of the Annual Board Meeting, SAR Annual Report (1958), 11.

37. Nancy Owen Lewis and Kay Leigh Hagan, *A Peculiar Alchemy: A Centennial History of SAR 1907–2007* (Santa Fe: School for Advanced Research Press, 2007), 70; Mitchel A. Wilder, "The Museum of New Mexico: A Study of Program and Operations, November 1958," School for Advanced Research Archive, AC 34.028.

38. Frank Zinn to Alexander V. Wasson, School for Advanced Research Archive, AC 24.028.

39. "Museum Board and Directorship Now on Full State Basis," *El Palacio* 66, no. 5. (1959), 154.

40. Peckham, Fox, and Lambert, "The Laboratory's Modern Era: 1947–1981," 37.

41. Fox, "Marjorie Ferguson Lambert: A Brief Biography," 3.

42. "Marjorie F. Lambert, Dedicated Delver," *Santa Fe Scene* (1962), 6–7.

43. Lambert to Fox, September 2, 1985.

Chapter 9

1. Lambert to Tisdale, July 25, 1990.
2. Stewart Peckham, Nancy Fox, and Marjorie Lambert. "The Laboratory's Modern Era: 1947–1981," *El Palacio*, 87, no. 3 (1981), 39.
3. Malinda Elliott, *The School of American Research: A History, The First Eighty Years* (Santa Fe, N.M.: School of American Research, 1987), 44.
4. Marjorie Lambert, Minutes of the Annual Meeting of the Board of Managers, SAR Annual Report (1959), 13–14.
5. Lambert, Minutes of the Annual Meeting of the Board of Managers, SAR Annual Report (1959), 13–14.
6. Boaz Long, Minutes of the Annual Meeting of the Board of Managers, SAR Annual Report (1960), 9.
7. Lambert to Tisdale, August 6, 1997.
8. The Cosgroves are best known for the excavation of the Swarts Ruin, located in New Mexico's Mimbres Valley, which they did from 1924 to 1927. For an overview of their work there, see Harriet S. and C. Burton Cosgrove, *The Swarts Ruin: A Typical Mimbres Site in Southwestern New Mexico*, with an introduction by Steve LeBlanc (Cambridge, Mass.: Peabody Museum Press, 2011); and Harriett Silman Cosgrove, C. Burton Cosgrove, and William White Howells, "The Swarts Ruin: A Typical Site in Southwestern New Mexico: Report of the Mimbres Expedition, Seasons of 1924–1927," *Papers of the Peabody Museum of American Archaeology and Ethnology, Harvard University, Volume 15 of the Papers of the Peabody Museum* (1932).
9. Lambert to Tisdale, August 6, 1997.
10. Marjorie F. Lambert and J. Richard Ambler, *A Survey and Excavation of Caves in Hidalgo County, New Mexico*, monograph no. 25. (Santa Fe, N.M.: The School of American Research, 1961), 2.
11. Lambert and Ambler, *A Survey and Excavation of Caves in Hidalgo County*, 18.
12. Lambert and Ambler, *A Survey and Excavation of Caves in Hidalgo County*, 37–40.
13. Lambert and Ambler, *A Survey and Excavation of Caves in Hidalgo County*, 77–78.
14. Polly Schaafsma, "Tlalocs, Kachinas, Sacred Bundles and Related Symbolism in the Southwest and Mesoamerica," in *The Casas Grandes World*, eds. Curtis F. Schaafsma and Carroll L. Riley (Salt Lake City: University of Utah Press 1999), 164–92.
15. Schaafsma, "Tlalocs, Kachinas, Sacred Bundles," 165.
16. Schaafsma, "Tlalocs, Kachinas, Sacred Bundles," 168.
17. Schaafsma, "Tlalocs, Kachinas, Sacred Bundles," 170–71.
18. Schaafsma, "Tlalocs, Kachinas, Sacred Bundles," 171.
19. Lambert and Ambler, *A Survey and Excavation of Caves in Hidalgo County*, 101.
20. Lambert and Ambler, *A Survey and Excavation of Caves in Hidalgo County*, 86.

21. Edward Weyer, Minutes of the Annual Meeting of the Board of Managers, SAR Annual Report (1960), 14–15.

22. Weyer, Minutes of the Annual Meeting of the Board of Managers, SAR Annual Report (1960), 14–15.

23. Weyer, Minutes of the Annual Meeting of the Board of Managers, SAR Annual Report (1960), 15.

24. Lambert to Tisdale, August 14, 1997.

25. SAR Annual Report (1961), 10.

26. Nancy Owen Lewis and Kay Leigh Hagan, *A Peculiar Alchemy: A Centennial History of the SAR 1907–2007* (Santa Fe, N.M.: School for Advanced Research, 2007), 74.

27. Lewis and Hagan, *A Peculiar Alchemy*, 75–76.

28. Lewis and Hagan, *A Peculiar Alchemy*, 73.

29. Lewis and Hagan, *A Peculiar Alchemy*, 75–76.

30. Lambert and Ambler, *A Survey and Excavation of Caves in Hidalgo County*.

31. Lewis and Hagan, *A Peculiar Alchemy*, 73.

32. See Paul Tosa, Matthew J. Liebmann, T. J. Ferguson, and John Welch, "Movement Encased in Tradition and Stone: Hemish Migration, Land Use, and Identity," in *The Continuous Path: Pueblo Movement and the Archaeology of Becoming*, eds. Samuel Duwe and Robert W. Preucel (Tucson: University of Arizona Press, 2019), 67. They provide an excellent overview of the migrations of the Hemish people from the Four Corners area to the Jemez Valley in what is today north-central New Mexico, where they stayed and established their own identity and way of life.

33. See David Grant Noble, *Ancient Ruins of the Southwest: An Archaeological Guide* (Flagstaff, Ariz.: Northland Press, 1981), 140.

34. Joe S. Sando, *Nee Hemish: A History of Jemez Pueblo* (Santa Fe, N.M.: Clear Light Publishing, 2008), 107.

35. Noble, *Ancient Ruins of the Southwest*, 141. The only report from this project was by Lansing B. Bloom in 1923, "The Jemez Expedition of the School," *El Palacio* 14, no. 2. (1923), 15–20.

36. Marjorie F. Lambert, "Mural Decorations in San Jose De Los Jemez Mission Church, Jemez State Monument, New Mexico," in "Collected Papers in Honor of Bertha Pauline Dutton," *Papers of the Archaeological Society of New Mexico*, 4 (Albuquerque: Archaeological Press, 1979), 181.

37. David Grant Noble, *Ancient Ruins and Rock Art of the Southwest: An Archaeological Guide* (Lanham, Md.: Taylor Trade Publishing 2015), 228

38. Lambert, "Mural Decorations in San Jose De Los Jemez Mission Church," 181.

39. Marjorie F. Lambert, "Spanish Influences on the Pottery of San Jose De Los Jemez and Giusewa, Jemez State Monument (LA 679), Jemez Springs, New Mexico," in "Collected Papers in Honor of Erik Kellerman Reed," *Papers of the Archaeological Society of New Mexico*, 6 (Albuquerque: Archaeological Press, 1981), 215–36.

40. Lambert, "Spanish Influences on the Pottery of San Jose De Los Jemez and Giusewa," 233.
41. Lambert, "Spanish Influences on the Pottery of San Jose De Los Jemez and Giusewa," 233–34.
42. Marjorie F. Lambert, unpublished, "Excavations at Twin Hills Site, Santa Fe County, New Mexico. A Preliminary Report of Research Conducted at LA 8866, Project 55.05, During June 6th–26th, 1967," *Laboratory of Anthropology, note no. 45* (August 1967).
43. Lambert to Tisdale, August 6, 1997.
44. Lambert to Tisdale, August 6, 1997.

Chapter 10

1. Lambert to Tisdale, July 10, 1997.
2. Lambert to Fox, September 2, 1985.
3. Lambert to Tisdale, July 20, 1990.
4. Lambert to Tisdale, July 20, 1990.
5. For an overview of the history of the Indian Arts Research Center through 2006, see Lewis and Hagan, *A Peculiar Alchemy*, 139–53.
6. Lambert to Tisdale, August 14, 1997.
7. Lambert to Tisdale, July 10, 1997.
8. The Native American Graves Protection and Repatriation Act is a federal law passed in 1990 to provide for the repatriation and disposition of certain Native American human remains, funerary objects, sacred objects, and objects of cultural patrimony. More information on the intent of Congress in passing this law can be found in US Senate Report 101–473. For a full reading of the law and implementing regulations, visit the website of the National Park Service at www .nps.gov. There you will also find information about the National NAGPRA Review Committee, a list of federally recognized tribes, the Annual Reports to Congress, and listing of Notices that have been published in the Federal Register regarding museum inventories and notices of intent to repatriate ancestral remains and items in museum collections to tribal nations making claims.
9. Lambert to Tisdale, July 10, 1997.
10. See Shelby Tisdale, *A Proposed Repatriation Policy for the School of American Research*, unpublished master's thesis, Department of Anthropology, University of Washington, Seattle (1985). Also see an article on the same topic by Shelby Tisdale, "The Status of Repatriation in Museums in the 1980s," in *The Concepts of Sacred Materials and Their Place in the World*, ed. George Horse Capture (Cody, Wyo.: The Plains Indian Museum, Buffalo Bill Historical Society, 1989).
11. Several books have been written since the passage of the Native American Graves Protection and Repatriation Act, including Chip Colwell's *Plundered Skulls and Stolen Spirits: Inside the Fight to Reclaim Native America's Culture* (Chicago: University of Chicago Press, 2017) and Kathy S. Fine-Dare's *Grave Injustice: The American Indian Repatriation Movement and NAGPRA* (Lincoln:

University of Nebraska Press 2002). For a legislative history leading up to the passage of NAGPRA, see C. Timothy McKeown's *In the Smaller Scope of Conscience: The Struggle for National Repatriation Legislation: 1986–1990* (Tucson: University of Arizona Press, 2012).

12. Lambert to Tisdale, July 10, 1997.
13. Nancy Fox, "Marjorie Ferguson Lambert: A Brief Biography," in "Collected Papers in Honor of Marjorie Ferguson Lambert," ed. Albert H. Schroeder, *Papers of the Archaeological Society of New Mexico*, vol. 3, no. 4 (1976).
14. Lambert to Tisdale, July 10, 1997.
15. An article was published in the *Santa Fe New Mexican* on April 24, 1926, regarding the opposition of the newly formed Old Santa Fe Association. A portion of their petition in response to this opposition is printed here.
16. Lambert to Tisdale, July 10, 1997.
17. Lambert to Tisdale, July 7, 1997.
18. Lambert to Tisdale, July 10, 1997.
19. Lambert to Tisdale, July 25, 1990.
20. Lambert to Tisdale, July 31, 1997.
21. Lambert to Tisdale, July 31, 1997.
22. Lambert to Tisdale, July 31, 1997.
23. Lambert to Tisdale, July 10, 1997.
24. Lambert to Tisdale, July 10, 1997.
25. An overview of the history of the Spanish Colonial Arts Society can be found on the Museum of Spanish Colonial Art website at http://www.spanishcolonial .org.
26. Lambert to Tisdale, July 10, 1997.
27. Lambert to Tisdale, July 10, 1997.

Chapter 11

1. Lambert to Fox, September 2, 1985.
2. Nancy Fox, "Marjorie Ferguson Lambert: A Brief Biography," in "Collected Paper in Honor of Marjorie Ferguson Lambert," ed. Albert H. Schroeder, *Papers of the Archaeological Society of New Mexico*, vol. 3 (1976), 3.
3. Lambert to Fox, September 2, 1985.
4. Lambert to Tisdale, July 24, 1997.
5. Lambert to Tisdale, July 24, 1997.
6. Lambert to Tisdale, July 24, 1997.
7. Lambert to Tisdale, July 31, 1997.
8. Lambert to Fox, September 2, 1985
9. Lambert to Fox, September 2, 1985.
10. Lambert to Tisdale, July 25, 1990.
11. Lambert to Tisdale, July 24, 1997.
12. Lambert to Tisdale, July 24, 1997.
13. Lambert to Fox, September 2, 1985.

14. Lambert to Tisdale, July 25, 1990.
15. Lambert to Tisdale, July 25, 1990.
16. Lambert to Tisdale, July 24, 1997.
17. Lambert to Tisdale, July 24, 1997.
18. Lambert to Tisdale, July 24, 1997.
19. Jeanne Shutes and Jill Mellick published a biography on Geronima Cruz Montoya titled *The Worlds of P'otsūnū: Geronima Cruz Montoya of San Juan Pueblo* (Albuquerque: University of New Mexico Press, 1996).
20. Lambert to Tisdale, July 25, 1990.
21. Lambert to Tisdale, July 24, 1997.
22. Lambert to Tisdale, July 25, 1990.
23. Lambert to Tisdale, July 24, 1997.
24. Lambert to Tisdale, July 24, 1997.
25. Lambert to Tisdale, July 24, 1997.
26. Lambert to Tisdale, July 25, 1990.
27. Lambert to Tisdale, July 24, 1997.
28. Lambert to Tisdale, July 24, 1997.
29. See Donald N. Brown's "Picuris Pueblo," in *Handbook of North American Indians, Southwest*, volume 9, vol ed. Alfonso Ortiz (Washington, D.C.: Smithsonian Institution, 1979), 268.
30. Lambert to Tisdale, July 25, 1990.
31. Lambert to Tisdale, July 24, 1997.
32. Brown, "Picuris Pueblo," 274.
33. Lambert to Tisdale, July 24, 1997.
34. Lambert to Tisdale, July 24, 1997.
35. Lambert to Tisdale, July 24, 1997.
36. Lambert to Tisdale, July 24, 1997.
37. Lambert to Tisdale, July 24, 1997.
38. Lambert to Tisdale, July 24, 1997.
39. Lambert to Tisdale, July 24, 1997.
40. Lambert to Tisdale, July 24, 1997.
41. Lambert to Tisdale, July 24, 1997.

Chapter 12

1. Lambert to Fox, September 2, 1985.
2. Nancy J. Parezo and Margaret A. Hardin, "In the Realm of the Muses," in *Hidden Scholars: Women Anthropologists and the Native American Southwest*, ed. Nancy J. Parezo (Albuquerque: University of New Mexico Press, 1993), 293.
3. Lambert to Tisdale, August 14, 1997.
4. Lambert to Tisdale, August 14, 1997.
5. Lambert to Tisdale, August 14, 1997.
6. Lambert to Tisdale, August 14, 1997.
7. Lambert to Tisdale, August 14, 1997.

8.   Lambert to Fox, September 2, 1985.
9.   Lambert to Fox, September 2, 1985.
10. Lambert to Fox, September 2, 1985.
11. Frederica de Laguna, *Voyage to Greenland: A Personal Initiation into Anthropology* (New York: W. W. Norton & Company, 1977).
12. Lambert to Tisdale, August 14, 1997.
13. See Cordell's "Women in the Southwest" and Shelby J. Tisdale's "Women on the Periphery of the Ivory Tower," in *Hidden Scholars*.
14. Lambert to Tisdale, August 6, 1997.
15. Samuel Duwe and Robert W. Preucel, eds., *The Continuous Path: Pueblo Movement and the Archaeology of Becoming* (Tucson: University of Arizona Press, 2019), xi.
16. Duwe and Preucel, eds., *The Continuous Path*, xi.
17. Leigh J. Kuwanwiiwma, T. J. Ferguson, and Chip Colwell, eds., *Footprints of Hopi History: Hopihinintiput Kukveni'at* (Tucson: University of Arizona Press, 2018), ix.
18. Nancy Fox, "Marjorie Ferguson Lambert: A Brief Biography," in "Collected Papers in Honor of Marjorie Ferguson Lambert," ed. Albert H. Schroder, *Papers of the Archaeological Society of New Mexico*, vol. 3 (1976), 4.
19. Fox, "Marjorie Ferguson Lambert: A Brief Biography," 5.
20. Linda S. Cordell is citing the interview that Marjorie did with Jennifer Fox for the Daughters of the Desert Oral History Project on September 2, 1985, in Santa Fe, New Mexico. See Linda S. Cordell's chapter, "Women Archaeologists in the Southwest," in *Hidden Scholars*, 214.
21. Lambert to Tisdale, July 20, 1990.
22. Marjorie F. Lambert, "Pojoaque Pueblo," in *Handbook of North American Indians, Southwest*, vol. 9, ed. Alfonso Ortiz (Washington, D.C.: Smithsonian Institution, 1979).
23. Parezo and Hardin, "In the Realm of the Muses," in *Hidden Scholars*, 293.
24. Fox, "Marjorie Ferguson Lambert: A Brief Biography," 5.
25. Lambert to Fox, September 2, 1985.
26. Lambert to Fox, September 2, 1985.
27. Lambert to Tisdale, August 14, 1997.

Bibliography

Amsden, Charles Avery. 1949. *Prehistoric Southwesterners from Basket-Maker to Pueblo.* Los Angeles: Southwest Museum.

Anonymous. 1929. The Field School Announcements 1929. *University of New Mexico Bulletin* 41 (10), no. 156.

———. 1930. Summer Field School. *El Palacio* 24 (2): 79–81.

———. 1931. Summer Field School at Chaco Canyon. *El Palacio* 31 (3): 29–37.

———. 1962. Marjorie F. Lambert, Dedicated Delver. *The Santa Fe Scene,* June 30, pp. 4–7. (Copy on file at the Museum of New Mexico History Library).

Babcock, Barbara, and Nancy J. Parezo. 1986. The Leading Edge: Women Anthropologists in the Native American Southwest, 1880–1945. *El Palacio* 92 (1): 41–49.

———. 1988. *Daughters of the Desert: Women Anthropologists and the Native American Southwest, 1880–1980.* Albuquerque: University of New Mexico Press.

Benedict, Ruth. 1946. *Chrysanthemum and the Sword: Patterns of Japanese Culture.* New York: Houghton Mifflin Harcourt.

Bloom, Lansing B. 1939. Edgar Lee Hewett: His Biography and Writings to Date. In *So Live the Works of Men, Seventieth Anniversary Volume Honoring Edgar Lee Hewett,* edited by Donald D. Brand and Fred E. Harvey, pp. 13–34. Albuquerque: University of New Mexico Press.

Browman, David L. 2013. *Cultural Negotiations: The Role of Women in the Founding of Americanist Archaeology.* Lincoln and London: University of Nebraska.

Brown, Donald N. 1979. Picuris Pueblo. In *Handbook of North American Indians, Southwest,* vol. 9, edited by Alfonso Ortiz, pp. 268–77. Washington, D.C.: Smithsonian Institution.

Caffrey, Margaret M. 1989. *Ruth Benedict: Stranger in a Strange Land.* Austin: University of Texas Press.

Carr, Malcolm, Katherine Spencer, and Dorianne Wooley. 1939. Navaho Clans and Marriage at Pueblo Bonito. *American Anthropologist* 41 (2): 245–57.

Chase, Richard. 1959. Ruth Benedict: The Woman as Anthropologist. *Columbia University Forum* 2 (3): 19–22.

Chauvenet, Beatrice. 1983. *Hewett and Friends: A Biography of Santa Fe's Vibrant Era.* Santa Fe: Museum of New Mexico Press.

Claassen, Cheryl. 1994. Introduction. In *Women in Anthropology*, edited by Cheryl Claassen, pp. 1–8. Philadelphia: University of Pennsylvania Press.

Colwell, Chip. 2017. *Plundered Skulls and Stolen Spirits: Inside the Fight to Reclaim Native America's Culture*. Chicago: University of Chicago Press.

Cordell, Linda S. 1993. Women Archaeologists in the Southwest. In *Hidden Scholars: Women Anthropologists and the Native American Southwest*, edited by Nancy J. Parezo, pp. 202–20. Albuquerque: University of New Mexico Press.

Cordell, Linda S., and Don D. Fowler, eds. 2005. *Southwest Archaeology in the Twentieth Century*. Salt Lake City: University of Utah Press.

Cosgrove, Harriet S., and C. Burton. 2011. *The Swarts Ruin: A Typical Mimbres Site in Southwestern New Mexico*, with an introduction by Steve LeBlanc. Cambridge, Mass.: Peabody Museum Press.

Cosgrove, Harriett Silman, C. Burton Cosgrove, and William White Howells. 1932. The Swarts Ruin: A Typical Site in Southwestern New Mexico: Report of the Mimbres Expedition, Seasons of 1924–1927. *Papers of the Peabody Museum of American Archaeology and Ethnology, Harvard University*, vol. 15.

Cotter, John L. 1958. Archaeological Excavation of Jamestown Colonial Historical Park and Jamestown National Historic Site, Virginia. *Archaeological Research Series 4*. Washington, D.C.: National Park Service, U.S. Department of the Interior.

Deacon, Delsey. 1997. *Elsie Clews Parsons: Inventing Modern Life*. Chicago and London: University of Chicago Press.

De Laguna, Frederica. 1977. *Voyage to Greenland: A Personal Initiation into Anthropology*. New York: Norton & Company.

Elliott, Malinda. 1987. *The School of American Research: A History, The First Eighty Years*. Santa Fe, N.M.: School of American Research.

Elliott, Michael L. 1982. Large Pueblo Sites Near Jemez Springs, New Mexico. *Cultural Resources Report 3* (November). Santa Fe: Santa Fe National Forest.

———. 1986. Overview and Synthesis of the Archaeology of the Jémez Province, New Mexico. *Archaeology Notes 51*. Santa Fe: Museum of New Mexico Office of Archaeological Studies.

———. 1993. *New Mexico State Monument: Jémez*. Santa Fe: Museum of New Mexico Press.

Ellis, Florence Hawley. 1989. *San Gabriel del Yunque: As Seen by an Archaeologist*. Santa Fe: Sunstone Press and Florence Hawley Ellis Museum of Anthropology at Ghost Ranch, Abiquiu, New Mexico.

Ferguson, Marjorie. 1931. The Acculturation of Sandia Pueblo. Unpublished master's thesis. University of New Mexico.

———. 1931. A Study of the Architecture of the Chaco Canyon Indians, the Province of Tusayan, and the Indians of the Seven Cities of Cibola. Unpublished report. Chaco Center Archives, University of New Mexico.

———. 1933. Preliminary Report on the Tecolote Ruin. *El Palacio* 34 (25–26): 196–98.

Fine-Dare, Kathy S. 2002. *Grave Injustice: The American Indian Repatriation Movement and NAGPRA*. Lincoln: University of Nebraska.

Fowler, Don D. 1999. Harvard vs. Hewett: The Contest for Control of Southwestern Archaeology, 1904–1930. In *Assembling the Past: Studies in the Professionalization of Archaeology*, edited by Alice B. Kehoe and Mary Beth Emmerichs, pp. 165–212. Albuquerque: University of New Mexico Press.

———. 2000. *A Laboratory for Anthropology: Science and Romanticism in the American Southwest, 1846–1930*. Albuquerque: University of New Mexico Press.

Fowles, Severin, and B. Sunday Eiselt. 2019. Apache, Tiwa and Back Again: Ethnic Shifting in the American Southwest. In *The Continuous Path: Pueblo Movement and the Archaeology of Becoming*, edited by Samuel Duwe and Robert W. Preucel, pp. 166–94. Tucson: University of Arizona Press.

Fox, Nancy. 1976. Marjorie Ferguson Lambert: A Brief Biography. In *Collected Papers in Honor of Marjorie Ferguson Lambert*, edited by Albert H. Schroeder. *Papers of the Archaeological Society of New Mexico* 3: 1–18.

Gacs, Ute, Aisha Khan, Jerri McIntyre, and Ruth Weinberg, eds. 1988. *Women Anthropologists: A Biographical Dictionary*. New York, Greenwood Press.

Gero, Joan. 1985. Socio-Politics and the Woman-at-Home Ideology. *American Antiquity* 50: 342–50.

Gifford, Carol A., and Elizabeth A. Morris. 1985. Digging for Credit: Early Archaeological Field Schools in the American Southwest. *American Antiquity* 500, no. 2 (April): 395–411.

Goldfrank, Esther. 1978. *Notes on an Undirected Life: As One Anthropologist Tells It*. Queens College Publications in Anthropology, no. 3. Flushing, N.Y.: Queens College Press.

Hare, Peter. 1985. *A Woman's Quest for Science: Portrait of Anthropologist Elsie Clews Parsons*. Buffalo, N.Y.: Prometheus Books.

Howard, Jane. 1984. *Margaret Mead: A Life*. New York: Simon and Schuster.

Irwin-Williams, Cynthia. 1990. Women in the Field: The Role of Women in Archaeology Before 1960. In *Women of Science: Righting the Record*, edited by G. Kass-Simon and Patricia Farnes, pp. 1–41. Bloomington: Indiana University Press.

Joiner, Carol. 1992. The Boys and Girls of Summer: University of New Mexico Archaeological Field School in Chaco Canyon. *Journal of Anthropological Research* 48: 49–66.

Jones, Courtney Reeder. 1995. *Letters from Wupatki*. Edited by Lisa Rappaport. Tucson: University of Arizona Press.

Kass-Simon, G., and Patricia Farnes, eds. 1990. *Women in Science: Righting the Record*. Bloomington: Indiana University Press.

Kehoe, Alice B. 1999. Introduction. In *Assembling the Past: Studies in the Professionalization of Archaeology*, edited by Alice B. Kehoe and Mary Beth Emmerichs, pp. 1–18. Albuquerque: University of New Mexico Press.

———. 1999. Professionals May Not Be Women. In *Assembling the Past: Studies in the Professionalization of Archaeology*, edited by Alice B. Kehoe and Mary Beth Emmerichs, pp. 115–19. Albuquerque: University of New Mexico Press.

Kehoe, Alice B., and Mary Beth Emmerichs, eds. 1999. *Assembling the Past: Studies in the Professionalization of Archaeology*. Albuquerque: University of New Mexico Press.

Kidder, Alfred V. 1924. *An Introduction to the Study of Southwestern Archaeology*. New Haven, Conn.: Yale University Press.

———. 1949. Introduction. In *Prehistoric Southwesterners from Basketmaker to Pueblo*, by Charles Avery Amsden, pp. xi–xvi. Los Angeles: Southwest Museum.

Lambert, Marjorie F. 1954. Paa-ko, Archaeological Chronicle of an Indian Village in North Central New Mexico (Parts I–V); The Physical Type of the Paa-ko Population (Part VI), by Spencer Rogers. *School of American Research Monograph*, no. 19.

———. 1956. Some Clay and Stone Figurines from the Mogollón Mimbres Area, Luna County, New Mexico. *El Palacio* 63 (January–December): 259–83.

——— (with Richard Ambler). 1961. A Survey and Excavation of Caves in Hidalgo County, New Mexico. *School of American Research Monograph*, no. 25.

———. 1979. Pojoaque Pueblo. In *Handbook of North American Indians, Southwest*, vol. 9, edited by Alfonso Ortiz, pp. 324–29. Washington, D.C.: Smithsonian Institution.

———. 1981. Spanish Influence on the Pottery of San Jose de los Jemez and Giusewa, Jemez State Monument (LA 679), Jemez Springs, New Mexico. In Collected Works in Honor of Erik Kellerman Reed. *Papers of the Archaeological Society of New Mexico* 6: 215–36.

———. 1985. The Wells in the Palace of the Governors Patio and the Excavation and Repair of Well I. LA 4451. In Southwest Culture History: Collected Papers in Honor of Albert H. Schroeder, edited by Charles H. Lange. *The Archaeological Society of New Mexico* 10: 207–22. Santa Fe: Ancient City Press.

Leckie, Shirley A., and Nancy J. Parezo, eds. 2008. *Their Own Frontier: Women Intellectuals Re-Visioning the American West*. Lincoln and London: University of Nebraska Press.

Lee, Dorothy. 1949. Ruth Fulton Benedict (1887–1948). *Journal of American Folklore* 62 (246): 345–47.

Lewis, Nancy Owen, and Kay Leigh Hagan. 2007. *A Peculiar Alchemy: A Centennial History of the School of American Research, 1907–2007*. Santa Fe: School for Advanced Research Press.

Lister, Florence. 1997. *Pot Luck: Adventures in Archaeology*. Albuquerque: University of New Mexico Press.

———. 2000. *Behind Painted Walls: Incidents in Southwestern Archaeology*. Albuquerque: University of New Mexico Press.

Love, Marian F. 1981. An Anthropologist Meets a Cowboy. *The Santa Fean* (December), pp. 38–39.

Mark, Joan. 1988. *A Stranger in a Strange Land: Alice Fletcher and the American Indians*. Lincoln: University of Nebraska Press.

Mathien, Frances Joan. 1992. Women of Chaco: Then and Now. In *Rediscovering Our Past: Essays on the History of American Archaeology*, edited by Jonathan E. Reyman, pp. 103–30. Aldershot, U.K.: Avebury Press.

McKeown, C. Timothy, 2012. *In the Smaller Scope of Conscience: The Struggle for National Repatriation Legislation: 1986–1990*. Tucson: University of Arizona Press.

Mills, Barbara J. 2005. Cultural Matters: The Impact of Field Schools on Southwest Archaeology. In *Southwest Archaeology in the Twentieth Century*, edited by Linda S. Cordell and Don D. Fowler, pp. 60–80. Salt Lake City: University of Utah Press.

Modell, Judith Schachter. 1983. *Ruth Benedict: Patterns of a Life*. Philadelphia: University of Pennsylvania Press.

Morley, Sylvanus Griswold. 1920. *The Inscriptions at Copan*. Washington, D.C.: Carnegie Institution of Washington.

Morris, Ann Axtell. 1933. *Digging in the Southwest*. New York: Doubleday, Doran and Company.

Noble, David Grant. 1981. *Ancient Ruins of the Southwest: An Archaeological Guide*. Flagstaff, Ariz.: Northland Press.

——, ed. 1984. New Light on Chaco Canyon. *Exploration: The Annual Bulletin of the School of American Research*. Santa Fe: School of American Research Press.

Parezo, Nancy J., ed. 1993. *Hidden Scholars: Women Anthropologists and the Native American Southwest*. Albuquerque: University of New Mexico Press.

——. 1993. Anthropology: The Welcoming Science. In *Hidden Scholars: Women Anthropologists and the Native American Southwest*, edited by Nancy J. Parezo, 3–37. Albuquerque: University of New Mexico Press.

——. 1993. Conclusion: The Beginning of the Quest. In *Hidden Scholars: Women Anthropologists and the Native American Southwest*, edited by Nancy J. Parezo, pp. 334–67. Albuquerque: University of New Mexico Press.

Parezo, Nancy J., and Margaret A. Hardin. 1993. In the Realm of the Muses. In *Hidden Scholars: Women Anthropologists and the Native American Southwest*, edited by Nancy J. Parezo, pp. 270–93. Albuquerque: University of New Mexico Press.

Parezo, Nancy J., Ruth Perry, and Rebecca Allen. 1991. *Southwest Native American Arts and Material Culture: A Resource Guide*. 2 vols. New York: Garland Publications.

Peckham, Stewart, Nancy Fox, and Marjorie Lambert. 1981. The Laboratory's Modern Era: 1947–1981. *El Palacio* (87) 3: 32–42.

Reid, J. Jefferson, and Stephanie M. Whittlesey. 2005. Seven Years that Reshaped Southwest Prehistory. In *Southwest Archaeology in the Twentieth Century*, edited by Linda S. Cordell and Don D. Fowler, pp. 47–59. Salt Lake City: University of Utah Press.

Reiter, Paul. 1938. The Jemez Pueblo of Unshagi, New Mexico: With Notes of the Earlier Excavations at "Amoxiumqua" and Giusewa. Part I and II. Monograph Series, vol. 1, no. 4–5. University of New Mexico and the School of American Research. Albuquerque: University of New Mexico Press.

Reiter, Paul, William T. Mulloy, and E. H. Blumenthal Jr. 1940. Preliminary Report of the Jemez Excavation at Nanishagi, New Mexico. *University of New Mexico Bulletin, Anthropological Series* 3 (3): 1–38.

Rossiter, Margaret W. 1982. *Women Scientists in America: Struggles and Strategies to 1940*, vol. 1. Baltimore and London: Johns Hopkins University Press.

———. 1995. *Women Scientists in America: Before Affirmative Action, 1940–1972*, vol. 2. Baltimore and London: Johns Hopkins University Press.

Schaafsma, Polly. 1999. Tlalocs, Kachinas, and Related Symbolism in the Southwest and Mesoamerica. In *The Casas Grandes World*, edited by Curtis F. Schaafsma and Carroll L. Riley, pp. 164–92. Salt Lake City: University of Utah Press.

Schroeder, Albert H. 1979. Pueblos Abandoned in Historic Times. In *Handbook of North American Indians*, vol. 9, edited by Alfonso Ortiz, pp. 236–54. Washington, D.C.: Smithsonian Institution.

Schwartz, Douglas W. 1984. Foreword. In New Light on Chaco Canyon. *Exploration: The Annual Bulletin of the School of American Research*, edited by David Grant Noble, pp. ix–xi. Santa Fe: School of American Research Press.

Shutes, Jeanne, and Jill Mellick. 1996. *The Worlds of Pótsünü: Geronima Cruz Montoya of San Juan Pueblo*. Albuquerque: University of New Mexico Press.

Simmons, Marc. 1979. History of Pueblo-Spanish Relations to 1821. In *Handbook of North American Indians*, vol. 9, edited by Alfonso Ortiz, pp. 178–93. Washington, D.C.: Smithsonian Institution.

Snead, James E. 2001. *Ruins and Rivals: The Making of Southwest Archaeology*. Tucson: University of Arizona Press.

———. 2005. Paradigms, Professionals, and the Making of Southwest Archaeology, 1910–1920. In *Southwest Archaeology in the Twentieth Century*, edited by Linda S. Cordell and Don D. Fowler, pp. 27–46. Salt Lake City: University of Utah Press.

Stanley A. Stubbs, Bruce T. Ellis, and Alfred E. Dittert Jr. 1957. "Lost" Pecos Church. *El Palacio* 64: 67–92.

Thomas, Chester A. 1969. Jean McWhirt Pinkley 1910–1969. *American Antiquity* 34: 471–73.

Thomas, Jeffrey Allen. 1999. "Promoting the Southwest: Edgar Lee Hewett, Anthropology, Archaeology and the Santa Fe Style." Unpublished PhD dissertation, Department of History, Texas Tech University, Lubbock.

Thompson, Raymond H. 2000. Edgar Lee Hewett and the Political Process. *Journal of the Southwest* 42 (2): 271–318.

Tichy, Marjorie. 1935a. The Material from Kuaua. *El Palacio* 38 (21): 119–22

———. 1935b. Puaray and Kuaua Cultural Material. *Annual Report of the School of American Research*. pp. 15–17.

———. 1936. Observations on the Mission Uncovered at Puaray. *El Palacio* 41: 63–66.

———. 1937a. The Excavation of Paa-ko Ruin: A Preliminary Report. *El Palacio* 42: 109–16.

———. 1937b. A Preliminary Account of the Excavation of Paa-ko, San Antonito, New Mexico. *New Mexican Anthropologist* 1 (5): 73–77.

———. 1937c. The Excavations at Paako. *Annual Report of the School of American Research*, p. 11, pt. 2.

———. 1938. The Kivas at Paako and Kuaua. *New Mexican Anthropologist* 2 (4–5): 71–80.

———. 1939. The Archaeology of Puaray. *El Palacio* 46 (7): 145–63.

———. 1944. Exploratory Work at Yuque-Yunque. *El Palacio* 51 (11): 207.

Tisdale, Shelby J. 1985. *A Proposed Repatriation Policy for the School of American Research.* Unpublished master's thesis. Department of Anthropology, University of Washington Seattle.

———. 1989. The Status of Repatriation in the 1980s. In *The Concepts of Sacred Materials and Their Place in the World,* edited by George Horse Capture. Cody, Wyo.: The Plains Indian Museum, Buffalo Bill Historical Society.

———. 1993. Women on the Periphery of the Ivory Tower. In *Hidden Scholars: Women Anthropologists and the Native American Southwest,* edited by Nancy J. Parezo, pp. 311–33. Albuquerque: University of New Mexico Press.

———. 2007a. Marjorie Ferguson Lambert (1908–2006). *Anthropology News* (April). American Anthropological Association.

———. 2007b. Marjorie Ferguson Lambert (1908–2006). *Journal of American Anthropological Research* 63 (2): 165–66 (reprinted with permission from *Anthropology News,* April. American Anthropological Association).

———. 2007c. Marjorie Ferguson Lambert: A New Mexico Archaeologist. *El Palacio* 112 (4): 20–24.

———. 2008. Marjorie Ferguson Lambert: Including American Indians and Hispanic Peoples in Southwestern Anthropology. In *Their Own Frontier: Women Intellectuals Re-Visioning the American West,* edited by Shirley A. Leckie and Nancy J. Parezo, pp. 181–207. Lincoln and London: University of Nebraska Press.

Toulouse, Betty. 1981. The Laboratory's Early Years: 1927–1947. *El Palacio* 87 (3): 6–13.

Vierra, Bradley J., and Stanley M. Hordes. 1997. Let the Dust Settle: A Review of the Coronado Campsite in the Tiguex Province. In *The Coronado Expedition to Tierra Nueva: The 1540–1542 Route Across the Southwest,* edited by Richard Flint and Shirley Cushing Flint, pp. 249–61. Niwot: University Press of Colorado.

Woodall, J. Ned, and Philip J. Perricone. 1981. The Archaeologist as Cowboy: The Consequence of Professional Stereotype. *Journal of Field Archaeology* 8: 506–8.

Index

Note: Page numbers followed by *f* indicates figures on the corresponding page.

About the Author

Shelby Tisdale, retired director of the Center of Southwest Studies at Fort Lewis College, is an award-winning author who has published more than forty book chapters, articles, and books on Southwest Native American art and women. She edited *Federico: One Man's Remarkable Journey from Tututepec to L.A.*, by Federico Jimenez Caballero (University of Arizona Press, 2021). She is now an independent scholar living in Tucson, Arizona.